MAKE MONEY TRADING
HOW TO BUILD A WINNING TRADING BUSINESS

JEAN FOLGER & LEE LEIBFARTH

Marketplace Books
Columbia, Maryland

Library of Congress Cataloging-in-Publication Data
Folger, Jean.
  Making money trading : how to build a winning trading business / Jean Folger and Lee Leibfarth.
    p. cm.
  ISBN-13: 978-1-59280-308-8
  ISBN-10: 1-59280-308-3
  1. Portfolio management. 2. Investment analysis. 3. Speculation. I. Leibfarth, Lee. II. Title.
HG4529.5.F65 2007
332.6068'1--dc22

                         2007031154

ISBN: 1-59280-308-3

ISBN 13: 978-1-59280-308-8

Printed in the United States of America.

 2 3 4 5 6 7 8 9 0

This book is dedicated to my parents, Ralph and
Carol, for their enduring support.
L.L.

To my parents, Tom and Linda, for their
encouragement; and to my daughter Evy who
is a constant source of inspiration.
J.F.

TABLE OF CONTENTS

FOREWORD
BY TONI TURNER

What makes a book worth reading? As a writer myself, I look for compelling, timely, and well-organized material presented in a reader-friendly style. As a trader and student of the financial markets, I look for valuable information that will make my journey in this arena a richer and more profitable experience.

To my delight, I've found that *Make Money-Trading: How to Build a Winning Trading Business*, has fulfilled my demands and expectations. Jean Folger and Lee Leibfarth have written an excellent and enjoyable book that offers a significant ROI (return on investment) in exchange for the time spent absorbing its high-quality content.

When I first started trading back in the mid-1990s, it was a free-for-all! The stock market exploded into a riotous bull market that hadn't been seen before. The budding Internet spewed forth stock information, and discount brokerages popped onto the landscape, offering low-priced commissions. From housewives to grandmas, from taxi drivers to CEOs, from auto mechanics to heart surgeons—everyone who could grab a few thousand dollars and open an online trading account became a "day trader."

Most of us who jumped headlong into the markets spent all our time looking for the next "hot stock." Risk-management was an unknown (unwanted?) term back then, as were any of the accompanying terms such as "risk-reward analysis," and "asset allocation."

And, although many of us spent huge blocks of time of time immersing ourselves in the markets, studying charts and executing trades, few of us took the time to treat our pastime as a real business. We just wanted to make big bucks.

Oh, the losses that could have been averted, and the profits that could have been generated, if traders could have read the common-sense concepts set forth in Folger and Leibfarth's pages back then!

Nonetheless, we are fortunate to have this book accessible to us now, and its pages are chock full of advice and strategic planning that when appropriately applied, can contribute to our success as traders and investors.

The subhead for this book, *How to Build a Winning Trading Business*, says it all. The content fulfills its promise by giving you a step-by-step plan for creating a trading career that can develops into a successful and profitable business.

This is not a "how to get rich by this Friday morning, early" book. In fact—and rightly so—the writers acknowledge that building an income-generating business through trading in the financial market can appear "daunting" (although attainable).

I heartily agree with their no-nonsense approach to this subject. Trading can be a difficult business, and the market takes no prisoners. The rewards, however, can be satisfying and are based on the willingness of the trader to educate him or herself, apply unwavering discipline, and use the best technology available.

Folger and Liebfarth also say that as with any worthwhile undertaking, those who want to develop a successful trading business need to realize that it demands a commitment of time: time for studying the markets, for studying the nature of risk, for implementing a business plan, for learning the tools of the trade, for developing a viable trading plan, for executing trades efficiently, and so forth. In other words, "learn before you burn." Amen.

Once the authors move through overall considerations and requirements, they approach trading as a business by first exploring its most formidable and perennially present enemy: risk.

The statement is sobering, but an entirely truthful one—as traders we will always be exposed to risk and we will always experience losses. It's the nature of the game.

Anyone who cannot stomach watching their account shrink in value may want to take up another occupation. To the degree that risk is understood, however, and to the extent that a disciplined trading plan is implemented, an account that's experienced a reasonable drawdown should easily bounce back to profitability.

To the authors' credit, they do not leave the subject of evaluating risk behind in the book's early chapters. They thread references to risk throughout the remainder of the text and apply it each aspect of trading.

Make Money Trading establishes another ongoing theme: that capital preservation should remain first and foremost in every trader's and investor's mind.

I often tell my students to ask themselves before entering each trade: Am I protecting my capital? If for any reason the answer is no, (think: lack of, or avoidance of, a protective stop, chasing a stock, overtrading, greed-driven share size), then the trader should remove his hand from his mouse and be grateful that what might have been a costly "joyride" was aborted.

When delving into more details of trading as a business, Folger and Leibfarth offer a wonderful analogy that brings our view of trading capital to a grassroots level: our trading capital is our inventory. Of course, if we protect our inventory from harm, and I would add—make sure our insurance policies (protective stop orders) are in good standing—then our inventory will grow over time and our business will flourish.

Make Money Trading moves forward in a logical and well-organized progression, from establishing overall trading business goals and defining objectives, to an evaluation process that includes historical modeling, forward performance testing, and live market testing. The trader's research and work in these areas, using the guidelines described in the book's chapters, should culminate in a fully developed trading plan. Of course, the plan's success will be put to the ultimate test in a live trading scenario that finalizes in a profit/loss statement.

Again, this book is all about the business of trading. It is up to the reader to explore and expand his or her knowledge of certain components of the process, such as candlestick trading technology, chart indicators and oscillators, volume signals and the interpretations of price patterns.

The challenge of coming to the end of a really good book is where to start—how to put all the great ideas in the pages into action. Even though I've been a trader and investor for more than sixteen years, I continue to learn from others. I will go back through this book's pages and revisit all the highlighted sentences and sections that drew my attention. Then I'll plan new strategies based on those ideas.

Was this book worth reading? Absolutely! Compelling, timely, well-organized and reader-friendly? For sure! I am confident that whether you're a trader or investor—novice or more experienced market veteran—*Make*

Money Trading will act as a valuable tool to help you develop your trading career into a successful—and winning—business!

Toni Turner

President, ToniTurner.com

Author
A Beginner's Guide to Day Trading Online
A Beginner's Guide to Short-Term Trading
Short-Term Trading in the New Stock Market

INTRODUCTION
WHAT IT MEANS TO BE AN INDEPENDENT TRADER

Every weekday morning at 9:30 sharp (Eastern Standard Time) the US financial markets come alive. While many of these markets have already been trading for hours on electronic and foreign exchanges, this is the time when market liquidity and volatility are at their peak. This is when the professional money managers and institutional traders who work at the exchanges get down to business. As independent traders, we do not see this action from the busy exchange floor, but from our computer monitors. We are screen based, independent traders.

Trading for a living has obvious appeal: working from home, being your own boss, and great profit potential. Many traders who make it over the hump—from struggling greenhorn to profitable business owner—find a great deal more than the obvious appealing. To some, the challenge of trading turns out to be one of the most appealing aspects of the business.

You are working typically by yourself, for yourself, against a lot of people doing the same thing. With such great autonomy comes great responsibility. You are responsible for everything that happens in your business, from deciding which markets to trade to actually pulling the trigger, and beyond. You have to plan well if you expect to make steady profits from trading.

Being a successful trader requires two steps: approaching trading as a business, and maximizing the available technology to your benefit. If you do these two things, you will greatly increase your chances of making it through another year of trading, and, eventually, becoming a self-sufficient, profitable trader.

Approaching trading as a business is integral to success because trading is a business. You wouldn't expect to become a pro golfer by reading a couple golfing magazines, and you shouldn't expect to become a good trader just because you read a few books or watched an infomercial on late-night television. A successful trading business requires a strategic plan that encompasses your actual business, and that includes your actual trading.

Your business plan includes things like short- and long-term goals, the amount of capital you will make available for the business, and what computer setup you will need. Your trading plan includes things like what instruments you will trade and how you will effectively trade them. Your trading plan needs to be absolutely specific and objective. Your plan should be so well laid out and comprehensive that you could hand it over to someone else and they could make a reasonable attempt at trading the plan.

In addition, it is important to understand that a good trading plan isn't just a set of rules that you think will work in trading, or a list of setups that you are fond of, or someone else's plan. A good trading plan has been researched, tested on historical data, tested in live markets, and evaluated at regular intervals—all by you.

You should expect to devote a significant amount of time to developing a viable trading plan. Most people don't have the requisite skills handy; they must be learned. Time will have to be dedicated to learning and understanding the market(s) that you wish to trade. You'll need to read about, apply and watch in a live market, different market indicators to discover which ones are most suited to your trading style and personality. You'll need to research technology, and find out how you can best use it to your advantage. You'll have to study the different methods of placing orders in the market, and practice placing orders so that it becomes second nature. You'll have to learn how to effectively backtest a trading strategy so that you can discover the potential merits (or lack thereof) of a system. You'll need to learn to accurately evaluate and compare trading plans so that you'll end up trading the best one. You'll have to know what to do, ahead of time, if you arc in the middle of a trade and you lose your Internet connection. You'll need to know how to stay organized so that you are prepared for tax time. These are just a few of the things that you will have to learn in order to develop a profitable trading plan, and business.

All of this may sound daunting, but it is realistic. And it is certainly attainable. All of the technology available to today's traders greatly reduces the amount of time is takes to develop a profitable trading system—just imagine (not that many years ago) charting the market by hand. The key is to plan well, and to utilize and maximize technology to meet the goals of your business.

MAKE MONEY TRADING
HOW TO BUILD A WINNING TRADING BUSINESS

CHAPTER 1
THE FUNDAMENTAL
CONCEPTS OF TRADING

An advertisement that ran in financial magazines posed the question, "A yacht or a surfboard, which will your investing get you?" While the intent of the ad is clear, my first inclination has always been to surf out on the waves rather than ride as a passenger on the yacht. This is not a reflection on my preference for adventure sports, but a metaphor for how active traders should view their place in the markets.

Let me explain; owning a large yacht requires a hefty bank account, with the owner and its passengers relying on the skill of the crew to safely navigate the waters. In most cases, this boat takes a significant amount of time to change course and must avoid shallow reefs, bad weather, and rough seas. This is comparable to handing an account to a money manager and sitting back as they take you on a ride. In some cases, a navigational error could cause serious damage to the expensive boat, much to the distress of the helpless owner.

The surfer on the other hand, thrives in the conditions that the yacht typically avoids. In sharp contrast to the yacht, anyone can own a surfboard; the challenge is becoming proficient at using it. The surfer must rely on his or her own skill, strength, and precision to navigate the rough waters and receives personal reward from the experience of "catching a great wave." Much like active trading, the surfer's passion and intensity will dictate the level of his or her ultimate success. While a yacht owner sits back and allows the crew to make navigational decisions, the surfer is responsible for his or her own performance. For those of us who have in interest in taking a more active role in managing our money...grab your board, the surf's up!

TRADING VS. INVESTING

For most of us, our first experience in the markets is through investing. The goal of investing, often referred to as buy-and-hold investing, is to build wealth over extended periods of time. This is typically accomplished through the buying and holding of a stock, or a basket of stocks, and allowing the price to fluctuate over time. After a period of years or decades, the investment will, in most cases, increase in value. These long-term profits may be further enhanced through compounding, or reinvesting the profits and dividends in additional shares of stock.

Trading involves the more frequent buying and selling of stocks or commodities with the goal of generating returns that outperform buy-and-hold investing. Trading profits are typically generated through buying at a low price and profiting from the subsequent sale at a higher price, all within a relatively short period of time. Figure 1.1 shows two price charts that compare the potential of trading versus buy-and-hold investing over the same time period. Notice that as the market fluctuates, the buy-and-hold investment may show significant losses (or drawdowns), such as the time period between 2000 and 2003. Conversely, a good trader will not only exit the market during these drawdown periods, but may take an opposing short position (described in Chapter 6—Placing Trades) that will allow profits from the descending price movement. It can be noted that any one of the nine individual trades shown on the bottom chart outperformed the buy-and-hold investment for the same time period. A

FIGURE 1.1

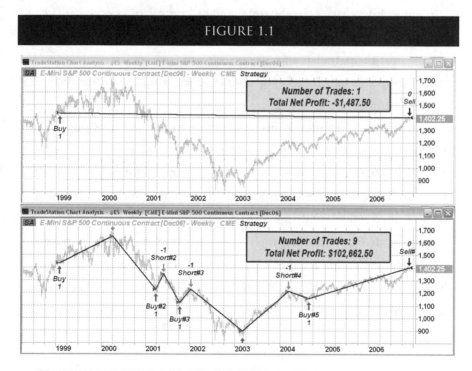

COMPARES THE RESULTS OF BUY-AND-HOLD INVESTING TO THE POTENTIAL
OF 9 INDIVIDUAL TRADES FOR THE SAME TIME PERIOD.

standard measure of the effectiveness of an investment or trading system is a comparison to the Standard and Poor's 500 Index, commonly referred to as the S&P. Effective trading plans are expected to consistently outperform the buy-and-hold performance of the S&P; performance is commonly expressed as a percentage gain or loss.

It is important to understand that trading is not investing. Trading and investing are two completely different animals. Successful traders have very defined, short-term profit goals and, as a result, must have a much more disciplined approach to the market. For some investors, a 10% annual return on their capital is deemed very acceptable, while a good trader may seek to gain a 10% return per month. In order to accomplish this, it is imperative that traders maintain tight control over potential losses by limiting their exposure to the market. Even if the market turns and goes against them, traders should not be in the market long enough to be significantly affected. In general, trading requires much greater precision than investing.

Trading also requires a different set of tools than investing. While investors can wait out less profitable positions, traders make profits (or take losses) within a shorter, predetermined amount of time. Traders focus mostly on the technical aspects of the markets, such as volume and relative price action, while investors tend to be more concerned with the fundamentals of the market, such as a company's profitability and earnings outlook. Trading requires close attention to the markets as well as a high degree of discipline and training. Trading is a business that requires an effective strategic plan.

Styles of Trading

Determining a trading style is the first step in building a trading plan. Trading style simply refers to the time frame or holding period in which stocks, commodities, or other trading instruments are bought and sold. Trading may take place over a wide variety of time frames, ranging from many years to just a few seconds. Trading styles are commonly broken down into four categories: position trading, swing trading, day trading, and scalping. Figure 1.2 compares these different trading styles. A trader must choose his or her trading style based on factors that include:

- Level of trading experience
- Time that can be dedicated to trading
- Risk tolerance
- Amount of capitalization or account size
- Personality

FIGURE 1.2

Trading Style	Time Frame	Holding Period
Position Trading	Long term	Months to years
Swing Trading	Short term	Days to weeks
Day Trading	Short term	Day only—no overnight positions
Scalp Trading	Extreme short term	Seconds to minutes— no overnight positions

TRADING STYLES MAY BE DEFINED BY THE HOLDING PERIOD OR TIMEFRAME IN WHICH POSITIONS ARE OPENED AND CLOSED.

Position trading refers to a relaxed style of trading in which trades are taken over a period of months to years. This style of trading attempts to identify technical trends in markets where large price movements are likely to occur. Position traders anticipate big price fluctuations or price breakouts over a relatively long time horizon. While position trading is a long-term type of trading most comparable to investing, all others are considered short-term methods.

Swing trading is the general category that defines the majority of active traders. This trading style involves taking trades (or positions) that last a few days or weeks, where a profit objective is often defined before the trade is entered. Swing traders will close a trade either after the profit objective is met, after a set amount of time, or if the trade is not moving in the intended direction. Although this style of trading involves greater precision than position trading, it does not necessarily require constant, minute-by-minute attention to the markets. Traders who do not have the ability to monitor their trades all day long often choose this type of trading.

Day trading refers to a style of trading in which all positions are closed by the end of the day. Unlike position or swing traders, day traders do not hold any trades overnight. In short, day traders attempt to profit from intraday price fluctuations and minimize risk through limiting their market exposure. Day traders often trade in relatively high volume, requiring them to borrow from their brokers (known as margin and explained in Chapter 4—The Tools of the Trade). Day trading requires actively monitoring the markets and managing trades throughout the day. While many longer-term traders consider this style of trading risky, responsible day trading can be a lucrative form of trading.

Scalp trading is an extremely active form of day trading that involves frequent buying and selling throughout the day. Scalpers typically trade in very large volume, and this requires a high level of market intuition and

FIGURE 1.3

Trading Style	System Name	Percent Winning Trades	2006 Annual Return	Initial Capital Required (000's)	Annual Return on $60,000 Account*
Position Trading	NDX Shadrach	53	127.5%	$50	$63,750.00
Position Trading	Trend Shark	53	90.1%	$50	$45,050.00
Position Trading	NDX Apednego	59	35.2%	$50	$17,600.00
Swing Trading	SeasonalST ERL	53.8	44.4%	$20	$66,600.00
Swing Trading	TZAR ES	61	40.1%	$30	$40,100.00
Swing Trading	MESA Notes	64.2	24.3%	$30	$24,300.00
Day Trading	Bounce EMD	57	48.5%	$10	$145,500.00
Day Trading	Bounce ERL	67.6	43.9%	$10	$131,700.00
Day Trading	Impetus eRL	58.3	12.4%	$10	$37,200.00

* Adjusted to apply the maximum amount of initial captial

THIS CHART COMPARES TOP PERFORMING COMMERCIALLY AVAILABLE
TRADING SYSTEMS FOR DIFFERENT TIME FRAMES.
—SOURCE: ATTAIN CAPITAL MANAGEMENT—

accuracy in placing trades. Scalp trades target the smallest intraday price movements and take place within seconds or minutes. Due to the level of precision that is required for this style of trading, it offers the greatest amount of risk and requires constant attention to the markets.

Generally speaking, as the holding period of a trading style decreases, the level of necessary precision and market awareness increase. The markets can be thought of as fractals since price fluctuations occur in all timeframes anywhere from monthly intervals to one-minute intervals. Figure 1.3 compares the annual trading performance of several commercially available trading systems and serves as a reference for the potential of different trading styles. Although the price movement of individual trades tends to be greater over longer timeframes, the greater frequency of trades in short-term trading creates plenty of profit potential.

In order for any style of trading to be successful, traders must find markets that offer the potential to make a reasonable profit. The two key elements that allow for successful trading are liquidity and volatility. Liquidity refers to the ability to easily enter and exit trades, while volatility refers to the amount of price fluctuation. As you can imagine, if you want to buy a stock but no one is willing to sell it, trading is not possible. Likewise, if you buy a stock and the price does not change, it will be difficult to make a profit. The trading instruments that we look for typically trade in high volume and make significant price swings. While many equate these markets with higher risk, these are simply the conditions that are needed for successful trading. Risk will be minimized in these markets using other tactics. Additionally, many modern traders prefer instruments that trade on all-electronic markets. This helps ensure that trades are executed quickly and efficiently since the trading is done via computers, and not on an actual exchange-trading floor.

Understanding Risk

Risk has many different meanings; in the context of trading, risk refers to the probability of losing money or trading capital. Risk is what trading is all about, or, more specifically, accurately managing risk. As a trader, you should be well aware of the risks involved in trading: you can lose all of the money in your trading account and even wind up owing more. It can happen, and it has happened to many unfortunate traders.

Before considering trading as a part-time or full-time business, you should make sure that you have the financial means to support yourself during the learning process and to adequately fund your trading account. It is extremely important that the money used for trading capital is money that you can afford to lose. Before proceeding along the path of trading, you should review the U.S. Securities and Exchange Commission's (the SEC's) risk disclosure statement and be aware of the rules and regulations involved in trading.

Throughout this book we will explore the different aspects involved with developing and trading a successful trading plan. By far, the most important element in this equation is accurately assessing the risk involved in any given trading method or system. The first step in evaluating risk is to understand exactly how much you could potentially lose, given the worst-case scenario. Traders should know exactly how much capital they are willing to risk on each individual trade long before pushing the "buy" button. This amount of trade risk can be expressed in risk units, or R. In addition, traders must also decide how much money they are willing to lose, known as maximum drawdown, before it becomes time to reevaluate a trading plan. Your loss potential should never be left to chance.

The best defense against complete disaster is education and planning. As a trader, it is your primary job to learn and understand as much as possible about the markets you are trading and how to control your potential losses. You must develop a careful plan that limits loss to an acceptable level if you ever hope to become profitable. Risk will always be there, and successful traders are constantly evaluating that risk by not just asking the question, "What can I win?" but first and foremost, "How much can I lose?"

Most of us tend be optimists. We spend more time thinking about good things than bad. In general, this is a pleasant trait, but in the trading context it can be dangerous. It is a lot of fun to think about the money that we can make trading, imagining ourselves on the deck of our boat, buying our second house, or driving a fancy new sports car. We are thinking about winning. As we will soon learn, trading is not just about winning.

Trading is mostly about losing. Not just losing, but learning from our losses, controlling our losses, and accepting our losses as a part of trading. Traders do not need to win more frequently than they lose to make money. In fact, many profitable trading systems only win about 40% of the time. The key is to make more money on each winning trade than you spend on losing trades (known as a +R advantage), as this allows traders to make money over time.

To understand risk, it is helpful to objectively measure this factor in order to establish and compare the elements of a trading plan. One of the most valuable measures of risk involves the concept of probability. In trading, we are never absolutely sure about the direction of the markets and we must rely on probability to help us understand the chances of making a correct decision. Probability can be expressed either as a decimal from 0.00 to 1.00, or as a percentage from 0% to 100%. A probability of 1.00 or 100% means an event will always occur, while a probability of 0.00 means the event will never happen. Keep in mind that when we analyze risk, we begin by looking at the probability of losing, and not just the probability of winning.

Let's examine some principles of measuring risk using the simple example of a repeated coin toss. If a gambler were to challenge you to bet $100 on a coin toss where you could double your money with a win, should you? In other words, a fair coin toss would determine if you won $100 by landing on heads or you owed $100 by landing on tails. This type of system does not provide us with any type of +R advantage and yields a high, 50% probability of losing our initial $100 bet. Many of us would choose wisely and not take this challenge.

> PROBABILITY OF LOSS = NUMBER OF
> NEGATIVE OUTCOMES (TAILS) /
> TOTAL NUMBER OF POSSIBLE OUT-
> COMES = 1 / (1+1) = .50 OR 50%

Now, the gambler changes the rules and offers you the ability to double your bet on the coin toss. This time, a heads will earn $200, with a tails still costing your initial $100. Mathematically, we now have a +R advantage and know that over time we could generate a profit. We look in our wallet and see two, crisp $100 bills. The question becomes, "Can we afford to play long enough to make a profit?"

Another concept that we must consider is that although we may have favorable rules, or a +R advantage, we must also be prepared to weather a string of consecutive losses (tails). The 50% probability of the coin toss would suggest that over a long period of time (100s or 1,000s of coin tosses) we should have a statistically similar amount of heads and tails, and thus see a significant profit. If we were to begin with several losses, however, we would not stay in the game long enough to show any profit since we would run out of money, ending up with a loss. This danger is referred to as being undercapitalized. Even with the 2-to-1 +R advantage, throwing seven tails during the first ten games will generate a loss. While this seems highly unlikely, let's take a closer look....

When tossing a coin ten times, there are 1,024 different possible outcomes for the heads-and-tails sequences. While there are only 120 outcomes with exactly seven tails, we must also consider the 45 outcomes with eight tails, ten outcomes with nine tails and one outcome where all ten throws are tails. In total, there are 176 possible outcomes for at least seven tails. This gives us a 17% probability, or roughly a one in five chance, that we will lose our money within the first ten throws.

> PROBABILITY OF LOSS (7 TAILS IN
> 10 THROWS) = 176 / 1024 = 17%

The question still remains, how much money do we need to have in order to responsibly take the gambler's coin tossing challenge? To answer this, we will use an important concept in both trading and gambling known as the probability of ruin. Probability of ruin allows us to measure the relationship between how much a trader is willing to risk versus the probability of losing everything. Losing everything is exactly what traders need to avoid. Understanding probability of ruin allows traders to make smarter decisions about bet or position sizing.

> PROBABILITY OF RUIN (FOR A COIN
> TOSS) = 1 / ((1 + ERA) ^ N)
> ERA = EXPECTANCY PER RISK UNITS
> (.5 FOR COIN TOSS EXAMPLE)
> N = UNITS OF INITIAL CAPITAL
> (INITIAL CAPITAL / INITIAL AMOUNT RISKED)

Figure 1.4 shows a graph of the coin toss example that relates the amount of the bet (as a percentage of the overall account size) to the probability of ruin. Notice that as the bet size becomes larger, the probability of ruin increases substantially. From our example, we have $200 of initial capital in our wallet and we must bet $100, or 50%. From the chart, we see that this relationship would give us a 44% probability of losing our

FIGURE 1.4

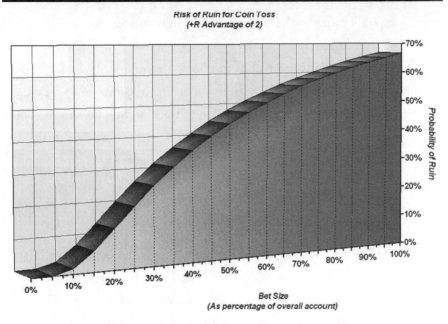

Risk of Ruin for Coin Toss
(+R Advantage of 2)

RISK OF RUIN FOR A COIN TOSS WHERE YOU CAN WIN TWICE
AS MUCH AS YOU RISK ON EVERY THROW.

entire $200 stake. This is not that much better than the 50% probability of the coin toss in the first example. While most players would find this to be too much risk, we now have tools that can help us stack the odds in our favor.

One way to use this information to our benefit is to first determine an acceptable probability of ruin and then decide how much capital is needed. For example, choosing a conservative 10% bet provides us with a much more comforting 2% probability of ruin; now the odds would be truly in our favor. While it would require $1,000 of initial capital to safely bet at this level, there is a 98% chance that we would become profitable because we are given a 2-to-1 +R advantage. Armed with this knowledge, I would run to the closest ATM, withdraw an additional $800 and continue to bet 10% of my capital as long as the coin-tossing gambler offered the game!

While trading is not exactly a game, the same rules apply. In fact, many of the formulas presented in this book are commonly used by modern portfolio managers and have been derived from gambling and gaming statistics. The bottom line is, before taking a trade, we should know exactly how much we are willing to risk. Understanding risk allows us to make decisions that will help us develop safer and more profitable trading plans.

POSITIVE EXPECTANCY

In the previous section, we looked at how we could control our losses. Now, we will examine how to win. In order for a trading business to be successful, it must be able to consistently make money over time. In trading, we can measure the potential of a strategy using a concept known as expectancy. Expectancy expresses the average amount that a trader can expect to win (or lose) per unit of risk. In order for traders to have any chance of making money, their systems must have a positive expectancy.

> EXPECTANCY = (PROBABILITY OF
> WIN* AVERAGE WIN) – (PROBABILITY
> OF LOSS* AVERAGE LOSS)

Using the coin tossing examples discussed earlier in the chapter, a game where we could win or lose an equal amount ($100) on a coin toss provides an expectancy of zero. Any system that has an expectancy of zero or less should be avoided; it is a losing system. The second coin-tossing example, however, provides a 2-to-1 +R advantage. A system that has a

50% probability of winning, an average win of $200 and an average loss of $100 would have an expectancy of $50. This is a moneymaking system and what is meant by positive expectancy.

EXPECTANCY = (.5 * $200) – (.5 * $100) = $50

Knowing this type of statistical information about a system allows us to make projections, such as how much profit is possible from the symmetric outcome (equal number of heads/tails) of 20 throws. This becomes a simple calculation of multiplying the expectancy by the number of games. Given the rules of this particular game, one could expect to make around $1,000 in 20 games.

Establishing positive expectancy in trading relies on two related components: probability of winning and R advantage. Both of these factors are critically important when developing and choosing a strategy on which to build a trading plan. In fact, these two factors provide another method of expressing expectancy, called risk-adjusted expectancy or ERA. In other words, expressing expectancy per unit of risk, instead of as a dollar amount, is often useful in comparing different systems. Multiplying ERA by the average dollar amount of risk (average loss) brings us back to the dollar value in which expectancy was originally defined.

ERA = (PROBABILITY OF WIN * R ADVANTAGE)
– (1 – PROBABILITY OF WIN)
ERA (FOR COIN TOSS EXAMPLE) =
(.5 * 2) – (1 – .5) = .5R OR .5

Probability of winning is the inverse of the probability of loss that we discussed in the previous section. While it seems that our goal should be to develop a trading plan that provides the greatest probability of winning possible, the reality is that this statistic depends mostly on trading methodology. A bigger probability of winning is not always better, or necessary. This is illustrated in the coin-tossing example where even a 50% winning system can provide excellent profit opportunity, if we have the right rules. It is most important to have a consistent and reliable probability of winning.

> **PROBABILITY OF WINNING = NUMBER OF WINNING TRADES / TOTAL NUMBER OF TRADES**

R advantage relates the amount of the expected return to the risk taken during an individual trade. Values greater than one are said to have a +R advantage since the amount of the return is a positive multiple of the amount of risk units taken (R).

> **R ADVANTAGE = EXPECTED RETURN / AMOUNT BEING RISKED {VALUES GREATER THAN 1: +R ADVANTAGE} {VALUES LESS THAN OR EQUAL TO 1: -R ADVANTAGE}**

As we have seen in the coin tossing examples above, having a +R advantage can be an essential factor in developing a profitable system. Developing trading rules that establish a +R advantage on every trade will help to build positive expectancy. It is important, however, to take the probability of winning into account as well. For example, planning a trade with a +R advantage of 4.5 sounds great (risking $100 to make $450), in theory. However, if the trades win less than 20% of the time, you will have a losing system. Figure 1.5 shows a table illustrating the profit/loss relationship between the probability of winning and R advantage. This table is calculated using the per dollar expectancy for 10 trades.

FIGURE 1.5

RValue	10%	20%	30%	40%	50%	60%	70%	80%	90%	100%
-2	($1,100.00)	($1,200.00)	($1,300.00)	($1,400.00)	($1,500.00)	($1,600.00)	($1,700.00)	($1,800.00)	($1,900.00)	($2,000.00)
-1.5	($1,050.00)	($1,100.00)	($1,150.00)	($1,200.00)	($1,250.00)	($1,300.00)	($1,350.00)	($1,400.00)	($1,450.00)	($1,500.00)
-1	($1,000.00)	($1,000.00)	($1,000.00)	($1,000.00)	($1,000.00)	($1,000.00)	($1,000.00)	($1,000.00)	($1,000.00)	($1,000.00)
-0.5	($950.00)	($900.00)	($850.00)	($800.00)	($750.00)	($700.00)	($650.00)	($600.00)	($550.00)	($500.00)
0	($900.00)	($800.00)	($700.00)	($600.00)	($500.00)	($400.00)	($300.00)	($200.00)	($100.00)	$0.00
0.5	($850.00)	($700.00)	($550.00)	($400.00)	($250.00)	($100.00)	$50.00	$200.00	$350.00	$500.00
1	($800.00)	($600.00)	($400.00)	($200.00)	$0.00	$200.00	$400.00	$600.00	$800.00	$1,000.00
1.5	($750.00)	($500.00)	($250.00)	$0.00	$250.00	$500.00	$750.00	$1,000.00	$1,250.00	$1,500.00
2	($700.00)	($400.00)	($100.00)	$200.00	$500.00	$800.00	$1,100.00	$1,400.00	$1,700.00	$2,000.00
2.5	($650.00)	($300.00)	$50.00	$400.00	$750.00	$1,100.00	$1,450.00	$1,800.00	$2,150.00	$2,500.00
3	($600.00)	($200.00)	$200.00	$600.00	$1,000.00	$1,400.00	$1,800.00	$2,200.00	$2,600.00	$3,000.00
3.5	($550.00)	($100.00)	$350.00	$800.00	$1,250.00	$1,700.00	$2,150.00	$2,600.00	$3,050.00	$3,500.00
4	($500.00)	$0.00	$500.00	$1,000.00	$1,500.00	$2,000.00	$2,500.00	$3,000.00	$3,500.00	$4,000.00
4.5	($450.00)	$100.00	$650.00	$1,200.00	$1,750.00	$2,300.00	$2,850.00	$3,400.00	$3,950.00	$4,500.00
5	($400.00)	$200.00	$800.00	$1,400.00	$2,000.00	$2,600.00	$3,200.00	$3,800.00	$4,400.00	$5,000.00

COMPARES THE RELATIONSHIP BETWEEN THE PROBABILITY OF WINNING AND THE R ADVANTAGE BASED ON PER DOLLAR EXPECTANCY OF 10 TRADES AND $100 OF RISK.

When planning individual trades, traders should aim for a +R advantage as high as possible while maintaining a reasonable percentage of profitable trades. In addition, external factors in trading such as slippage and commissions (discussed in Chapter 8 –Evaluating and Comparing Trading Plans) will close the gap between your risk and return levels, and must be considered. Most successful trading plans achieve a 40%-60% probability of winning. Using this as a guideline, +R advantage ratios need to be 1.5 or greater. In general, traders should look for a consistent, mid-level probability of winning with a high +R advantage.

It can be noted that scalp traders often employ a high-risk day trading tactic that is opposite to most other styles of trading. Scalpers rely on a high probability of winning trades (70% – 80%) and a very low R advantage, often risking more than they make on any individual trade. In order to make this style of trading profitable, scalpers must trade in large volume, thus increasing their overall risk. While having such high winning percentages may seem very appealing to newer traders, only very experienced traders should attempt this style of scalp trading since it requires absolute precision. Even a small mistake can result in significant losses. For new traders attempting this style of trading, it can be like crossing a busy interstate while blindfolded.

OPTIMAL RISK

Whenever we trade, there is no guarantee that we will make money. Each individual trade is somewhat of a gamble that may result in a loss, causing us to deplete our capital. We are constantly trying to strike a balance between the amount of risk we take versus what we stand to gain.

In some cases, we may think of not only trading in terms of risk, but everyday life as well. Most of us make choices each day that are the outcome of risk to reward analysis. Should I drive all the way across town to hear a short concert? Should I risk not being prepared for work on Monday to take a relaxing weekend trip? Should I chance gaining weight to indulge in a delicious chocolate cake? The point is that by practicing thinking in terms of what you are risking versus what you stand to gain, it will help you make clearer trading decisions and will be a key indicator for determining your individual trading style.

A basic financial principle is the more risk you take, the greater the potential for profit. Taking this principle to the extreme, however, has been the downfall of many traders. Our primary goal in this business is to protect our capital, and too much risk can create disastrous results. Conversely, not taking enough risk will keep us from trading at a level that will generate significant profits. Developing a profitable trading plan requires us to become responsible risk takers and to establish reasonable tolerances for risk.

This brings us back to the coin-tossing game where we can win twice as much as we risk for each throw (+R advantage of 2). For this round, however, the gambler allows us to bet whatever amount we would like, but limits our play to 10 coin throws. Additionally, we are limited to only betting with the $200 that is currently in our wallet. How much of the $200 should we bet?

From the previous sections we know two things: (1) the game has the ability to generate profits (positive expectancy), and (2) if we bet too much of the overall account size, we will go bankrupt (risk of ruin). This game has now become a much better simulation for the position sizing decisions that we are faced with in actual trading. Before we determine how much to bet, we must first decide how to bet. While it may seem easiest to select a set amount of money to bet and continue betting that amount, known as constant position sizing, this will not maximize our statistical +R advantage. Instead, betting a consistent percentage of our capital, referred to as fixed-percentage betting, will allow us to scale our trading to the conditions. In other words, as our profits grow, so does the amount that we will be betting. This allows us to risk more as we make more, and vice-versa.

Figure 1.6 shows two graphs representing the probable outcomes of 10 coin tosses using the above rules. The curve represents the fixed-percentage relationship between bet size and profit, while the rectangular block in the background shows the initial capital of $200 as a reference. As we can see, the risk and profit relationship does not follow a straight line, as many may think. In other words, more risk does not necessarily equate to greater profits, as this only occurs when bet sizes are between 0 and 25%. In fact, if we bet more than 50% in our coin tossing system, we begin to lose money, and drop below our initial $200.

From the curve, we can see the maximum profit is $360 and occurs at a bet size of 25%, this is known as the level of optimal risk (sometimes referred to as optimal f—a term and concept made popular by the work of Ralph Vince). Risking slightly more or less than 25% creates a sharp decline in the amount of profit for the system. From this information, we can deduce that in order to maximize our profits, we should risk $50 on our initial coin toss and continue to risk 25% as our capital grows.

> OPTIMAL RISK = ERA / R ADVANTAGE
> OPTIMAL RISK (COIN TOSS EXAMPLE) = .5 / 2 = 25%

Earlier in the chapter we introduced the concept of risk of ruin, and we can now analyze this coin tossing system by referring back to Figure 1.4.

FIGURE 1.6

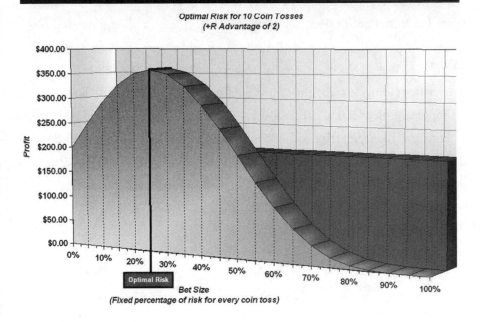

Optimal Risk for 10 Coin Tosses
(+R Advantage of 2)

FIGURE 1.6 SHOWS THE OPTIMAL RISK LEVEL FOR THE COIN TOSSING GAME.

If we compare the optimal risk percentage of 25%, we see that this system would have a 20% probability of ruin. While this level of risk will statistically optimize the profit potential of this system, the one-in-five chance of losing our entire $200 stake may be too high for many. Remember, just because a system has a 50% chance of winning does not guarantee that a consecutive string of losing coin tosses will not occur. Most would elect to bet less than 25% and find a point that would yield good profits with less probability of ruin. Knowing this information about a system allows us to build an effective trading plan around our individual risk tolerances.

Throughout this chapter, the importance of understanding risk was discussed as an inescapable part of the trading business. For our examples, we have used an ideal model of a coin toss. In real trading, however, neither the probability of winning nor the +R advantages of a system is fixed, and we must adjust our formulas to account for this. We will explore the specific trading application of probability of ruin, optimal risk, and other important metrics in Chapter 8—Evaluating and Comparing Trading Plans. For now, managing risk will become our primary challenge in building a profitable trading business and designing an effective trading plan.

CHAPTER 2
THE BUSINESS OF TRADING

As a business, trading has many advantages that include being your own boss, low startup costs, a flexible schedule, and virtually unlimited income potential. Trading certainly offers the opportunity to have a thriving part-time or full-time business. The key to developing a successful trading business, or any type of business for that matter, is good planning.

Many people are lured into the trading business without knowing what the business really entails. Some prospective traders even begin trading large positions without having developed any type of logical business or trading plan. Any business embarked on with such impulsiveness and lack of foresight is likely to fail.

Unfortunately, there is also lot of deception associated with learning the business of trading. A quick Internet search or the myriad late night infomercials will have you convinced that generating a huge income from the financial markets is easy. Or, that anyone with enough money to fund a trading account can double his or her money within a short amount of time. Here are some facts about the trading business:

- Most traders that begin a trading business (about 90%) fail within the first year.

- There is no such thing as easy money.

- There is no such thing as a trading system that has zero risk.

- There is no such thing a system that wins all of the time.

- Most successful independent traders are not "filthy rich," but generate a comfortable income.

Trading is not for everyone, nor is it easy. It is a business that requires constant research, evaluation, and discipline. There are no guarantees or insurance with the trading business, and people who are considering trading should make sure they have both the personality and the financial means to take on this type of business activity. Some of the questions that you should ask yourself before pursuing a part-time or full-time independent trading business include:

- Am I driven to succeed?

- How do I handle losing?

- How well can I take criticism?

- Can I stick to a plan?

- Do I have the support of my family?

- How do I deal with stress?

Those traders who are able to weather the learning curve and the inevitable account drawdowns often go on to achieve considerable financial success. Trading is a business that is well suited for focused, responsible risk takers.

First, it is important to view trading as a part-time or full-time business, and not a hobby. As a hobby, trading would be frustrating and very expensive. Just dabbling in trading will keep traders from gaining the proficiency and experience needed to become consistently profitable. Although trading can be fun and exciting, it is still a business—one that can be very profitable and rewarding when approached from the proper perspective.

Profitable business owners seek to stay in business for the long haul, and understand that get-rich-quick schemes often lead to failure. As a business, trading may not always provide a short-term profit. Winning trades are not considered net profit, since they have to be combined with trading losses and other expenses to develop the overall profit or loss of a trading business. It is the difference between the gross trading profit and expenses over time that creates the overall net profit (or loss) for the business. It is only over time that a business will develop a substantial profit, and successful traders have to take this long-term view. Figure 2.1 shows a performance report for a trading plan broken down into months. Although this system showed a large loss during the first month and a net loss during two months of the time period, it managed to achieve an annual total net profit of $76,050.00. Statistics such as these help us develop a comprehensive business plan.

Developing a trading plan as part of an overall business plan may seem like a daunting task, especially to novice traders. Trading, however, offers a unique advantage that is not available to most other businesses: the ability to accurately test trading plans on historical market data, a

FIGURE 2.1

Period	Avg. Net Profit	Return on $50,000 Account	Percent Profitable
January	($9,290.00)	-18.58%	0.00%
February	$7,900.00	19.41%	50.00%
March	$540.00	1.11%	37.50%
April	$20,070.00	40.83%	100.00%
May	$10,960.00	15.83%	66.67%
June	$0.00	0.00%	0.00%
July	$12,760.00	15.91%	100.00%
August	($4,850.00)	-5.22%	0.00%
September	$7,140.00	8.11%	100.00%
October	$12,400.00	13.02%	80.00%
November	$18,110.00	16.83%	100.00%
December	$310.00	0.31%	100.00%
Totals	$76,050.00	151.48%	63.64%

THIS PERFORMANCE REPORT SHOWS MONTHLY PROFIT AND LOSS
STATISTICS FOR A TRADING SYSTEM.

process known as backtesting. Backtesting allows a simulation of a trading plan on past market data.

Imagine making plans to open a new store and projecting how much inventory you would need for the first year. Now imagine you have access to records showing exactly what items would have sold during the previous five years, had your store been open in the same location. Although this wouldn't guarantee your store would sell the exact items again in the upcoming year, it would provide a realistic starting point for inventory projections. The historical records could also prove or disprove the viability of your business plan.

Developing a trading plan around historical testing can offer you the same type of valuable statistical information that will help in developing an overall strategic business plan. Throughout the following chapters we will extensively use this method of historical backtesting in our development of a trading plan. Using modern trading software and historic market data, we can accurately test the merits of a trading plan before we actually risk money trading it.

If you are considering becoming a part-time or full-time trader, there are some important challenges along the way. The first is developing realistic expectations for yourself, your business, and your ability to learn. This is not a profession at which you will become skilled overnight. Traders who push themselves into trading too soon or without a well-researched trading plan often find themselves back at the beginning, but with a lot less money in their accounts. Take the time to research and plan your business, as these are essential steps in your overall success as a trader.

PROTECTING CAPITAL

The primary goal in a trading business is to protect trading capital. This is, by far, the most important concept of successful trading and building a consistently profitable trading plan. The fact is, without money to trade with, your business is bankrupt. Game over. Once a trading account has been lost or significantly depleted it can take a very long time and a lot of stress to start over. Get it right the first time by planning well enough to protect your most valuable asset: your trading capital.

Trading capital can be thought of as inventory. Similar to a retail store, once an inventory is considerably reduced, so is the ability to generate profits. We cannot sell retail products that we do not have (there is no backordering in trading). Traders are limited to the money in their accounts (including margin limits, discussed in Chapter 4—The Tools of the Trade) to buy or sell in the financial markets.

Unfortunately, the primary business goal for many new traders is simply to make money. This can be a dangerous goal since it causes many of these traders to take unnecessary risks and burn through their initial trading capital. Don't get me wrong; making a profit is an important part of trading and is, in fact, our secondary business goal. But we should always keep the big picture in mind by controlling our losses.

Early in my trading career, a mentor gave me the advice, "Before you can make money, you must first learn how not to lose money." At the time, this was not very well received and sounded more like an ancient proverb than useful trading advice. Over time, however, I have learned that this very simple phrase carries great meaning. I have found myself muttering this phrase during tense trading moments. The fact is, if you can actively trade without depleting your initial capital, you are well on your way to trading success.

Now that we understand the importance of protecting capital, we will discuss how to accomplish this important task. There are two primary methods that traders can employ to protect their capital and actively control losses: responsible position sizing and the use of a stop loss.

POSITION SIZING

Before placing a trade, traders must specify the amount of shares or contracts that they intend to buy or sell. This is an important factor in protecting capital. As a general rule, traders should begin trading with small position sizes and work up to trading larger positions. This allows traders to build up their trading skills and their trading accounts. Traders may take frequent losses while learning to trade and developing a trading plan. Keep in mind that losses aren't always a result of your trading strategy: pilot error accounts for a notable amount of trading losses, especially in the early days of a trading career. Order entry mistakes are common, and more than a few traders have bought when they meant to sell, and vice versa. Large losses at the beginning of a trading career can be devastating because traders will not have the same amount of capital to trade with later on.

Once a trading plan has been developed that has produced profits and given consistent results, then it's time to think about increasing position sizes. This is known as an anti-martingale betting system, and it allows us to take greater risk when trading with our profits than with our initial capital. This is similar to the concept of fixed percentage betting that was introduced in Chapter 1—The Fundamental Concepts of Trading. This type of system allows traders to objectively choose a position size to trade with, maintaining the primary goal.

STOP LOSSES

The second method of controlling loss is known as a stop loss. A stop loss is a simple limit to how much capital you are willing to risk on any one trade. A stop loss is a type of order that can be placed in the market at the same time that a trade is initiated, and should only be a small percentage of the overall trading account value. The stop loss amount is determined prior to entering the trade, and if the trade goes the wrong way and reaches that predetermined amount, the trade will be closed. Although most of us think of losing as a bad thing, a stop loss is an essential tool that limits losses. It is recommended that you always trade with a stop loss.

In Chapter 1—The Fundamental Concepts of Trading, we introduced the importance of having a +R advantage in our trading plan. One meth-

FIGURE 2.2

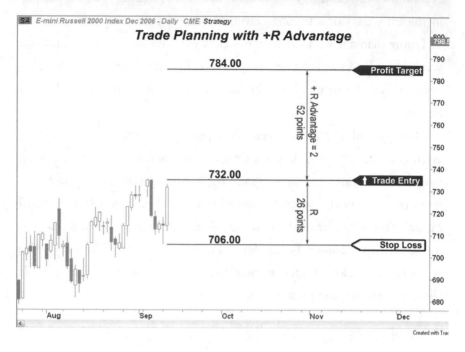

A PRICE CHART SHOWING A POTENTIAL TRADE WITH A PROTECTIVE
STOP LOSS AND A +R ADVANTAGE OF 2.

od of creating a consistent +R advantage is through the use of a carefully
placed stop loss. While there are many methods of determining the placement for a stop loss, each provides us with a measurable distance from our
trade entry point. Setting a second order that will close the position for a
profit, known as a profit target, will allow us to create a trade with a known
+R advantage. Figure 2.2 shows a trade-planning example with location of
a trade entry, the stop loss, and the profit target. Notice that the distance
between the trade entry and the profit target is twice the distance as that
between the entry and the stop loss. This provides a +R advantage of 2 for

this trade. While there is no guarantee that this trade will reach the projected profit target, we know that the maximum amount we can expect to lose on this trade is 26 points. This type of trade planning can be critical to establishing positive expectancy.

GETTING AN EDUCATION

Many aspiring traders may envision a time when they can sit in front of their high-speed computers, fueled by adrenaline, and rely on their instincts and quick reactions to make money in the markets. While this vision may not be entirely unrealistic, the time commitment involved in creating those instincts and quick reactions is significant and can be greatly underestimated. In addition, most successful traders are not fast paced, adrenaline junkies, but responsible risk takers who have spent a considerable amount of time learning about and researching the markets and their individual trading plans. These traders are typically very familiar with the statistics of their trading plans and track their individual trades with some type of journal for later analysis. These successful traders remain students of the market.

As stated earlier, about 90% of people entering the trading business fail within the first year. I believe that the largest reason for this low success rate can be attributed to a lack of trader education. Although most traders go into the business with great enthusiasm and a willingness to succeed, few accurately estimate the length of time it takes to learn the business. With many professions, there is a significant learning curve that often requires many years of formal training before it is even possible to legitimately enter the business. In trading, you do not need a degree in finance or an MBA to try your hand at buying and selling stocks or commodities. Many people assume the ease of entry into this profession translates into a business that is easy to learn. Unfortunately, trading is not an easy business to learn, nor is it intuitive.

Possibly the most difficult part of learning to trade is the lack of binary feedback. In most learning situations, you are rewarded when you perform correctly and, conversely, given criticism for doing something wrong. In trading, you can do everything right and still lose money on a trade. Even worse, you could completely ignore your trading plan, blow through your stop loss, and still wind up making money on that individual trade. You can see how learning in this way can be confusing and very expensive. It is only over time and with consistency that you will be rewarded for good trading.

New traders cannot rely on instinct or intuition to make market-timing decisions. Instead, they must rely on a trading plan that is developed using historical research, one that employs consistent logic and sound money management principles. Good trading is having the discipline to always follow your trading plan.

We have already discussed how important it is to protect our capital; strictly following your trading plan is what allows you to do just that. A good day of trading should not be measured by how much money you make but by how well you followed your plan. If you have correctly position-sized, taken every trade that your trading plan alerted you to, and followed your money management strategy, then you have achieved perfect trading. Discipline is a vital factor in profitable trading and learning to develop a successful trading plan.

So the question remains, how do we start to develop a profitable trading plan? The first recommendation is to look at the startup costs of trading not just in terms of initial trading capital, but also by how much time you can afford to invest in learning the business. This can be a much

FIGURE 2.3

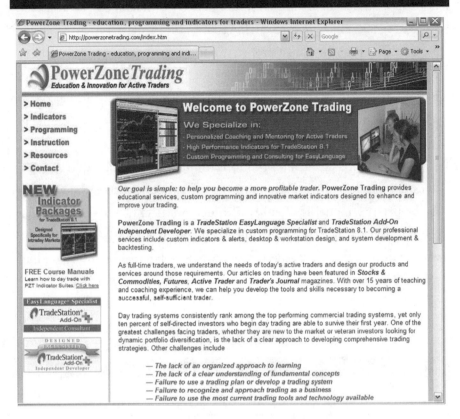

ONLINE TRADING SCHOOLS CAN INTRODUCE THE BUSINESS OF DAY TRADING.

more significant investment than simply funding a trading account. Your time should be viewed as risk capital or time that you can afford to be without an income.

The next step is to develop an educational path. This may include reputable trading schools, instructional chat rooms, seminars, or private coaching/mentoring. Although these will add to the initial expense of the business, they can be a critical step in minimizing the time it takes to develop a successful trading business. When considering an educational service, spend some time researching and comparing services. Typically, services that promise "huge profits," "no risk systems" or require you to consistently subscribe to their recommendation service should be avoided. Before paying for an educational service, you should talk with the service provider to make sure they teach a trading methodology that is compatible with your trading style and account size.

Using an organized approach to learning is critical, and developing a schedule or educational plan will make the process much more efficient. A competency model is often used to determine critical levels along the learning spectrum, such as the one displayed in Figure 2.4. Recognizing where you fall along this spectrum can help self-paced learners build an effective educational plan. This is where a trading mentor or coach can be

FIGURE 2.4

LEVEL 1	LEVEL 2	LEVEL 3	LEVEL 4
Unconscious Incompetence	Conscious Incompetence	Conscious Competence	Unconscious Competence
This is where learning begins. Traders at this level are not aware of the skills or behavior needed to become successful traders.	Traders have developed an awareness of the skills that are needed to become successful traders. Books, seminars or a trading coach can help bring these skills into focus for the trader.	At this level traders can now trade with reasonable competence but must think about doing it. Trading does not yet happen naturally.	These traders can trade instinctively and no longer have to think about it. Through much repetition, trading has become natural. This is the level of mastery

A COMPETENCY MODEL APPLIED TO TRADING.

very helpful. Learning requires us to take something that is complex and break it down into a series of attainable steps. Each of these steps should be linked together in a logical order known as a progression. It is through this progression that we will be able to advance through the different competency levels. Setting goals is the first logical step in developing this process, and traders should have the answers to these key questions written down in a journal or notebook:

- What are my long-term trading goals, other than specific financial goals?

- What are my short-term trading goals, other than specific financial goals?

- What do I hope to gain from trading, other than money?

Since there are so many elements to learn and understand in trading and developing a trading plan, it is important to prioritize the key aspects. Understanding your own personal learning style is essential to building an effective educational plan. Traders often find that they will learn a lot about themselves during this process, and having the answers to these questions will be helpful:

- What do I consider to be my greatest weaknesses?

- What are my strengths?

- How have I excelled in the past?

- What tools/methods do I need to learn?

- How much time and money am I willing to risk?

Another key tool is a trading journal, shown in Figure 2.5, which logs individual trades and acts as a trading diary. Traders should write down

FIGURE 2.5

Date	Symbol	Shares/Contracts	Reason for Trade	L/S	Entry Price	Exit Price	Profit (Loss)	Notes
9/13 - 9/22	ER2U06	4	L2 Buy	L	702.90	704.90	800	Great support off MA
9/22 - 10/3	ER2Z06	4	S1 Sell	S	704.90	688.90	6400	Took a little heat, then nice move
10/4 - 10/4	ER2Z06	4	L1 Buy	L	694.00	710.00	6400	Quick move - fun trade
10/10 - 10/13	ER2Z06	4	S1 Sell	S	721.50	734.60	(5240)	Trade against me right away couldn't penetrate MA
10/13 - 10/17	ER2Z06	4	L2 Buy	L	734.60	745.20	4240	Good resitance from DTL Time to get out!
10/17 - 11/1	ER2Z06	4	S1 Sell	S	745.20	729.20	6400	Faily slow trade... nice push through MA
11/6 - 11/7	ER2Z06	4	L1 Buy	L	727.10	743.10	6400	Beautiful Trade
11/15 - 11/28	ER2Z06	4	S1 Sell	S	759.80	743.80	6400	Little bouncy

A TRADING JOURNAL IS A VALUABLE LEARNING TOOL.

every trade, making sure to provide information for each one. It is important to review this journal at regular time intervals (weekly or monthly), as this can be an important tool for evaluating progress and establishing additional goals.

While learning the business of trading is hard work, that doesn't mean that the process cannot be fun and rewarding. It is important to maintain a positive attitude and lifestyle throughout the learning process as this will help to avoid frustration. It may sound a bit hokey, but adopting a positive mantra such as, "I will learn to develop a profitable trading plan," can help push through difficult points while learning. A good education is, by far, the most important tool in developing a profitable trading plan and a profitable trading business.

RESEARCHING THE BUSINESS

Most of us could not imagine opening a new retail store without having extensive knowledge of the products that we were planning to sell. Yet, many new traders try each year to start a trading business without having a thorough understanding of what they are buying and selling. Sure, it sounds easy to buy something and then sell it for more than you paid for it. It is the detailed subject knowledge and expertise, however, that separates the successful businesses from the bankrupt. Whether you choose to have $50,000 in retail inventory or in a trading account, it is a business. Successful business owners use more than just the retail value of their products to determine pricing. They must understand their intended market. They must also realize when to cut their losses by selling a product at a loss in order to generate money to reinvest into other types of products that are more popular and can consistently sell at a good profit. This type of decision-making is critical to a successful business and requires experience, education, and practice. Trading is no different than any other type of retail business. Business owners who wish to be successful must have a professional, systematic approach and be willing to thoroughly research their intended markets. Research is an important component in the trading business.

For most, trading is a one-person business, yet it requires two distinctly different roles: that of a strategist and that of a market trader. While both aspects are critically important, each requires a different set of skills and responsibilities. It is important that traders be able to differentiate between the two distinctly different roles that are required of the trading

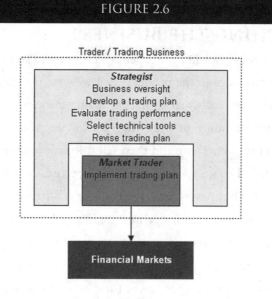

FIGURE 2.6

Trader / Trading Business

Strategist
Business oversight
Develop a trading plan
Evaluate trading performance
Select technical tools
Revise trading plan

Market Trader
Implement trading plan

Financial Markets

THE STRATEGIST AND THE MARKET TRADER MAKE UP
THE TWO ESSENTIAL RESPONSIBILITIES OF A
TRADING BUSINESS.

business. Figure 2.6 shows a graphical model of these two important functions associated with a successful trading business.

The strategist must see the "big picture" and is responsible for the overall planning of the business, including the development of the trading plan. In addition, the strategist must set a risk limit with regard to how much can be lost on any given trade, and overall, before the trading plan is revised. Another responsibility for the strategist is maintaining the trading account and selecting the technical tools that the trader will use. Essentially, the strategist is the chief operating officer (COO) for a trading business.

The market trader's responsibilities are a much more defined: to interact with the markets and follow the trading plan exactly. This requires having complete confidence in the trading plan and executing each trade precisely according to the rules of the plan. Market traders don't care if they lose a trade; they are well aware that over time the trading plan has a positive expectancy, and they know the thresholds for the plan. As long as the market is open and trading can take place, the market trader is on duty. Everything that the market trader does should be written down in the trading journal for later evaluation; any changes or revisions to the trading plan fall under the jurisdiction of the strategist.

STRATEGIST + MARKET TRADER = TRADER

As mentioned above, both of these roles are necessary for building a successful trading business. While most of us have a stronger inclination for one role over the other, too much emphasis on just one aspect of the trading business can create a significant imbalance. For instance, some traders who enter the business look at trading as simply a new job. They only want to focus on placing trades and being participants in the markets. They prefer to be told how to trade, often looking to purchase a trading plan or follow an advisory service. Unfortunately, without having formulated a trading and business plan of their own, these market traders will most likely fail. They seem to constantly change their tactics and are always looking for a better system. The fact is, they must customize their business and trading plans to meet their specific goals, account size, and risk tolerance. By developing the skills necessary to becoming good strategists and establishing long-term or strategic business goals, they will greatly increase their chances of developing a profitable trading business.

Conversely, some people will focus on developing a trading business solely around historical data and performance reports, without much regard for developing trading skill. These strategists often view market trading as a menial task that is necessary to implement their overall financial goals. They often have a difficult time removing themselves from the stress of actual trading. As traders, they tend to overanalyze each trading decision and may not allow themselves to follow their own trading plan. They must separate their roll as a strategist and focus on developing their skills as a market trader in order to build a successful business. For them, this means turning off the analytical part of their brains and focusing on the task at hand...good trading. As mentioned earlier, good trading simply means following the trading plan.

Having a strong inclination for one role over the other is not necessarily a bad thing, as long as you realize your preference or bias towards one role. Understanding your personal inclination as a business owner allows you to structure your trading business around your particular strengths. For instance, people who tend to be primarily a market trader may find it helpful to select a more active style of trading (such as day trading) on which to base their trading plan. Strong strategists may elect to use some form of trade automation (explained in Chapter 6—Placing Trades), to

FIGURE 2.7

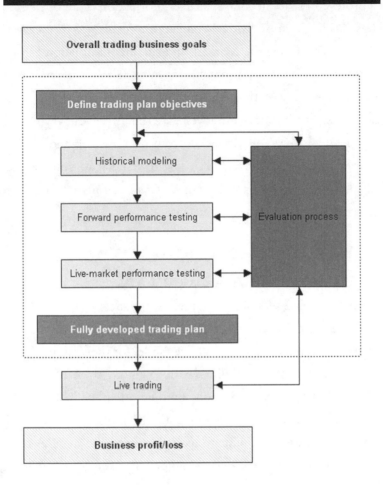

SHOWS A STRATEGIC PLANNING MODEL FOR A TRADING BUSINESS.

keep them from second guessing their trading rules and help them execute their trades according to their trading plans.

Developing a successful trading business, just like any other business, requires time and hard work. Most importantly, traders (the unified strategist and market trader) should be willing to substantiate every aspect of their business and trading plans by doing their own research. Trading is not a profession that encourages shared information or an open exchange of ideas. Trading is an individual competition (explained further in Chapter 3—Getting to Know the Market), and sharing information can make a trading plan or system less profitable, or even destroy the system's profitability all together. For this reason it becomes even more important to develop your own business and investigate things on your own.

The reality is this: you have to do your own research and the research is an ongoing process. Nobody is going to hand it to you. People who have had past careers or backgrounds that required performing thorough research often make outstanding traders.

Building a Strategic Plan

A strategic plan serves as a map to lead traders from where they are now to where they would like to be in the future. This type of planning allows traders to build a comprehensive model for their trading businesses as well as providing the most direct path to getting there.

Notice that the area surrounded by the dotted line in Figure 2.7 represents the specific steps in developing a trading plan. The overall model illustrates a path to developing a successful trading business. A thorough strategic plan includes the following components: a mission statement, objectives, goals, and a trading plan. In addition, a strategic plan should be:

- Written
- Concise
- Based on accurate research

A strategic plan should allow enough time to be successfully implemented. Traders who rush into trading or that trade positions that are too large will more than likely have problems.

A mission statement explains the reason for a part-time or full-time trading business. While it may seem obvious that trading is about making money in the financial markets, we still need to answer the question, "Why choose trading to make money?" There are certainly many other businesses that are less competitive or may fall into an area in which you currently have more experience and expertise. For some, the answer may be in the flexibility that trading offers or the desire to manage your own investments. In any event, traders need to be able to clearly and simply define this important question.

Objectives set out areas of emphasis that are critical to the success of the business. These areas of emphasis outline what type of trading activities should be pursued. This includes both current and prospective trading activities and, for new traders, should include an educational component as well.

The importance of establishing goals has been mentioned earlier in this chapter. For a strategic plan, these should include both long-term and short-term goals. Monthly, quarterly, one-year, and five-year goals should all be taken into consideration and will allow traders to outline the strategy for reaching these goals. It is recommended to first set long-term goals and then set short-term goals. In this way, the short-term goals act as steps toward achieving the long-term goals.

A trading plan is an essential element of a strategic plan that addresses the specific trading aspects of the business. This plan is based on thorough research and addresses the implementation of all of the previous goals. In essence, this is the action plan of how we will achieve our mission.

FIGURE 2.8

Trading Business Profit and Loss	Aug	Sep	Oct	Nov	Dec	2006
Winning Trades	$0	$14,280	$49,600	$54,330	$310	$265,512
Losing Trades	($4,865)	($7,150)	($37,225)	($36,235)	($5)	($189,662)
Commisions	($15)	($10)	($25)	($15)	($5)	($200)
		—	—	—	—	—
Trading Costs	($4,880)	($7,160)	($37,250)	($36,250)	($10)	($189,862)
Gross Trading Margin	($4,850)	$7,140	$12,400	$18,110	$310	$76,050
Operating Expenses:						
Payroll	$4,167	$4,167	$4,167	$4,167	$4,167	$50,000
Platform Fees	$100	$100	$100	$100	$100	$1,200
Exchange Fees	$35	$35	$35	$35	$35	$420
Internet Service	$45	$45	$45	$45	$45	$540
Phone/Cell Service	$80	$80	$80	$80	$80	$960
Insurance	$200	$200	$200	$200	$200	$2,400
Other	$175	$175	$175	$175	$175	$2,100
	—	—	—	—	—	
Total Operating Expenses	$4,802	$4,802	$4,802	$4,802	$4,802	$57,620
Profit Before Taxes	($9,652)	$2,338	$7,598	$13,308	($4,492)	$18,430
Taxes Incurred	$0	$1,428	$2,480	$3,622	$62	$18,038
Net Profit	($9,652)	$910	$5,118	$9,686	($4,554)	$392

SHOWS A PROFIT AND LOSS STATEMENT FOR A SMALL, INDEPENDENT TRADING BUSINESS.

Just writing down this type of information can help traders understand the time and financial requirements for developing a successful trading business. Figure 2.8 shows a hypothetical profit and loss statement for a small, full-time independent trading business. These numbers represent the same trading plan that was illustrated in Figure 2.1. While the trading profits (after commissions) still amount to $76,050 for 2006, the business only shows a $392 overall net profit after accounting for operating expenses, a nominal "salary," and taxes. While it may be safe to say that most traders begin trading only as a part-time business, this shows the importance of seeing the big picture. Planning these types of business expenses can provide a more realistic projection and can help answer important question such as:

- How much money will I need in my trading account?
- What type of returns do I need to generate from trading?
- How long can I afford to learn the business?
- What type of salary can I hope to generate from trading?
- Should I pursue trading as a full-time or part-time business?

A strategic plan should not be confused with a trading plan. A trading plan is an essential element of a strategic plan that addresses the specific trading aspects of the business. While the majority of this book will discuss building a successful trading plan, it is important for traders to also consider the bigger picture of developing an overall business. As we discussed in Chapter 1, even an outstanding and well implemented trading plan can result in ruin if it is undercapitalized or not planned correctly. An overall strategic plan will help traders develop an important overview of their trading businesses.

CHAPTER 3
GETTING TO KNOW
THE MARKET

Before we talk about how to make money in the financial markets, it is important to understand how these markets actually work. This chapter can be considered a quick-start guide to help traders understand this highly competitive atmosphere. Building a business around profiting from inefficiencies in the financial markets literally means beating someone else. In order for you to make money trading, someone else has to lose it; short term trading is a zero sum game. The only market participants that never lose money are the brokers and the exchanges. Traders must compete with other traders for their profits.

To understand the markets, we must first take a look at what really drives the market. While primarily guided by supply and demand, we must also consider the investor emotions that lead to market inefficiencies: fear and greed. While this may sound like a cliché, it is the emotional factor that allows for short-term trading opportunities in the market. At this point you may be wondering how we can profit from this emotional factor in the market. We do it by teaching ourselves to take all emotion out of our trading. Our trading decisions should be based on good research and planning, not on what we may feel at the moment. Establishing and following a trading plan is what allows us to take advantage of emotionally driven markets and make profits.

THE STOCK MARKET

STOCK EXCHANGES

Most people who refer to the "market" are usually talking about the US equities market, or stock market. The US stock market is composed of three primary exchanges where trading takes place: the New York Stock Exchange (NYSE), the American Stock Exchange (AMEX), and the NASDAQ Stock Market (NASDAQ), which combined list approximately 7,000 individual stocks. Stocks can be thought of as little pieces of a publicly-traded company that can be bought and sold. Stocks are broken down into units called shares and each individual share of a stock has a tangible value. The exchanges can then be thought of as the exclusive retailers for those companies. Much like the Wal-Marts, Sears, and K-marts of the trading world, the NYSE, AMEX, and NASDAQ represent enormous retail markets where companies compete to sell their stock.

Also similar to the sale of goods in a store, stocks have both a wholesale and retail value. These are known in the trading world as the bid and ask prices. As a retail trader (one who does not work at an exchange), we must typically purchase a stock at its retail price (the ask price) and when we wish to sell it, we can only sell it through the exchange at its wholesale price (the bid price). Similar to purchasing a brand new car and driving it off the lot, you cannot sell that car for exactly what you paid for it unless the supply or demand for that vehicle significantly changes. In addition, retail traders cannot buy directly from an exchange but must go through a broker who will buy or sell shares of a stock on our behalf in exchange for a commission.

The difference between the bid and ask price is called the bid-ask spread and, along with the trading volume, this reflects a stock's liquidity. Trading volume is the number of shares that have been bought and sold during a particular time period (daily volume is calculated from the beginning of the day's trading session). Typically, traders look for stocks that have a very small bid-ask spread and trade in relatively high volume as this will ensure that if you want to buy or sell a particular stock, someone else will be willing to sell it or buy it from you. This is what is meant by liquidity.

Figure 3.1 shows a time and sales screen from a highly liquid stock, Microsoft (MSFT). This shows the amount of buying and selling taking place as soon as it happens. Since each transaction is matching a buyer to a seller, "buy" or "sell" is relative to the last price at which a transaction has occurred. In other words, if the last sale occurred at the ask price (retail value) of the stock we can assume that it is being bought; if the last sale occurred at the bid price (wholesale value), we can assume that it is being sold. Since we know the bid and ask prices (shown at the top), we can tell that someone just bought 100 shares at a price of $29.92 per share, since this transaction occurred at the ask (retail) price. In addition, we can see a very small $0.01 difference between the bid and ask prices for this stock that shows that there is very little 'markup' for the price of this stock. Prices can continue to fluctuate between the bid price and ask price

FIGURE 3.1

Symbol	Bid T...	Last	Bid	Ask	Vol Tot
MSFT	⬇	29.92	29.91	29.92	11,029,813

Time	Price	Size	Condition	
12:26:17 PM	29.92	100	At Ask	
12:26:16 PM	29.92	100	At Ask	
12:26:12 PM	29.92+	100	At Ask	
12:26:12 PM	29.91	200	At Bid	
12:26:12 PM	29.91	100	At Bid	
12:26:10 PM	29.91	200	At Bid	
12:26:10 PM	29.91	950	At Bid	
12:26:10 PM	29.91	150	At Bid	
12:26:10 PM	29.91	200	At Bid	
12:26:09 PM	29.91-	1500	At Bid	
12:26:07 PM	29.92	100	At Ask	

A TIME AND SALES SCREEN DISPLAYS ALL OF THE REAL-TIME
TRANSACTIONS FOR A STOCK. (CREATED WITH TRADESTATION)

without the overall value of the stock changing; this simply represents the normal buying and selling that can take place.

At this point, you may be wondering what makes the price of a stock fluctuate. This is where trading volume and a good sales associate come in. At the NYSE and AMEX, each individual stock has its own auction taking place with its own specific auctioneer, known as a specialist. At the NASDAQ, sales associates are called market makers and their job is to create liquidity for their individual stocks by creating and selling their own inventory and pricing the stock at a value that will initiate buying and selling. Essentially, specialists and market makers are responsible for lining up buyers with sellers by adjusting the price of the stock depending on the current supply and demand. They do this by setting the price for their stock, and carefully watching as market participants line up to buy or sell that stock. If more participants are lining up to buy, they will increase the price of the stock to attract more sellers (who will sell because the increase in the stock's value will allow them to profit). Once the amount of buyers is equal to the amount sellers, the market has reached a point of efficiency where everyone is happy and the value of the stock is considered "fair." If all of the sudden the higher price creates another imbalance and begins to attract more sellers than buyers, however, the value of the stock will go back down. These types of dynamic supply and demand imbalances can be seen most clearly by viewing the intraday market depth data (also known as a Level 2 screen) as seen in Figure 3.2.

The Level 2 screen of General Electric (GE) stock in Figure 3.2 shows two shaded columns representing the amount of market participants buying versus those who are selling. The column labeled "ID" shows the market participant's identification, indicating from whom we could buy or sell. The bid, ask, and size columns list what is currently available. We can see from the top price lines that there are significantly more market participants willing to sell at the ask price of $37.55 than are willing to buy at

FIGURE 3.2

Symbol	Bid Tick	Bid	Ask	Last	Trd Size	Net Chg	Vol Tot
GE	⇧	37.54	37.55	37.55	200	-0.42	8,440,300

ID	Bid	Size	Time	ID	Ask	Size	Time
NYSE	37.54	1100	10:37:43 AM	NASD	37.55	6600	10:37:44 AM
ARCX#	37.53	6500	10:37:43 AM	ARCX#	37.55	8000	10:37:44 AM
NASD	37.53	6800	10:37:43 AM	NYSE	37.55	15300	10:37:44 AM
CHXE	37.50	500	10:34:15 AM	CHXE	37.65	300	10:29:51 AM
CINN#	37.41	100	10:34:13 AM	CINN#	37.75	100	10:16:48 AM
PHLX	1.00	100	09:11:04 AM	PHLX	100.00	100	09:11:45 AM

A LEVEL 2 SCREEN FOR GENERAL ELECTRIC (GE) SHOWS BUYERS ON THE LEFT SIDE, SELLERS ON THE RIGHT. (CREATED WITH TRADESTATION)

the bid of $37.54. These white price zones are known as the inside bid and ask since they represent the best prices currently available for buying and selling. From this information, we can assume that this market is trying to initiate short-term buying since there seems to be greater supply than demand. This may often create a short-term price drop as there are greater bid sizes lining up to buy at the shaded price level of $37.53. This type of price action occurs continually in most stocks throughout the day.

Although the NYSE, AMEX, and NASDAQ essentially do the same thing (as do many other stock exchanges in the US and around the world), there are several differences between these major exchanges. The NYSE, commonly referred to as the "Big Board," is the oldest, most prestigious stock exchange, and was founded in 1792. It is located on Wall Street in downtown New York City and lists approximately 2,800 individual stocks, mostly from the industrial and manufacturing sectors. The NYSE lists its stocks as one, two, or three letter abbreviations (such as "GE" or "IBM") and uses a system where transactions occur live between traders and specialists. Trading on the floor of the NYSE is a hybrid system, part electronic and part auction. In the NYSE, there are several rooms with "posts" representing the different equities. In order to buy or sell a NYSE stock, or listed stock as they are called, someone must physically place an order with a specialist on the floor of the exchange.

In contrast, the NASDAQ is an all-electronic marketplace that consists of a telecommunications network that does not have a physical trading floor. NASDAQ stocks are typically listed as four letter abbreviations ("JAVA" or "INTC") and include many technology-oriented stocks. Although the NASDAQ was only started in 1971, it lists approximately 3,200 companies and surpassed the NYSE in 1994 in annual share volume.

While the AMEX is owned by NASDAQ, its structure is more similar to the NYSE. The AMEX uses specialists to conduct its auction-like trading live on a trading floor. While most AMEX companies are smaller than the NYSE or NASDAQ companies, they list over 800 individual stocks and have become the primary trading location for Exchange Traded Funds (see the ETF section later in this chapter).

If you have ever watched a ticker symbol scroll by or watched a financial news network such as CNBC, you may have noticed how stock prices appear, as shown in Figure 3.3. In this case, each stock is represented by a three or four letter abbreviation followed by the quantity and price for the last sale of the stock. An up arrow, usually in green, means the stock price is higher than its previous day's value, while a down arrow, usually in red, means that the stock is down on the day. The second stock shown in Figure 3.3, for instance, shows that a transaction for General Electric (GE) has just occurred for 15,000 shares at a price of $37.97. Additionally, we can tell that this stock is down $0.03 from yesterday's trading session. While this can provide very basic information about the current state of a stock price, unless we know the bid or ask price, we cannot determine if the stock is being bought or sold.

Individual stocks have long been the trading instruments of choice for many traders. Stocks are simple to understand and have become very easy to trade through the popularity of online brokers who offer discount commission fees. Individual stocks can also carry high levels of risk. This can

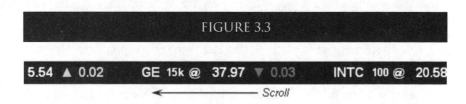

FIGURE 3.3

5.54 ▲ 0.02   GE 15k @ 37.97 ▼ 0.03   INTC 100 @ 20.58

←——————— Scroll

A STOCK TICKER REPRESENTING THE LAST SALE, QUANTITY OF THE
SALE AND THE NET CHANGE IN DAILY PRICE FOR EACH STOCK
SYMBOL THAT SCROLLS BY.

FIGURE 3.4

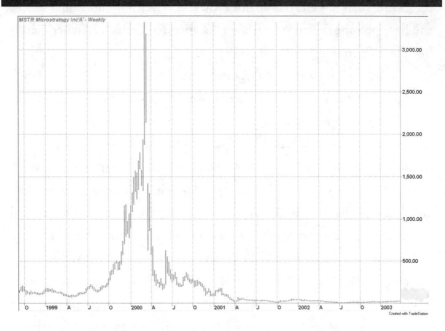

THIS DAILY PRICE CHART OF MICROSTRATEGY INC. SHOWS A DRAMATIC PRICE DROP FROM $3,330.00 PER SHARE ON 3/10/00 TO JUST $4.40 PER SHARE ON 7/26/02. (CREATED WITH TRADESTATION)

be illustrated most vividly during the late 1990s when the stock market was making a significant rally with the popularity of technology stocks. This boom created a wave of hysteria that brought online trading to the forefront of the American financial landscape. What had long been the sole domain of institutional and professional traders working at the exchanges had become accessible to anyone who had a computer and a funded trading account. Many aspiring traders quit their jobs with the intentions of making millions of dollars trading the stock market.

The stock market craze was short lived, and by 2001 many prospective day traders had lost huge amounts of money during the subsequent fall. One such tech stock, Microstrategy, shown in Figure 3.4, fell from just over $3,300 per share to about $4. The wild speculative investing was over and the stock market settled. While retail investing and trading continue to shape the face of the stock market, corporate scandals and increased market competition have created an atmosphere requiring much more caution. It should be noted that once you own shares of an individual stock, it is possible for that company to go bankrupt and for the stock to lose all of its value. This may leave investors holding onto shares of a stock that they cannot sell simply because no one else wants to buy them. This is an example of what is meant by risk in the stock market.

While stocks still offer opportunities to the retail trader, there are many other trading instruments that may be better suited to modern active trading. Although most of these instruments are based on the stock market, they may offer fewer restrictions, have greater liquidity and may require less research than trading individual stocks. In the following sections of this chapter, we will discuss many of these instruments and how they can be used in building a trading plan.

STOCK MARKET INDICES

It is important to understand the relationship of stock indices to the overall market. Stock indices, also known as cash indices, are collections of stocks that are tracked and combined into a statistic that can be used to represent the strength of an exchange, trading sector, or similar market capitalization. While market capitalization refers to the amount of money that it would take to buy every share of an individual stock, there are hundreds of different indices that are used around the world, and are calculated and maintained by various institutions. These cash indices may contain anywhere from 30 to over 6,700 individual stocks and can provide us with an important method of gauging the movement of the overall market. The three major cash indices for the US financial markets are the Dow-Jones Industrial Average Index, the NASDAQ Composite Index, and the Standard and Poor's 500 Index (or S&P 500).

The Dow-Jones Industrial Average Index, commonly abbreviated DJIA, is composed of 30 of the largest and most liquid stocks in the world, primarily from the NYSE. A price-weighted average is used to calculate the index, which simply adds the prices of the 30 stocks and divides by a predetermined divisor. The Dow has become the most well-known cash index in the world.

The NASDAQ Composite Index, abbreviated NAS, consists of over 4,800 stocks and represents the strength of the overall NASDAQ exchange. Although this cash index is often confused with the NASDAQ-100 Index, which is composed only of the top 100 non-financial NASDAQ companies, the NASDAQ Composite Index is an important metric for gauging the overall NASDAQ marketplace. This is a capitalization-weighted index, meaning that price fluctuations in larger companies have a bigger effect on the index than the same price fluctuation in a smaller company.

The S&P 500 Index, or SPX, is a capitalization-weighted index that tracks a combination of 500 large-cap stocks. A committee decides which 500 stocks to include in this versatile index. The S&P 500 is often used

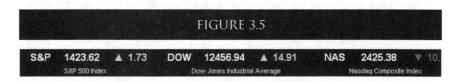

FIGURE 3.5

| S&P | 1423.62 | ▲ 1.73 | DOW | 12456.94 | ▲ 14.91 | NAS | 2425.38 | ▼ 10. |
| | S&P 500 Index | | | Dow Jones Industrial Average | | | Nasdaq Composite Index | |

THIS TICKER SHOWS THE LEVELS OF THE MAJOR US CASH INDICES SHOWING THEIR CURRENT VALUES AND DAILY NET CHANGE.

FIGURE 3.6

Index	Extremely Bearish	Bearish	Neutral	Bullish	Extremely Bullish
Dow Jones Industrial Average (Daily Change)	-75 or Lower	-75 to -35	35 to -35	35 to 75	75 or Higher
Nasdaq Compsite Index (Daily Change)	-20 or Lower	-20 to -15	15 to -15	15 to 20	20 or Higher

THE DIFFERENT LEVELS OF DAILY CHANGE FOR TWO MAJOR CASH INDICES, AND THE CORRESPONDING MARKET SENTIMENT.

to gauge the trend and strength of the overall US financial markets and is an important reference used by individual traders and money managers to track their comparative performance.

The daily change in these cash indices is often used to point out the strength or weakness in the broad market on any given day. Most news networks run a continuous ticker with the major cash indices throughout the day. The up or down arrows shown in Figure 3.5 indicate the current intraday direction of these cash indices. As these numbers get larger and the direction of multiple cash indices coincide, they can show strong trends in the overall market. Figure 3.6 illustrates the general market sentiment as the daily changes in the DJIA and the NAS achieve different levels. For example, if the DJIA is down more than 75 points from the previous day's trading session, it indicates an extremely bearish market sentiment; if the NAS is up more than 20 points from the previous day's trading session, it indicates an extremely bullish market sentiment.

While a single number represents each of these indices, there is no way to actually trade a stock index without owning shares of every component stock in that index. Since it is not practical for most of us to buy and sell shares of 500 different stocks in order to trade the S&P 500 index, there are many different funds, futures contracts, and other investment products based on these important stock indices. We will look at many of these in detail, as they can be important tools for traders.

EXCHANGE TRADED FUNDS

Exchange traded funds, or ETFs, have become a popular trading instrument among both traders and investors. ETFs trade like an individual stock but represent the strength of an entire index instead of a single company. Originally introduced by the AMEX in 1993, ETFs represent the holdings of many different individual stocks. The most popular ETFs follow the major US stock indices and include the NASDAQ 100 Trust Shares or "cubes" (QQQQ) that follows the Nasdaq-100; the Standard and Poor's Depository Receipts or "spiders" (SPY) that follows the S&P 500; the iShares Russell 2000 Index (IWM); and DIAMONDS Trust or

FIGURE 3.7

Symbol	Description	Index ETF is Based on	Exchange	Price per Share (as of 1/1/07)	Average Trading Volume* (shares)
QQQQ	Nasdaq-100 Trust Ser 1	Nasdaq 100	NASDAQ	$43.18	106,767,731
SPY	S&P Dep. Receipts	S&P 500	AMEX	$141.67	65,802,068
IWM	iShares Russell 2000 Index Tr.	Russell 2000	AMEX	$78.19	46,257,628
DIA	Diamonds Trust, Series 1	Dow Jones Industrial	AMEX	$124.60	7,047,810

A COMPARISON OF POPULAR EXCHANGE TRADED FUNDS.

"Diamonds" (DIA) that follows the Dow Jones Industrial Average. Figure 3.7 shows a comparison of these popular ETFs.

ETFs have many distinct advantages for retail traders, including the ability to control risk through diversification. This simply means that having stock in many individual companies offsets some of the risks involved in trading one individual stock. Given the worst-case scenario of a company in which you own stock going bankrupt, an ETF would not lose its entire value, and thus, gives you an element of protection. Another advantage to trading ETFs is liquidity; this can be most easily seen through the tight bid-ask spreads and high volume. The ETFs mentioned above typically trade with very high volume, as seen in the bid and ask sizes on the Level 2 screen in Figure 3.8. Notice that there are over 25,000 shares available at the bid size and about 3,000 at the ask (with a bid size of 17,000 next in line), and with an extremely tight spread of only one cent. This high liquidity within this ETF means that it is easy to enter or exit a position.

FIGURE 3.8

Symbol	Bid Tick	Bid	Ask	Last	Trd Size	Net Chg	Vol Tot
SPY	⇑	141.40	141.41	141.40	100	0.03	32,273,400

ID	Bid	Size	Time	ID	Ask	Size	Time
NYSE	141.40	1000	11:25:43 AM	CINN#	141.41	600	11:25:44 AM
NASD	141.40	2400	11:25:48 AM	ARCX#	141.41	100	11:25:46 AM
CINN#	141.40	2600	11:25:48 AM	NASD	141.41	600	11:25:48 AM
ARCX#	141.40	19700	11:25:52 AM	AMEX	141.41	1700	11:25:50 AM
AMEX	141.37	2200	11:25:34 AM	NYSE	141.41	100	11:25:52 AM
CBOE	141.10	15000	11:25:33 AM	CBOE	141.69	17000	11:25:30 AM
CHXE	137.84	100	09:30:52 AM	CHXE	143.90	100	09:30:46 AM

THIS LEVEL 2 SCREEN OF THE STANDARD AND POOR'S DEPOSITORY RECEIPTS (SPY) SHOWS THE LARGE VOLUME IN THE SIZE OF BOTH THE BID AND ASK LEVELS OF AN ETF. (CREATED WITH TRADESTATION)

An additional advantage to trading ETFs is that there is no uptick rule on short sales. Short selling is the opposite of traditional buying and selling of an instrument with the intention of profiting from a rising value (also known as a long trade). Short selling (or selling short) means selling first and buying later in the hopes of profiting from the falling price of an instrument, and is described in greater detail in Chapter 6—Placing Trades. While many brokers offer a list of individual stocks that can be used in short selling, there is a well-known rule that only allows short sales on an uptick in the stock's price. ETFs do not have this restriction and traders can go short just as easily as they can go long.

ETFs can provide good opportunities for trading; and, due to their popularity, just about every online broker now offers access to them. ETFs have also become widely accepted with longer-term investors and, in many cases, are taking the place of more traditional mutual funds.

The Futures Market

Futures Exchanges

The futures market began in the US around 1850 as a means of trading commodities (such as corn, cotton, and wheat). This type of market provided a method for farmers to get the money necessary for planting and harvesting their crops and, in turn, the farmers agreed to sell their produce when it was harvested at a particular price. This type of a contract still provides farmers and buyers with a level of protection. Farmers can plan on the future sale of crops; buyers can plan on the future purchase of goods. Futures (commodities and financial instruments) are traded in units known as contracts and do not have a tangible value since the underlying commodity may not yet exist.

Unlike stocks, futures contracts are not issued but are formed when one party buys a contract (takes a long position) from another party who sells a contract (takes a short position). The number of contracts that traders are long must equal the number of contracts that traders are short. Futures trading always takes place through the exchange, and the exchange becomes the counterparty for all trades.

Futures are traded on many different exchanges with each exchange typically specializing in a particular type of commodity. The two primary futures exchanges are the Chicago Mercantile Exchange Group (CME Group) and the New York Mercantile Exchange (NYMEX). The CME Group concentrates primarily on agricultural products, interest rates, and financial futures, while the NYMEX specializes in petroleum products and metals. It should be noted that the CME Group is the result of the recent merger between the Chicago Mercantile Exchange (CME) and the Chicago Board of Trade (CBOT).

While a bit more complex than the stock market, it is important to understand the dynamics of futures markets because they provide many unique opportunities for short-term trading. Futures contracts state the price that will be paid on a date in the future, known as the contract month and year, in which the contract is set to expire (usually the third Friday of the expiration month). No more trading can occur after the expiration date, and the contract will be settled. At this point, plans are made for delivery of the commodity or a cash settlement. Since futures trades are always projected forward there may be multiple contracts for the same commodity or instrument being traded simultaneously but with different contract months. Typically, it is the closest contract month that has the greatest liquidity and is most actively traded. In addition, some futures will have a rollover date in which the liquidity switches from one contact to another. Traders must use the correct futures symbols, as shown

FIGURE 3.9

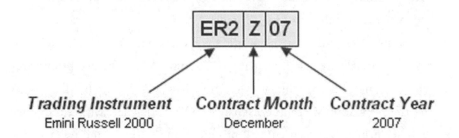

Trading Instrument   **Contract Month**   **Contract Year**
Emini Russell 2000   December   2007

FUTURES SYMBOLS MUST INCLUDE THE FUTURES TRADING INSTRUMENT SYMBOL, THE CONTRACT MONTH, AND THE CONTRACT YEAR.

FIGURE 3.10

January	February	March	April	May	June
F	G	H	J	K	M
July	August	September	October	November	December
N	Q	U	V	X	Z

A DECODER FOR FUTURES CONTRACT MONTHS.

in Figure 3.9, as the contract month and year will periodically change. A symbol that defines a specific futures contract has three parts: the instrument symbol (typically a two to four letter and/or number combination), the contract month (a special one-letter code), and the contract year (the last two digits of the year). Figure 3.10 shows the letter code for each futures month.

Similar to stock market trading, futures have a bid and an ask price. These values do not represent the amount of money that you must pay, rather a value that is relative to the commodity or financial product that is being traded. While the minimum price fluctuation of stocks is typically $.01, futures contracts use ticks to represent the minimum price movements, and this value will differ for each commodity or financial instrument.

The market depth for futures is typically displayed as a price ladder instead of the Level 2 screen used to analyze stocks, and is shown in Figure 3.11. This price ladder displays the current price, bid, ask, and market depth as a series of vertical cells. In this case, the last price appears in black with the size to the left of the price, and shows that one contract sold for 1421.50, with 237 contracts at the inside bid of 1421.50 and 80 contracts at the inside ask at 1421.75. This type of display may also be used to enter orders or manage trades and is described in detail in Chapter 6—Placing Trades.

Similar to ETFs, all futures contracts can be instantly shorted and, as mentioned above, every long position must be matched with a short. Possibly the biggest advantage for trading futures, however, is the amount of leverage that a trader has access to. Unlike stocks and ETFs, futures traders do not need to front all of the money for the futures contact that they are buying or selling. Therefore, the margin (borrowing) requirements in a futures account is significantly less and allows futures traders to use

FIGURE 3.11

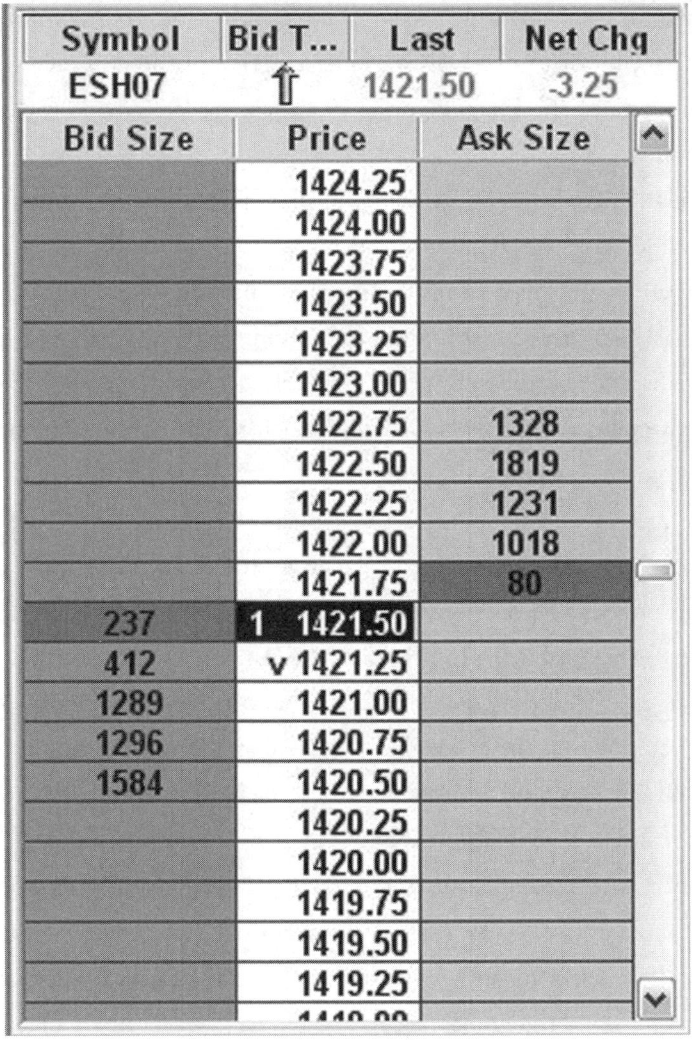

Symbol	Bid T...	Last	Net Chg
ESH07	⇑	1421.50	-3.25

Bid Size	Price	Ask Size
	1424.25	
	1424.00	
	1423.75	
	1423.50	
	1423.25	
	1423.00	
	1422.75	1328
	1422.50	1819
	1422.25	1231
	1422.00	1018
	1421.75	80
237	1 1421.50	
412	v 1421.25	
1289	1421.00	
1296	1420.75	
1584	1420.50	
	1420.25	
	1420.00	
	1419.75	
	1419.50	
	1419.25	
	1419.00	

THIS PRICE LADDER SHOWS THE MARKET DEPTH FOR THE E-MINI S&P 500 MARCH 2007 FUTURES CONTRACT. (CREATED WITH TRADESTATION) large amounts of leverage. Although over leveraging is something to be avoided, responsibly used leverage can allow futures traders to generate greater profit using less initial capital (but keep in mind this can also generate greater losses).

STOCK INDEX FUTURES

Although the futures markets began primarily as a means to sell commodities, the first stock index futures contract began trading in 1982. Since its inception, stock index futures have taken off to become some of the most actively traded instruments in the world. There are currently full-sized futures contracts based on seven major indices, with the largest being on the S&P 500. Much like ETFs, stock index future contracts allow traders to buy and sell the strength of an entire cash index without having to own every individual stock.

Stock index futures tend to track closely the cash indices on which they are based, but with slight deviation. This deviation between the futures and cash indices is known as the premium and often occurs when trader sentiment is bullish or bearish. As traders develop a positive bias and expect higher stock prices, they will buy index futures, pushing the futures price above the cash index, or at a premium. As traders anticipate lower stock prices, the opposite will occur, bringing the futures price below the cash index.

While stock index futures trade in much the same manner as any other futures contact, they must be settled in cash (since they are not based on an actual commodity). Unlike traditional futures contracts, stock index futures trade both during daytime exchange trading hours and after hours on electronic networks. Each stock index future trades on a multiple of the underlying cash index and has a particular tick value. A full-sized S&P 500 stock index futures contract, for instance, trades at a multiple of

$250 times the index with a minimum tick size of .10, with each full point being valued at $250. If a trader bought a full-sized S&P contract and its value increased by two points, he or she could sell the contract for a $500 profit (less commissions).

E-MINI INDEX FUTURES

Launched in 1997, the E-mini index futures are the smaller cousins of the full-sized stock index futures and trade around-the-clock on all-electronic networks. These extremely liquid trading instruments are much more affordable to smaller investors and traders than the full-sized stock index futures contracts. The E-mini S&P 500 futures contract, for instance, is one-fifth the size of the full-sized S&P 500 futures contract, and has a multiplier of $50 times the index, with each point being valued at $50.

FIGURE 3.12

Symbol	Description	Index ETF is Based on	Size	Months Traded	Minimum Fluctuation	Average Trading Volume* (contracts)
ES	E-mini S&P 500	S&P 500	$50 x Index	H, M, U, Z	.25 = $12.50	1,004,120
NQ	E-mini Nasdaq 100	Nasdaq 100	$20 x Index	H, M, U, Z	.5 = $10.00	281,339
ER2	E-mini Russell 2000 Index	Russell 2000	$100 x Index	H, M, U, Z	.1 = $10.00	164,795
YM	mini-sized Dow Futures ($5)	Dow Jones Industrial	$5 x Index	H, M, U, Z	1 = $5.00	101,130

SPECIFICATIONS FOR E-MINI FUTURES CONTRACTS.

E-minis have become the primary market for many active traders, especially day traders. They offer some distinct advantages over both individual stocks and ETFs. One major advantage is that the all-electronic trading networks provide transparency in the markets as well as a fast and reliable method of placing trades. Transparency means that traders can see exactly which market participants are buying or selling. Since we are somewhat at a disadvantage when trading on exchanges where there are live auctions taking place (and we are not physically on the trading floor), electronic markets level the playing field by offering all participants an equal advantage. Another important benefit to trading the E-mini futures is that the volatility of this market creates excellent potential for profit, while maintaining very tight bid-ask spreads (usually around 1 tick). Figure 3.12 shows the specifications for four of the major financial E-mini contracts.

THE FOREX MARKETS

FOREIGN EXCHANGE

Foreign exchange (forex or FX for short) is another instrument that is popular among today's traders, and is the largest, most liquid financial market in the world. It is the arena where one nation's currency is exchanged for another's. Although currency in some form or another has been around since recorded history, the basis for the forex market may have started in 1875 with the creation of the gold standard monetary system. The idea behind the gold standard was for governments to guarantee the conversion of currency into a specific amount of gold, and vice versa. Essentially, a currency would be backed by gold. During the late nineteenth century, all the major economic countries had established an amount of currency that would be equivalent to an ounce of gold. Eventually, the difference in price between two currencies for an ounce of gold became the exchange rate for those two currencies. This signified the first standardized method of currency exchange in history. Today, currencies need to be exchanged to conduct business and foreign trade. Import/export businesses could not operate without exchanging currencies; individuals who travel internationally must exchange currencies to pay for things in different countries. The global need for currency exchange, the advent of online trading and the ever-increasing level of sophistication in trading technology have all contributed to the growth of the forex markets in recent years.

One of the biggest attractions to forex trading is its stability. With the equivalent of about $1.9 trillion in transactions daily, it is virtually impossible for the forex markets to get pushed around, even by the big players. There is simply so much market depth that one institution would have a difficult time creating a serious impact on the market. For traders, that means that some of the whipsaws characteristic of lesser-traded instruments are not typical in the forex arena.

Another benefit in forex trading is its round-the-clock availability and liquidity. Unlike stocks and futures, the forex market has no physical location and no central exchange, allowing it to operate 24 hours a day. Since forex is a popular trading instrument around the world, it remains active throughout most of the day. As US markets close, other markets in the world open, allowing liquidity nearly 24 hours a day. Traders who are unable to trade during US market hours still have access to liquid instruments after hours with forex.

In addition to its stability and round-the-clock availability, forex is intriguing to individual investors due to its ultra-high leverage. Traders can enter large positions with practically nothing in their trading accounts. For

FIGURE 3.13

EUR / USD		USD / JPY		GBP / USD		USD / CHF	
Bid	Ask	Bid	Ask	Bid	Ask	Bid	Ask
1.3084	1.3087	119.26	119.29	1.9437	1.9441	1.2321	1.2325

THE FOUR "MAJORS" ILLUSTRATE TYPICAL BID-ASK
SPREADS IN FOREX TRADING.

example, traders with $1,000 in their accounts can control a position of $100,000, referred to as having 100:1 leverage. Since daily currency fluctuations in forex are quite small, this leverage is used to amplify the value of potential price moves. As with any leverage or margin, caution should be used.

Forex is always traded in currency pairs. When a currency is quoted, it is done in relation to another currency. The value of one currency is reflected through the value of another. For example, if you want to know the exchange rate between the Euro (EUR) and the US dollar (USD), the quote would be:

EUR/USD = 1.3232

The currency on the left (EUR, in this case) is the base currency; the currency on the right (USD, in this case) is called the quote or counter currency. The value of the base currency is always one unit, and the quoted currency is what that one unit equals in the other currency. In our example:

1 EURO = 1.3232 US DOLLARS

As with most other trading, there is a bid and an ask price in forex. These are in relation to the base currency. When buying (going long) a currency pair, the ask price refers to the amount of quoted currency required to buy one base unit. When selling (going short) a currency pair, the bid price refers to how much of the quoted currency will be obtained when selling one unit of the base currency. The difference between the bid and the ask (the bid-ask spread) is measured in pips (which stands for percentage in point). Forex is typically advertised as "commission free" trading and this spread is where your broker makes a commission (transaction fee). Figure 3.13 shows an example of a forex quote screen, and illustrates the bid-ask spreads typical to the forex markets.

Every forex instrument has its own pip value and a corresponding dollar value for each pip. We can see from Figure 3.14 that when trading the EUR/USD currency pair, the minimum change in price (or pip value)

FIGURE 3.14

Symbol	Description	Terminology	Exchange Rate (as of 1/2/07)	Pip Value (basis point)	Dollar Value of Pip*
EUR/USD	Euro and US Dollar	Euro	1.3232	0.0001	$1.00
USD/JPY	US Dollar and Japanese Yen	Dollar-Yen	118.59	0.01	$0.84
GBP/USD	British Pound and US Dollar	Sterling	1.9649	0.0001	$1.00
USD/CHF	US Dollar and Swiss Franc	Dollar-Swiss	1.2148	0.0001	$0.82

* BASED ON 10,000 UNIT CONTRACT TRADE
SPECIFICATIONS FOR THE "MAJORS" IN THE FOREX ARENA.

is 0.0001, with each pip valued at $1.00 (based on a 10,000 unit contract trade). In other words, a one pip change in value is equivalent to a $1.00 change in price value with this particular contract.

The vast majority of forex trading involves the four "Majors":

- EUR/USD (Euro and US dollar)
- USD/JPY (US dollar and Japanese yen)
- GBP/USD (British pound and US dollar)
- USD/CHF (US dollar and Swiss Franc)

Forex can be traded on the spot market or the futures market. The spot market is the most popular, since it is the underlying asset for the futures market. When people refer to the forex market, they usually are referring to the spot market.

FIGURE 3.15

Symbol	Description	Currency Pair Contract is Based on	Trading Unit	Months Traded	Minimum Fluctuation
ED	EuroFX Futures	EUR/USD	125,000 Euro	H, M, U, Z	.0001 = $12.50
JY	Japanese Yen Futures	USD/JPY	12,500,000 Japanese Yen	H, M, U, Z	.000001 = $12.50
BP	British Pound Futures	GBP/USD	62,500 British Pounds	H, M, U, Z	.0002 = $12.50
SF	Swiss Franc Futures	USD/CHF	125,000 Swiss Francs	H, M, U, Z	.0001 = $12.50

SPECIFICATIONS FOR FOUR OF THE MOST POPULAR FOREX FUTURES MARKETS.

In contrast to the spot market, the futures market does not trade actual currencies. Instead, it deals in contracts that are traded based on a standard size and settlement date in public commodities markets, such as the Chicago Mercantile Exchange Group. Similar to other futures markets, forex futures contracts have specifications such as the contract trading unit, delivery and settlement dates, and minimum price fluctuations, as shown in Figure 3.15.

CHAPTER 4
THE TOOLS OF THE TRADE

TECHNOLOGY AS A TOOL

Throughout this book, we emphasize the two keys to building a successful trading plan: taking a business-like approach to trading and effectively employing technology. Electronic trading has been around for a while, but the tools that are available to modern traders are constantly improving and evolving. This provides traders with faster access to information, more methods of analyzing data, and powerful software that assists in actual trading. Using outdated technology puts a trader at a severe disadvantage; however, old school trading methods (those that are tried and trued) can still be effective, especially when enhanced with current technology. Keep in mind that trading is a competition, and you had better believe that other traders are using top-of the line computers with the fastest internet connections possible, reliable online brokers, and powerful trading software. As with any business, becoming competitive means keeping up with technology.

FIGURE 4.1

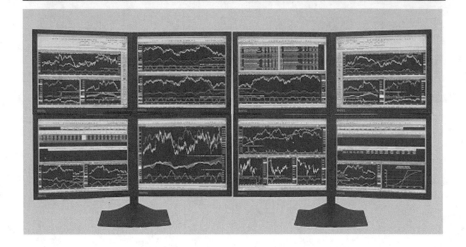

A MONITOR ARRAY FROM TRADINGCOMPUTERS.COM

It wasn't long ago that traders would have to pick up the phone and call their brokers just to make a simple trade. They would then wait while the broker called the order into one of the floor traders who were physically at the exchange that could buy or sell the order. As you can imagine, trading this way was much more time consuming, and in fast moving markets, trades could move away from your entry criteria long before the order was even placed. Fortunately, trading in the 21st century has become much more efficient. Faster computers, high-speed Internet, all-electronic markets, and direct access trading have all helped the independent retail trader. Additional technologies, such as trade automation, innovative market research tools, and the ability to quickly test trading systems on historical data, have given us even more powerful tools to work with. Technology is a definite edge in today's trading world.

FIGURE 4.2

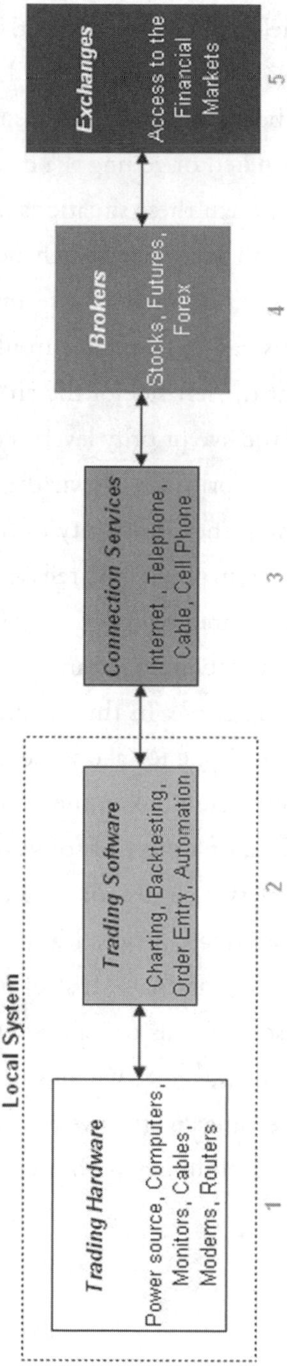

THE CHAIN OF TECHNOLOGY NECESSARY FOR MODERN TRADING.

Technology, nevertheless, is another area that can introduce significant risk to a trading plan. When technology fails or we use it incorrectly, we lose money. Imagine being in a trade and losing your Internet connection, having a software conflict, or getting the dreaded "blue screen" while your computer seizes. Although these situations may occur at some point, we want to be prepared and minimize the chances of losing money due to technology failures. Figure 4.2 shows the technology chain that is typically used in trading. This can be a helpful troubleshooting reference, as we should always begin at the left side of the chain and troubleshoot our way to the right. Each of the five priority levels is critically important since they each affect the higher priorities down the line. In addition, as we move along these five levels, the complexity of troubleshooting increases. Since trading is all about controlling risk, reliability is the key word when choosing and setting up our trading tools.

For most of us, trading technology can be overwhelming at first and can require a steep learning curve. In this chapter we describe why these tools are important, and we hope to take some of the mystery away from deciding which tools to use. Each link in the technological chain, whether it is a computer, a data feed, or a piece of software, calls for a high level of understanding and awareness in order for it to become an effective tool. You should give yourself adequate time to learn and understand each piece of technology in your trading arsenal. Most of us do not enjoy spending hours reading detailed user manuals or waiting on hold for technical support, but it is a reality of the business. We must first master the technology of trading before it can become an effective tool. During the process, keep reminding yourself that, "Technology is your edge."

SETTING UP A TRADING DESK

FIGURE 4.3

A BASIC TRADING DESK SET-UP.

A computer is the primary tool for a trader. This is where all of the action takes place: the market analysis, the testing, and the actual trading. Many new traders expect to simply load some software onto their home computer and start trading. This can be a recipe for disaster. Although today's computers are designed to perform a multitude of tasks, a trading computer needs to be optimized for just one thing: trading! That means, more than anything else, that your trading computer must be reliable. One of the most important decisions you can make regarding your trading computer is to plan to use it just for trading. This should not be a family computer, nor should it have any unnecessary programs running on it. This is a business machine that should stay pure, fast, and healthy.

A trading computer does not need to be a high-end gaming computer (nor should it be). It should be a dependable, multi-core PC with a high-speed Internet connection, capable of running multiple applications and able to support multiple monitors. Although Macintosh computers are reputable and very reliable machines that are less prone to virus attacks, there is currently very little trading software and support available for them. The machine of choice for trading is the PC.

As with any recommendation having to do with computers or software, traders should look for the fastest processor and the maximum amount of memory they can afford. Traders should expect to spend about $1,500 - $3,000 on a trading computer (including monitors). Since computer technology evolves so quickly, we will only give general computer recommendations in an attempt to not outdate this book before it goes to print.

Trading computer recommendations:

- IBM compatible PC with a multi-core processor
- As much Random Access Memory (RAM) as the computer will hold
- Video card capable of handling at least two monitors
- Most current Windows-based operating system
- Updated Antivirus software
- Updated Spyware/Adware detection software
- Uninterruptible Power Supply (UPS) Backup
- At least two flat screen monitors (17 to 21 inch)

- High-speed Internet connection (DSL or Cable)

- No wireless connections such as Internet, keyboard, or mouse

- Absolutely no non-essential software or data such as games, videos, or music

Traders should use at least two monitors for trading: one for charts, and one for order execution. This type of a setup allows a trader to watch both active trades and market action without having to switch back and forth between windows. An example of electronic trading workspaces, or screens, can be seen in Figure 4.4. Setting up efficient workspaces allows for a higher level of situational market awareness. You may need more monitors depending on your trading style or how many charts you plan to analyze. Some professional traders like to have one monitor for each instrument that they trade, as well one for order entry. Multiple monitors

FIGURE 4.4

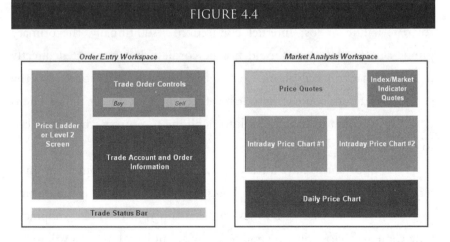

A VISUAL DESCRIPTION OF MULTIPLE TRADING WORKSPACES. A SOFTWARE EXAMPLE OF THESE SCREENS CAN BE SEEN IN FIGURES 4.5 AND 4.7.

require special video cards that accommodate multiple displays. For a basic trading computer, a video card should support a minimum of two monitors; others may be added to the computer later on.

You will also need a high-speed Internet connection. DSL and cable are great options as they are typically fast and reliable. Satellite connections are not good for trading since they often have a lag time (as much as 20 seconds), and can be unreliable during bad weather. Dial-up connections are quite scary for a trader due to the possibility of slow fills and spotty charting from the slower connection speeds. Many traders choose to have both a primary Internet source and a back-up source.

Traders should avoid any wireless connections, as this will add another link in the technology chain that can fail. Wireless Internet, keyboards, speakers, or any other peripheral that is not hardwired into your computer should be avoided. Remember, reliability, speed, and accuracy are the key features of our trading technology.

Trading desks should always have a telephone with each broker's phone number programmed into the speed dial in case of a computer/software failure or lost Internet connection. Additionally, the primary phone at a trading desk should not be cordless, but connected directly to a phone jack. A cell phone is an important back up as sometimes the reason an Internet connection is lost is the same reason your phone line is dead. It is no fun to have to look for a phone to borrow when you need to exit a trade.

It is important to have a back-up battery for your computer—an uninterruptible power supply or UPS. You should have one that is big enough to grow with your trading business and can run your essential equipment long enough to close out any trades. Think about how long you will want/need to keep your computer running if you lose power, and shop for your UPS based on this, as well as the number of inputs you will need.

Many traders like to have a television close to their desks with financial news. This allows traders to keep abreast of any reports or news that may create short-term moves in the market. While it is not recommended to base any trading decisions on news events, most institutions, exchanges, and brokerage houses, have a monitor with CNBC playing in the background.

It is a good idea to understand your whole computer set-up before you begin trading. You should know how to reboot your computer, reconnect your Internet, and check your network connections. It is also important to perform routine maintenance on your computer, including the removal of unnecessary files, defragmenting the hard drive, and installing regular system updates. Later in the book, we will talk about creating a troubleshooting guide and trading binder for your trading desk (Chapter 9—Live Trading).

PURCHASING/LEASING TRADING SOFTWARE

The sheer amount of trading software on the market today is overwhelming. Each claims to do something a little different that will provide you with a unique edge, leading to higher profits. Most software companies offer a free demonstration or a free trial offer to persuade you to use their products. Just trying out all of the software options available could take well over a year. There are also great differences in price between trading software packages, ranging from free to over $10,000. You might be asking yourself, "What exactly can all this software do?" Let's start by focusing on what we absolutely need in trading software.

The first thing we need is a market analysis platform that has the ability to create price charts and display price quotes (shown in Figure 4.5).

For traders, charts are the windows to the world. These charts allow us to see the market action graphically and are what we use to make trading decisions. Market analysis platforms require a data feed into the market that allows access to current information (typically, in less than a second). This type of software permits traders to view the live trading that is occurring during active market hours. It is critically important that the data is accurate, as this will be our primary means of making trading decisions.

Market analysis platforms typically come in two different varieties depending on your style of trading. These include end-of-day (EOD), or

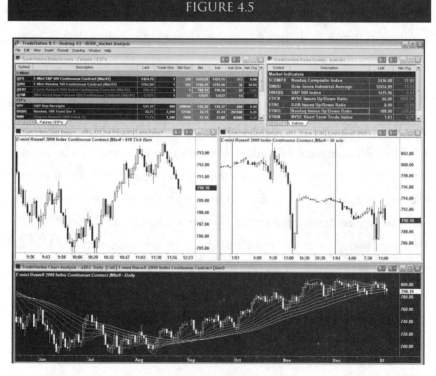

A PROFESSIONAL MARKET ANALYSIS PLATFORM ALLOWS TRADERS TO SEE THE PRICE ACTION AS IT OCCURS. (CREATED WITH TRADESTATION)

delayed data versions, which are geared toward longer-term or position traders who do not require constantly updating data. Shorter-term swing and day traders, however, require real-time data versions (often referred to as the professional version) that will instantly update as conditions change in the market. Traders should look for a market analysis platform that offers the ability to apply technical indicators to their charts, as well as the capability to create custom indicators and studies (these are discussed in Chapter 5—Charting the Market).

The next piece of software that is important in developing a trading plan is a backtesting application. This type of software applies trading systems to historical market conditions and calculates performance characteristics. This type of functionality is often included in a market analysis package and does not require additional software for this task. Testing a trading plan on historical data could be accomplished manually by scrolling back through historic price charts and writing down each possible trade entry and exit; however, using a backtesting application makes this process much more efficient and accurate. This type of software (seen in Figure 4.6) often requires some programming on the part of the user in order to describe the rules of the trading system. Once programmed, the software applies the rules to the market(s) and charting intervals that the user specifies, and automatically calculates the performance results. This software also requires a data feed to provide accurate historical market data. Backtesting applications are an essential component in the design and evaluation of a successful trading plan.

An additional feature that is often available with backtesting software is the ability to automate a system based on the rules developed through backtesting (described in Chapter 6—Placing Trades and Chapter 9—Live Trading).

FIGURE 4.6

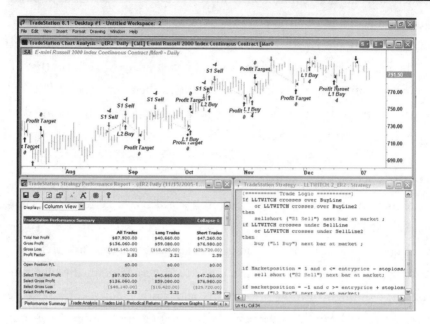

A BACKTESTING APPLICATION ALLOWS TRADERS TO TRY OUT TRADING SYSTEMS ON HISTORICAL DATA. ONCE THE RULES FOR THE SYSTEM ARE PROGRAMMED, PERFORMANCE STATISTICS FROM THAT SYSTEM CAN BE VIEWED AND ANALYZED. (CREATED WITH TRADESTATION)

Finally, traders need an order execution program that allows communication with their brokers, and which places trades in the market (shown in Figure 4.7). Most direct access brokers offer their clients proprietary order execution software as a benefit of funding an active account. This type of software allows traders to specify what markets they wish to trade, how the order is routed to the market, and also how to confirm each trade. Additionally, this software calculates profit and loss (P&L) from each day of trading as well as a host of useful statistics about the performance characteristics of actual trading.

ORDER EXECUTION SOFTWARE ALLOWS TRADERS TO QUICKLY AND
EFFICIENTLY BUY AND SELL STOCKS, FUTURES, OR FOREX.
(CREATED WITH TRADESTATION)

Order execution software should be easy to use but may require some time to gain familiarity with it. For this reason, many brokers offer a trade simulator that allows traders to practice trading with a demo account. It is important to feel comfortable with your order entry software before beginning live trading, as this will become the direct trading tool.

Most high-end trading software packages offer an element of programmability that permits traders to customize their indicators, studies, or strategies to meet specific trading needs. This often requires becoming familiar with the programming language of the trading platform. While most of us do not consider ourselves programmers (nor do we all wish to be), learning the basics can be a very helpful skill. Custom indicators and strategies can be purchased, or they can be programmed for you, typically at a rate of $75.00 - $100.00 per hour. Knowing how to do at least basic programming, however, is a helpful skill and one that is worth the effort in learning.

Market analysis, back testing, and order execution programs are essential; however, additional software exists for other trading specific tasks, such as pre-designed trading systems, custom indicators, trade automation (discussed in Chapter 9—Live Trading), and portfolio analysis. You can think of each individual program as a different tool for your trading toolbox. Each tool takes time to learn, and it is best to first develop a specific need for a tool, instead of purchasing it first and then trying to invent a reason to use it. Keep in mind that no one is going to sell you a magic program that will turn you into a great trader. You are not going to build a mansion just because you bought a $10,000 hammer; you have to first study carpentry and then learn how to use a host of other complementary and important tools.

When deciding on your essential programs, you should focus on reliability, accuracy, and speed. Having a fast data feed is useless unless you are getting accurate data. Similarly, using bad data in historical testing can give you false results when evaluating an overall system.

While some trading software is sold as a complete package, most is leased on a monthly basis. Additionally, it is important to maintain a relationship with the software vendor, as there are often essential upgrades (or newer builds) that are necessary to maintain its greatest functionality. It should be noted that since trading software requires an active data feed to the markets, this will add a regular expense to a trading business. Typically, traders should plan to spend about $100 - $200 a month for reliable software and data subscriptions.

While some software packages offer specific functions, more and more are using an integrated approach and are offering all of the necessary features in one package. Some brokerages even incorporate market analysis, back testing, order execution, and automation for their clients, all in one package.

Below is a list of software companies providing market analysis and backtesting packages:

TradeStation	www.tradestation.com
NinjaTrader	www.ninjatrader.com
Tradecision	www.tradecision.com
eSignal	www.esignal.com
Qcharts	www.qcharts.com
MetaStock	www.metastock.com
Strategy Center	www.cybertrader.com
RealTick	www.realtick.com
Sierra Chart	www.sierrachart.com

CHOOSING A BROKER

Brokers are an essential partner in the trading business and allow us to interact with the markets. As retail traders, we cannot buy or sell directly at the exchanges, and must look to a broker to act as an intermediary, allowing us to trade stocks, futures, or forex. Brokers charge a fee, known as a commission, to execute trades on our behalf. Since the accuracy of trade executions and the cost of commissions directly affect our business, choosing the right broker is an important decision. As with any component in the chain of trading technology, reliability and accuracy are the most important factors.

Stock, futures, and forex brokers are abundant, and you will need to do some research before choosing one. Several trading magazines publish yearly broker guides that offer helpful information. It is a good idea to call a prospective broker and get a feel for the type of customer service you can expect to receive. Things to consider when choosing a broker include:

- Do they service markets that you want to trade (i.e. stocks, futures, or forex)?

- How efficient is their customer service?

- What are their hold times when calling?

- What are their commissions and fees, including "hidden charges"?

- Do you need them to provide a data feed?

- Do they provide their own order execution software, and is there a platform fee?

- Do they provide a simulator to gain familiarity with their software?

- How do they handle order execution?

- What are their margin requirements? (Discussed later in this chapter)

Brokers come in three different varieties: full service, online, and direct access:

FULL SERVICE BROKERS

Full service brokers offer a variety of services in addition to market access. These services include research and advice that may include trading recommendations, retirement planning, or tax tips. In exchange for their services, full service brokers will charge a substantial commission. These include the traditional, well-known brokers such as Merrill Lynch, Smith Barney, or Charles Schwab. Buying or selling through a traditional full service broker usually means calling them over the phone, and is more appropriate for investing rather than trading.

Over the past few years, however, a new type of full service broker has developed which allows for trader-assist system trading. Trader-assist system trading is an alternative form of investing that allows traders to purchase or lease commercial trading systems that are traded and monitored by the broker. These systems can range in style from day to position trading, and once traders agree to the terms of the system, they are in for the ride. Much like traditional full service brokers, these brokers (who may also be money managers) offer research tools and statistics to help traders select a system or portfolio of trading systems. These full-service trader-assist system brokers include:

Robbins Trading Company	www.robbinstrading.com
Attain Capital Management	www.attaincapital.com
Daniels Trading	www.danielstrading.com

ONLINE BROKERS

Online brokers have become increasingly popular with self-directed investors and active traders. Online brokers offer access to the markets via the Internet and charge significantly smaller commissions than do full service brokers. Online brokers typically offer only stock/ETF trading and do not offer advisory services, but may include online or software research tools for their clients. Online trades are executed at much greater speeds than a full service broker, with some even advertising trade executions as fast as a few seconds. While these brokers offer more reasonable commission pricing and trade execution speeds than full service brokers, they are still not the primary brokers for short-term active traders, including day traders. Online brokers do not offer the fastest connection to the markets, their commission pricing is usually not scalable to position sizes (online brokers usually charge a fixed rate for commission, regardless of the amount of shares or contracts), and very few online brokers offer access to the futures and forex markets. Popular online brokers include:

TD Ameritrade	www.tdameritrade.com
E*Trade	www.etrade.com
Scottrade	www.scottrade.com
Fidelity Investments	www.fidelity.com

DIRECT ACCESS BROKERS

Direct access brokers allow clients to trade directly with a stock or futures exchange. This is the broker of choice for active traders who want to focus on speed and order execution. This type of broker may offer stock, futures, and forex access and will not provide research or advisory services, except for a data feed that provides instant price quotes. Direct access brokers offer low commission rates that are based on the amount of trading volume (amount of shares or contracts traded over a time period). These brokers offer some type of order execution software that allows clients to instantly place trades in the market. Some order entry software includes an application program interface, or API, that allows charting or front-end software to be programmed to place or manage trades automatically (this is discussed in Chapter 9—Live Trading).

Using a direct access broker requires learning how to use their software and knowing the specific type of orders that are available. Trading with a direct access broker is serious business and should be approached in that manner. Below is a list of a several direct access stock, futures and forex brokers along with their web addresses:

TradeStation Securities	www.tradestation.com
MB Trading	www.mbtrading.com
Mirus Futures	www.mirusfutures.com
PFG Direct	www.pfgbest.com
Global Futures	www.globalfutures.com
Interactive Brokers	www.interactivebrokers.com
CyberTrader	www.cybertrader.com

Forex Only Brokers:

Forex Capital Markets	www.fxcm.com
Global Forex Trading	www.gftforex.com
CMC Markets	www.cmcmarkets.com

SETTING UP A TRADING ACCOUNT

Establishing a trading account is a decisive step in starting a trading business. There are a few important concepts that new traders must understand when opening a trading account. The first is that stocks, futures, and forex trade differently and often require specific brokers. Make sure you are using the correct broker for the type(s) of instruments that you will be trading. In addition, traders who wish to day trade stocks or ETFs have additional restrictions that require a higher minimum account balance to be maintained (this is discussed later in this section).

Opening a trading account is a relatively easy task. This usually involves filling out a variety of forms, providing your signature to indicate that you acknowledge the risks of self-directed investing, and planning a method of transferring money. Many brokers offer the ability to do this electronically via their websites. Once funded, a trading account can be approved and activated in as little as three business days.

Active traders should not open a cash account, but what is called a margin account. Margin is essentially a loan that a broker gives you towards purchasing stock shares, futures contracts, or foreign currency. The concept of margin varies somewhat between stocks, futures, and forex because stock and forex trading requires purchasing a tangible entity (a part of a company or a foreign currency) and futures trading involves buying or selling a contract whose obligation will be met at an upcoming date. Margin for stock or forex trading is defined as borrowed money, while futures margin is considered an initial deposit, or an "earnest money" deposit, required for entering into a contract. Margin can be a bit confusing at first and should be fully understood before trading begins. Brokers often have their own margin requirements in addition to the guidelines that are already in place for the industry. For stock traders, the Federal Reserve Board sets the minimum allowable margin requirements, known as Regulation T or Reg T. Minimum margin requirements for futures contracts are known as performance bonds and are set by the exchanges that trade those instruments or commodities. Forex margin is established by the individual brokerage. In addition, day trading has much different margin requirements than traditional overnight trading. Figure 4.8 shows the important levels and terminology used to define margin requirements.

FIGURE 4.8

	Minimum Margin	Initial Margin	Maintenance Margin	Margin Call
	Below this amount, brokers cannot allow any trades on margin	Amount that traders must pay with their own money	Minimum amount that must be maintained in a margin account	Occurs if the account falls below the maintenance margin amount
Stocks (Overnight)	$2,000 (Reg-T) Margin Rate: 2:1	50% of the purchase price (Reg-T)	25% of the total market value of all stock shares in the account (Reg-T)	Traders must deposit additional money into the account or close existing positions
Stocks (Pattern Day Trade)	$25,000 (NASD & NYSE) Margin Rate: 4:1	25% of the purchase price (NASD & NYSE)	$25,000 (NASD & NYSE)	Occurs whenever account equity falls below $25,000
Futures (Overnight)	Varies by broker initial account balance, typically $5,000	Varies by contract and date. Example: E-Mini S&P 500 $3,500 per contract (Performance Bond)	Varies by contract and date. Example: E-Mini S&P 500 $2,800 per contract (Performance Bond)	Traders must deposit additional money into the account or close existing positions
Futures (Intraday)	Varies by Broker Initial account balance typically $5,000	Varies by broker. Example: E-mini S&P 500 $1,000 per contract	Varies by broker. Example: E-mini S&P 500 $1,000 per contract	Traders must deposit additional money into the account or close existing positions
Forex	Varies by Broker Initial account balance typically $5,000 Margin Rate: 100:1	Market price / margin rate. Example: EUR/USD (1.3232 * 100,000 units) / 100 margin rate = $1,323.20	Market price / margin rate. Example: EUR/USD (1.3232 * 100,000 units) / 100 margin rate = $1,323.20	Traders must deposit additional money into the account or close existing positions

MARGIN DEFINITIONS AND REQUIREMENTS VARY FOR STOCKS, FUTURES AND FOREX TRADING.

A margin account is necessary for any type of short-term trading activity because a trade must be cleared before the transaction becomes official, and that process can take several days. In the case of intraday trades, traders would have to fund the combined value of every transaction that they make (not just profits or losses, but the complete value) for multiple days in order to continue trading. This would be the retail equivalent of having to buy an entire inventory every time we wanted to profit from the sale of just one item. For this reason, brokers offer margin to provide the ability to place multiple round turn trades while trades are still being cleared. Round turn trades refers to the combination of trades that encompass entering and exiting a position, returning to a neutral, or flat, position.

Another essential reason for margin is the ability to sell short. Selling short requires traders to begin a trade by borrowing shares of a stock or futures contracts from a broker (using margin) and then selling them. Traders must then buy back the stock or futures contracts (known as buying to cover) when they wish to flatten or close out the trade. In this way, traders can profit from falling prices as easily as they can from the traditional buying and selling.

A third and important reason for margin is that it allows traders to use leverage. Leverage allows us to buy more stock shares or futures contracts than we could afford with the money in our trading account alone. Brokers require a minimum amount of funds in an account, or minimum margin, for traders to be able to use margin. A day trading margin rate for stocks, for instance, is four times the account value. This would allow a trader with a $30,000 trading account to buy $120,000 worth of stock (this is also known as buying power). Futures intraday margin requirements for E-mini contracts can be as small as $500 per futures contract, which would allow a trader with a $30,000 trading account to buy up to 60 contracts. When trading with this kind of leverage, a single point move on the E-mini S&P 500 Index would generate a $3,000 profit or loss. Forex brokers typically offer a staggering 100:1 margin that would allow a trader with a $30,000 account to buy up to $3,000,000 in foreign currency.

While leverage can be an important tool used to generate greater profits, as previously stated it can also generate significant losses, and should be used with extreme caution and consideration. Trading close to maximum margin rates is a recipe for disaster, as brokers will monitor the overall value of your account. If, for instance, traders elect to use substantial margin and the underlying stock or futures contract moves against them (loses value), they will be issued a margin call. A margin call is a demand from your broker that you add more money to a trading account in order to meet the minimum margin requirement. If this call is not met, the broker will close out your position (without consulting you) in order to ensure that you can pay back the margin.

The "pattern day trader" (PDT) designation was established in September 2001 by the NASDAQ and NYSE. Pattern day traders are those traders who make four or more day trades within a consecutive five-day period, where the number of day trades accounts for more than 6% of the total trades taken during the time period. This classification requires stock and ETF day traders to maintain minimum account equity of $25,000 at the beginning of each trading day. In addition, if a margin call is issued (referred to by many brokers as a daytrade call), a day trader has five business days to deposit funds before their account is halted from any additional trading. The Securities and Exchange Commission, the government agency that regulates the stock market, enforces these restrictions.

Using a margin account comes with a great responsibility, as traders must know how much money is required at any given time to avoid a margin call. Futures and forex accounts, in particular, allow for substantial leverage and should be watched very carefully. Traders should never use the maximum buying power that a broker will allow, as this could lead to catastrophic losses. It is advised that newer traders begin trading without significantly leveraging their accounts.

CHAPTER 5
CHARTING THE MARKET

Previous chapters in this book have explored the physical dynamics of the market. This chapter will take a detailed look at what supply and demand really look like in an active market. For traders, price charts offer the most accurate view of market action and provide a means of making objective trading decisions. Using high-performance charting techniques, we can quickly spot market inefficiencies that can be exploited for a profit. As traders, the faster we see these opportunities, the more potential there is to make money and minimize losses.

This chapter will also introduce the concept of technical analysis, which is a method of analyzing market movement based on past price and volume activity. Technical analysis is a very important element in short-term trading and trading plan development. We encourage you to spend time researching this very important topic. It should also be noted that while many traders implement only commonly used technical methodology, having a slightly different and more innovative view of the markets can give traders an edge. As we will see in Chapter 7—Developing a Trading Plan, thinking outside the box and using non-traditional methods of technical analysis is a very important skill.

CHART TYPES

BARS AND CANDLESTICKS

Price charts simply provide a history of price and volume over a specified interval. This visual history of price action is only as useful as the data that is used to create it. In other words, a charting platform must have accurate and consistent data in order to provide traders with reliable charts. Since price charts are the primary means of making trading decisions, they must be dependable. Once data is received by a market analysis platform, the prices can be displayed in a variety of charting methods. Price charts are two-dimensional graphs that display price along the vertical axis, and the charting interval along the horizontal axis. In order to have useful price charts, an interval must be selected that reflects a snapshot of the price fluctuations for a given period. For each interval, several data points are recorded that include the price at which the interval began (Open), the highest price during the interval (High), the lowest price during the interval (Low), and the last price during the interval (Close). In addition, the number of shares or contracts traded during the interval (Volume), and the elapsed time for the interval (Time in minutes) are recorded.

The two most common ways to display price data are a bar chart and a candlestick chart, as seen in Figure 5.1. Of these two charting methods, candlestick charts are the most useful to traders (and as such, we will usually refer to candle bars or candlestick charts when discussing charting methods). Originally used in Japan by rice traders over a century ago, candlestick charts are easy to understand and can give valuable information about the direction of price. On a candlestick chart, a single candle bar represents an individual interval. The thin, vertical line is called the wick (or shadow) of the candle, and represents the highest and lowest prices that occurred during the interval. The thicker part of the candle is called the body and represents the opening and closing prices for that candle bar. Candlesticks can be displayed on a chart in a variety of color

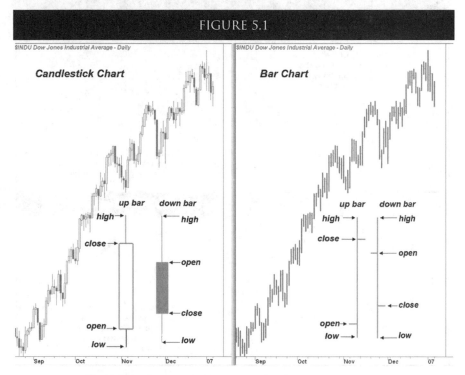

FIGURE 5.1

CANDLESTICK AND BAR CHARTS DISPLAY PRICE ACTION
OVER A GIVEN INTERVAL. (CREATED WITH TRADESTATION)

combinations, or as a single color with open or closed bars. The latter method for displaying candle bars uses an outline of the body for up candles (where the close is higher than the open), and a filled in body for the down candles (where the close is lower than the open). When setting up a candlestick chart, the candles should be big enough to identify quickly and have a sharp contrast from the background of the chart. Chart background colors are best kept neutral to allow good distinction from the individual candle bars. White, gray or black are good colors for chart backgrounds.

FIGURE 5.2

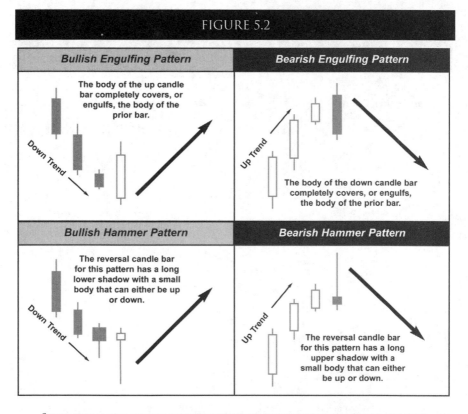

SOME COMMON CANDLESTICK PATTERNS THAT FORM ON PRICE CHARTS.

Another advantage to using candlestick charts is the ability to easily spot price patterns that may be indicative of a reversal or a weakening trend. Patterns can be formed either by comparing the size of the body to the wick on a single candlestick or by comparing several different candlestick bars. While candlestick patterns work great in hindsight (as do many technical market theories), it is important to realize that when used alone, they can be unreliable during real-time trading. This is because patterns can change drastically during the formation of the current candlestick bar. It is only after a candle bar has completely formed (and printed), that a candlestick pattern can be confirmed. For instance, a pattern may clearly form during the day on a daily chart, only to change by the end of the day. This type of pattern recognition is best suited for end of the day (EOD) technical analysis. Additionally, candlestick patterns work best when combined with other technical tools or indicators. Figure 5.2 shows several candlestick reversal patterns that occur regularly in just about every market and interval.

CHART INTERVALS

Choosing a charting interval is an important factor in developing a trading plan, as strategies are often built around a specific chart. In general, bigger chart intervals will represent longer-term styles of trading and vice versa for smaller chart intervals. Chart intervals can be monthly, weekly, daily, or a variety of intraday timeframes. By far, the most common charting interval is the daily chart, where each bar or candlestick represents one day of trading. While this is has become the standard interval, there are many others that can be used in combination with a daily chart to gain a more thorough view of the markets.

Figure 5.3 shows three different charts of the "cubes" (symbol: QQQQ) where the shaded areas are magnified and shown in detail on the next chart to the right. These three charts represent (from left to right) daily, 30-minute and 5-minute chart intervals. While monthly, weekly, or daily interval charts provide insight into the longer-term direction of the market, it is also useful to monitor a variety of intraday charts as well. Much like using a microscope with multiple lenses, traders may use the broad magnifications to find possible trading opportunities, and then increase the lens magnification to pinpoint high-probability trade entries. In general, the more confirmation multiple charts provide for a price move,

FIGURE 5.3

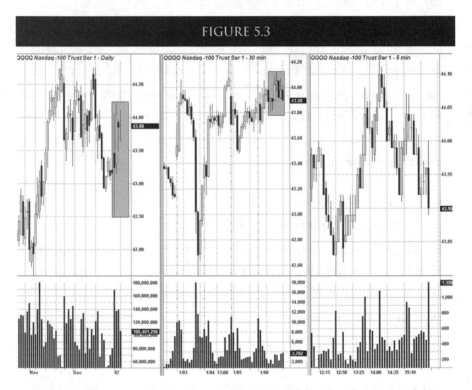

THESE MULTIPLE INTERVAL CHARTS FOR QQQQ PROVIDE A MORE DETAILED PICTURE THAN CAN A SINGLE CHART. THE TRADING ACTIVITY SHADED IN THE LEFT CHART IS EXPANDED AS THE ENTIRE MIDDLE CHART; THE TRADING ACTIVITY SHADED IN THE MIDDLE CHART IS EXPANDED AS THE ENTIRE RIGHT CHART. (CREATED WITH TRADESTATION)

the better the chance of a successful trade. Once in a trade, monitoring a longer interval price chart can help traders stay in a trend longer and avoid getting pushed out by short-term price fluctuations or pullbacks.

Intraday charts are particularly important to swing and day traders. Intraday chart intervals can be either time- or data-based. Time-based price charts are specified in minutes, such as 60-, 15- or 5-minute charts. This type of chart prints a new bar or candlestick at the end of every time interval. On a 5-minute chart, for instance, a candle bar will print at 9:35, 9:40, 9:45...and continue until the close of the market, regardless of the volume or trading activity. Traders can select any minute interval for the charts, and often a volume graph is added along the bottom of charts to show the amount of trading activity that is contributing to a price move. Typically, price moves that occur under higher volume tend to be more enduring.

During the past few years, as retail trading technology continues to evolve, charting platforms and data providers have begun to offer new types of intraday charting intervals. These new methods include the option of viewing price action from various data intervals instead of just time. While many traders continue to use time-based charts in everyday trading, tick and volume charts offer some unique advantages. Unlike time-based charts, tick and volume charts close at the end of a specified data interval, regardless of the time that has elapsed. Tick charts plot prices for a specific number of transactions, while volume charts record the prices for a specified number of contracts or shares traded. Tick and volume charts often paint a more accurate picture of market action by showing the effect that the number of transactions or the volume has on price. This means that you can quickly determine the amount of trading taking place just by glancing at a chart and noting the number of candle bars during a particular time interval. As more candle bars print within a set amount of time, it indicates an increase in volatility, as seen in Figure

FIGURE 5.4

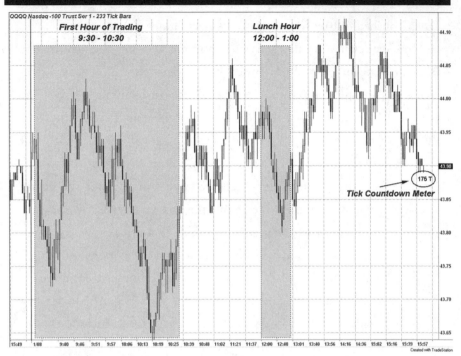

THIS 233- TICK CHART OF QQQQ SHOWS TWO SHADED AREAS, EACH REPRE-
SENTING ONE HOUR OF TRADING BUT WITH SIGNIFICANTLY MORE VOLUME
DURING THE OPENING HOUR THAN THE LUNCH HOUR. THE NUMBER ON THE
RIGHT IS A COUNTDOWN METER THAT REPRESENTS THE NUMBER OF TRANSAC-
TIONS REMAINING IN THE CURRENT BAR. (CREATED WITH TRADESTATION)

5.4. Additionally, tick and volume charts can point out important price
patterns that time-based charts often miss.

When using tick or volume chart intervals, a countdown meter (sometimes referred to as a timer) should be used to display the number of ticks
or volume remaining in the current candle bar. A countdown meter acts
like a price display on a gas pump, and allows traders to judge the flow of
the market by the speed at which the price scrolls by. Since tick and vol-

ume charts are not time-based, a candle bar could take just a few seconds or several hours to print. Looking inside a bar using a countdown meter allows a trader to gain instantaneous information about the condition of the market. As the countdown meter progresses faster, this can be used to gauge the immediate increase in market activity without having to wait for several bars to print. Conversely, when the numbers on the countdown meter advance slowly, or are not moving at all, it can help traders stay out of a sluggish market. The EasyLanguage code for a countdown meter can be found in Appendix B.

At this point, you might be wondering what intraday chart intervals are the most useful. This is much like declaring your favorite color; it will differ for everyone. For time-based intraday charts, common minute intervals include:

> 1, 3, 5, 10, 15, 30, 60 AND 120 –
> MINUTE INTERVALS

For data-based intervals where there is practically an unlimited number of options, Fibonacci numbers can be used to establish rough guidelines for tick and volume intervals. Fibonacci numbers are a series of numbers that begin with zero and one, and are calculated by adding the two most recent numbers to get the next:

> 0, 1, 1, 2, 3, 5, 8, 13, 21, 34, 55, 89, 144, 233, 377,
> 610, 987, 1597, 2584...

Originally described by Leonardo of Pisa (otherwise known as Fibonacci) in 1200, Fibonacci numbers and ratios appear frequently in nature, geometry, and statistics. Most importantly, traders love them and find uses for these numbers whenever possible. Whether or not they accurately describe or predict the behavior of the markets, they provide a good statistical relationship on which to base a tick or volume interval. Traders should try to find intervals that accurately portray the intraday dynamics of their chosen markets. Additionally, instruments that trade at significantly different volumes may require different chart intervals.

SUPPORT AND RESISTANCE

Now that we have described some methods of viewing price action using charts, we will look at techniques for determining what price might do next. This is where it starts to get fun! The fundamental concept behind this type of technical analysis is support and resistance. Support can be thought of as a floor under trading prices, while resistance is the ceiling. As prices move outside of these levels it is much like climbing onto the roof of a house, and what was once resistance (the ceiling) now becomes support (the roof). Prices often will hover around these areas (known as consolidation) before moving up or down to the next level. These levels of support and resistance occur on every chart interval with larger chart intervals having the most significance. Figure 5.5 illustrates how price resistance can often become support.

This concept is important in developing high probability trading plans. Once traders can pinpoint an area of support or resistance, it provides valuable potential trade entry or exit points. Regardless of trading methodology, these trade entry or exit points can provide relatively low risk trades with a positive +R advantage. This is because as price reaches a point of support or resistance, it will typically do one of two things: bounce back towards its original direction or break out from the direc-

FIGURE 5.5

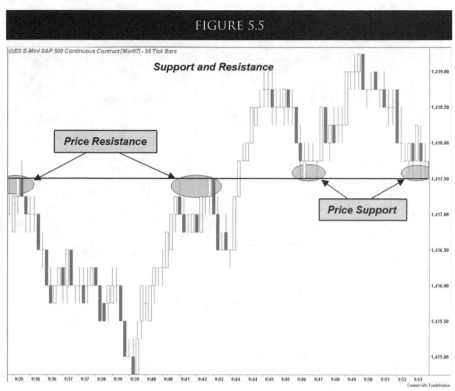

THIS 55-TICK CHART OF THE E-MINI S&P SHOWS HOW RESISTANCE AND SUP-
PORT LEVELS MAY BE DETERMINED. (CREATED WITH TRADESTATION)

tion from which it came (often dynamically). In either event, traders can "bet" on a direction and quickly determine whether they are correct. If price moves immediately against them, they can use a protective stop loss to take a small loss on the trade. However, if price moves in the intended direction, this often leads to a move that is many times greater than the stop loss amount, yielding the all-important +R advantage.

This type of trade planning can be seen in Figure 5.6 where an area of resistance is used to plan a long trade entry. Since price has recently found support just below the trade entry point, this recent support level makes

FIGURE 5.6

RESISTANCE AND SUPPORT LEVELS CAN BE USED TO PLAN TRADE
ENTRIES AND EXITS. (CREATED WITH TRADESTATION)

a good location to place a stop loss. Longer-term resistance levels can be used to plan the location of a profit target. Comparing the distance between the trade entry and the profit target, with the distance between the trade entry and the stop loss allows traders to determine a +R advantage, and verify if the trade is worth the risk.

TRENDLINES

Possibly the easiest way to spot trends and see support and resistance on a price chart is with trendlines. Trendlines are straight lines drawn on

FIGURE 5.7

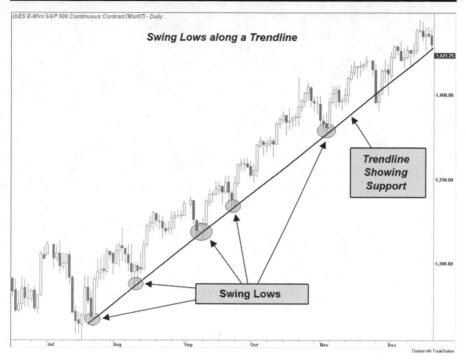

@ES E-Mini S&P 500 Continuous Contract [Mar07] - Daily

Swing Lows along a Trendline

1,423.75

1,400.00

**Trendline
Showing
Support**

1,350.00

1,300.00

Swing Lows

Jul   Aug   Sep   Oct   Nov   Dec

Created with TradeStation

SWING LOWS ARE USED TO DRAW A TRENDLINE SHOWING
LEVELS OF SUPPORT. (CREATED WITH TRADESTATION)

a chart connecting points where prior price reversals have occurred, typically projecting into the future, or the right-hand edge of the screen. These
price reversals may be easily spotted by zooming out on a price chart and
looking for Vs or inverted Vs. These turning points are known as swing
lows and swing highs and can be seen in Figures 5.7 and 5.8, respectively.

Trendlines may be angled (known as up or down trendlines) or horizontal. The slope of a trendline defines the phase of price movement for
the chart, and is shown in Figure 5.9. Markets are said to be in an up
trending phase (or an uptrend) if they are making higher swing highs and

FIGURE 5.8

@ES E-Mini S&P 500 Continuous Contract [Mar07] - Daily

Swing Highs along a Trendline

Swing Highs

Trendline Showing Resistance

Created with TradeStation

SWING HIGHS ARE USED TO DRAW A TRENDLINE SHOWING LEVELS
OF RESISTANCE. (CREATED WITH TRADESTATION)

higher swing lows. This would mean that two trendlines could be drawn
(one connecting swing highs, one for swing lows) that would both have
positive slopes and form an upward channel of price movement. Likewise,
a down trending phase occurs when prices form lower swing lows and
lower swing highs, creating trendlines with negative slopes and a downward price channel. Horizontal trendlines (with a slope at or very close to
0) show periods of consolidation or market indecision where price is not
trending at all.

FIGURE 5.9

@ER2 E-mini Russell 2000 Index Continuous Contract | Mar0 - Daily

Down Trend: Prices are making lower swing lows and lower swing highs

Price Channels

Up Trend: Prices are making higher swing lows and higher swing highs

690.00
680.00
670.00
660.00
650.00
640.00
630.00
620.00
610.00

Mar   Apr   May   Jun   Jul
Created with TradeStation

PRICES MAY BE IN AN UP OR DOWN TREND DEPENDING ON THE SLOPE OF THE TRENDLINES. (CREATED WITH TRADESTATION)

Trendlines are an important tool for analyzing market activity and can provide another method of making trading decisions. As price returns to a trendline (known as testing the trendline) it will do one of two things: bounce back in the direction from which it came, or break through. Trendlines become stronger as more swing highs or swing lows occur along the same line. In many cases, stronger trendlines provide greater opportunities for big price moves resulting from a break of the trend line. These moves can by very dynamic and are referred to as price breakouts. It should be noted that trendlines often show one key price that is acting as strong support or resistance. Price levels that create support or resistance on multiple chart intervals (especially longer-term chart intervals) can pinpoint important trading opportunities.

Drawing trendlines takes practice and can be somewhat subjective. As a starting point, trendlines are most significant if at least three swing highs or lows fall along the same line. In many cases, price will make three swings in a particular direction before either breaking through or falling back. Also, not all highs and lows need to be considered when drawing

FIGURE 5.10

A CHANNEL BREAKOUT CAN BE SEEN ON THIS 1597-TICK CHART
OF THE E-MINI RUSSELL. (CREATED WITH TRADESTATION)

trendlines since a rouge transaction (a sale significantly above or below the market) can create an artificial swing.

Similar to candlestick patterns, trendlines form patterns that may be indicative of large price moves. These patterns often trigger during a candle bar and are easily spotted by comparing the price of the current candle bar with the trendlines drawn on a chart. These patterns include a channel breakout and a triangle pattern. A channel breakout can be seen in Figure 5.10 and is formed as price breaks out above or below two parallel (or close

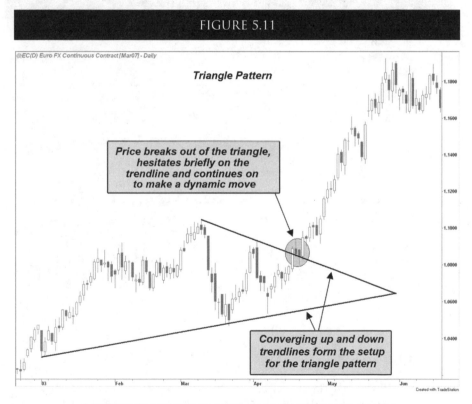

FIGURE 5.11

A TRIANGLE PATTERN FORMED ON A DAILY CHART OF THE EURO FX FUTURES. (CREATED WITH TRADESTATION)

to parallel) trendlines. The price will often stall at the trendline that it broke out from before making a dynamic move away from the price channel.

A triangle pattern (sometimes referred to as a pennant) can be seen in Figure 5.11 and forms as two trendlines converge, creating a consistently smaller support and resistance channel in which price can move. On intraday charts, at least one of these trendlines should trace back to the previous day's trading session forming this setup. Similar to a channel breakout, once price breaks one of these trendlines, it may stall slightly at

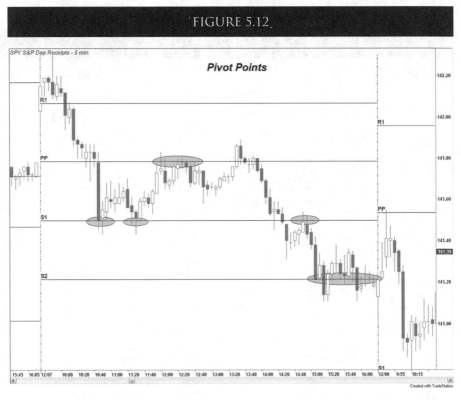

PIVOT POINTS PROJECT LINES OF POTENTIAL SUPPORT AND
RESISTANCE; PRICE WILL OFTEN STALL OR REVERSE AS IT REACHES
THESE POINTS. (CREATED WITH TRADESTATION)

the triangle formation before making a much larger move. Triangle patterns can be a powerful precursor to fast, explosive price moves.

PIVOT POINTS

Pivot points are a type of technical indicator calculated by averaging a previous day's high, low, and closing prices. Originally calculated by floor traders and market makers at the exchanges, pivots points project support and resistance levels. Pivot points are overlaid on a price chart and appear as horizontal lines that correspond to a price value, as illustrated in Figure 5.12. Unlike trendlines, pivot points attempt to predict areas of support and resistance based on prior trading sessions. Pivots are only effective at establishing areas of support and resistance if price respects them by stalling at that pivot level. Without this confirmation, pivots do not have much use and they should be disregarded.

While there are many variations of pivot point calculations available, the concept behind interpreting these points is similar. Pivot points can be used to determine the overall market trend by tracking price movements above or below the central pivot point, as described in Figure 5.13. As price crosses over the central pivot, it indicates a bullish market, favoring long positions, while crosses below the pivot favor short positions. Additionally, prices often hover between the first support and resistance levels (S1 and R1), but breakouts from these levels typically lead to moves that reach the next subsequent level of support or resistance. Pivot points are a helpful tool for creating profit targets and stop points.

While the basic formula for calculating pivot points is given below, also included is a pivot point calculation that uses the Fibonacci relationship. This type of pivot can be a helpful tool when applied to the index and forex markets. The EasyLanguage code for these pivots is included in Appendix B.

FIGURE 5.13

Pivot Level	Description
R2	Second Resistance Level - Price often finds strong initial resistance at this level. Prices that break above this level often maintain their upward momentum and continue higher throughout the day.
R1	First Resistance Level - Prices often find resistance at this level and bounce back toward the pivot. Once this level is broken, however, it often leads to an upward move to the R2 level.
PIVOT	Average of previous day's High, Low, and Close. Strong support or resistance. As price moves above this line, wait to buy until after a pullback. If price moves below this line, look to go short after a rally. Price will often oscillate above and below this line until a range is formed and a breakout occurs. Potential profit targets are R1 and S1.
S1	First Support Level - Prices often find support at this level and bounce back toward the pivot. Once this level is broken, however, it often leads to a fast, downward move to the S2 level.
S2	Second Support Level - Price often finds strong initial support a this level. Prices that fall below this level often maintain their downward momentum and continue lower throughout the day.

THIS CHART DESCRIBES THE FIVE MAJOR PIVOT POINTS. IT SHOULD BE NOTED THAT PIVOT POINT CALCULATIONS ARE RELATIVE TO THE SESSION TIMES IN WHICH TRADING OCCURS. FOR INSTANCE, PIVOT POINTS FOR STOCKS ARE CALCULATED DURING THE NORMAL EXCHANGE HOURS OF 9:30 AM AND 4:00 PM EST, BUT FUTURES AND FOREX TRADE DURING MULTIPLE SESSION TIMES. IN THE CASE OF E-MINI FUTURES AND FOREX, PIVOT POINTS SHOULD BE CALCULATED BASED ON THE SPECIFIC SESSION TIMES IN WHICH MOST TRADING TAKES PLACE.

Standard Pivot Point Calculation	Fibonacci Pivot Points
R3 = Pivot + R2 - S2	R3 = Pivot + ((H – L) * 1.000)
R2 = Pivot + R1 - S1	R2 = Pivot + ((H – L) * 0.618)
R1 = (Pivot * 2) - L	R1 = Pivot + ((H – L) * 0.382)
Pivot = (H + L + C) / 3	Pivot = (H + L + C) / 3
S1 = (Pivot * 2) - H	S1 = Pivot - ((H – L) * 0.382)
S2 = Pivot - R1 + S1	S2 = Pivot - ((H – L) * 0.618)
S3 = Pivot - R2 + S2	S3 = Pivot - ((H – L) * 1.000)

H = Yesterday's High, L = Yesterday's Low, C = Yesterday's Close

FIBONACCI RETRACEMENTS

Earlier in this chapter, we introduced Fibonacci numbers. Retracements are another application where these numbers have become useful. Fibonacci (Fib) retracements are a method of measuring past price movements in an attempt to make a statistical projection of where price may go. In other words, Fib retracements allow us a way of estimating where future price may find support or resistance.

A retracement refers to the tendency of price to pull back after a strong market move. These retracements occur on every charting interval and occur whenever price makes a big move in a certain direction, reaches a point of exhaustion, and inevitably falls back. While these retracements, or pullbacks, may simply act as speed bumps as price continues in its original direction, they may also initiate a complete reversal in price.

Fib retracements measure the strength of the initial price move by establishing the beginning and end of the price move using the swing highs and lows. Once these points are established, prices are projected that represent different percentages of the original move. This is where Leonardo of Pisa comes in and attempts to establish statistically significant ratios for each of these projections.

The Fibonacci series has special values that keep showing up in unexpected places, such as the logarithmic spiral in a nautilus shell and the double helix of the DNA molecule. An important relationship in this series is known as the "Golden Section" or 0.618, which describes the ratio between any Fib number and the next highest Fib number (after the first

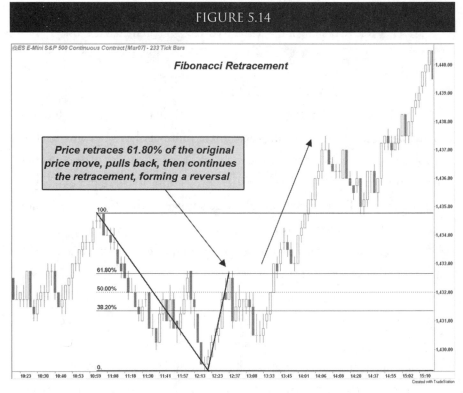

FIGURE 5.14

A FIB RETRACEMENT APPLIED TO A 233-TICK CHART OF THE E-MINI S&P SHOWS A DEEP PULLBACK (61.8%) THAT EVENTUALLY BECOMES A REVERSAL. (CREATED WITH TRADESTATION)

four calculations). This ratio is rounded into a percentage and subtracted from 100% to create the key Fib levels of 61.8% and 38.2%. A 50% retracement level is also added to form the final indicator, which typically appears as a series of horizontal lines projected to the right hand side of a price chart. In this way, each of these Fib levels can be directly related to a price.

A popular application of Fib retracements is to estimate the strength of a pullback by comparing the amount of the retracement to the Fib ra-

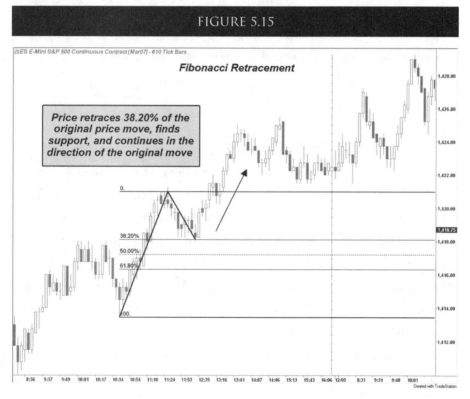

FIGURE 5.15

A FIB RETRACEMENT IS APPLIED TO A 610-TICK CHART OF THE E-MINI
S & P SHOWING A SHALLOW PULLBACK (38.2%) THAT CONTINUES ALONG ITS
ORIGINAL DIRECTION. (CREATED WITH TRADESTATION)

tios, shown in Figures 5.14 and 5.15. Retracements that only reach 38.2% of their original trend show a strong tendency to maintain the trend and go higher, while a 61.8% retracement often leads to a change in direction. 50% retracements display market indecision that can go either way. In addition, prices regularly find support or resistance when approaching the 0% or 100% levels as these swing highs and lows established the initial trend.

Another application of Fib retracements is to apply them to multiple chart intervals (of the same instrument). As instances of price levels coincide from different charts, known as Fib clusters, they often become key areas of support or resistance. While the jury may still be out on why Fib ratios are so effective, it is remarkable how often they point out important relationships in the market.

TECHNICAL INDICATORS

Technical indicators are tools that can offer traders a unique perspective on market activity. An indicator can either be overlaid on an existing price chart or displayed on its own, usually just below the main price chart. Most technical indicators are based on price action over a given amount of time (or look back period), and use some type of mathematical calculation or formula to determine a value. Technical indicators are used to help traders quickly determine optimal market conditions, and can be useful tools in developing the rules of a trading plan.

It is up to each trader to determine how best to use technical indicators, as well as which indicator(s) to use. Most commonly available indicators allow for an element of customizing simply by changing input values. Input values are user-defined variables (such as look back period or type

FIGURE 5.16

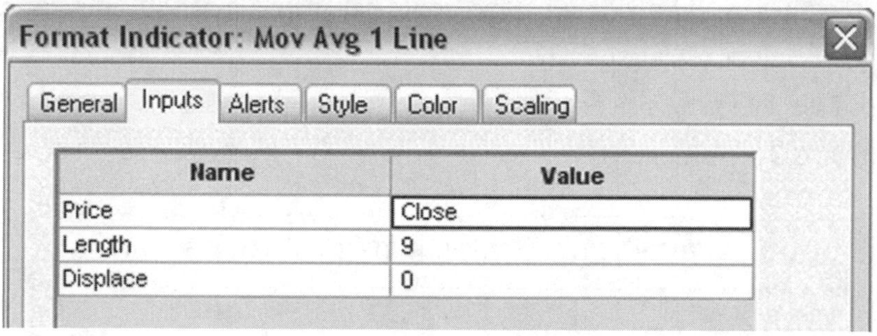

Format Indicator: Mov Avg 1 Line   ☒

| General | Inputs | Alerts | Style | Color | Scaling |

Name	Value
Price	Close
Length	9
Displace	0

AN INDICATOR FORMATTING WINDOW IN TRADESTATION FOR
A SIMPLE MOVING AVERAGE DISPLAYS THE VALUES THAT USERS CAN EASILY
CHANGE. (CREATED WITH TRADESTATION)

of price data) that modify the behavior of an indicator. Changing input values can give an indicator much different values and point out different market conditions. Figure 5.16 shows a window in a charting platform used to modify an indicator's input values.

MOVING AVERAGES

A moving average provides a reference for where price has been and in which direction it is moving. It is used to smooth out market "noise" and help determine if price is in trend. The most basic moving average is known as a simple moving average (SMA) and is formed by adding up a specified number of past prices and dividing by the total number of prices. Two input values are used in the calculation of a SMA: the type of price (high, low, open or close) and the look back period. The type of price that is most commonly used to calculate a SMA is closing price, while the look back period refers to the number of price bars that will be used in the averaging. Shorter periods react faster to changes in the price, while longer-term periods are slower to react. For example, adding the last five closing prices and dividing by five would calculate a 5-period simple moving average of closing price:

Last 5 closing prices (in order of least to most recent): 707.8, 707.1, 707.0, 707.3, 707.1

$$SMA = (707.8 + 707.1 + 707.0 + 707.3 + 707.1) / 5 = 707.26$$

An exponential moving average, or EMA, is similar to a SMA but gives more value (or weight) to the most recent prices in the look back period. This type of moving average reacts faster to recent price moves and follows price action more closely. The following formula shows the calculation for an EMA and a sample calculation for a 5-period EMA using the above data:

EMA = P + [K x (C - P)]

C = CURRENT PRICE

P = PREVIOUS PERIOD'S EMA (A SMA IS USED FOR THE FIRST PERIOD'S CALCULATION)

K = SMOOTHING CONSTANT = 2 / (1 + N)

N = NUMBER OF PERIODS FOR THE EMA

EMA = ((707.8 * 1) + (707.1 * 2) + (707.0 * 3) + (707.3*4) + (707.1 * 5)) / 15 = 707.18

A double exponential moving average (DEMA) is a combination of a single exponential moving average and the second derivative of the exponential moving average (that is, an EMA of another EMA). A DEMA provides a faster method of averaging that tracks price much more closely than either an EMA or SMA. This can be a valuable tool for intraday analysis where having less lag between the price and an indicator is important. A DEMA can be derived using the following formula:

> DEMA = (2 * EMA) - (N PERIOD EMA OF EMA)
> N = NUMBER OF PERIODS FOR THE EMA

THE EASYLANGUAGE CODE FOR THE DEMA IS INCLUDED IN APPENDIX B.

Figure 5.17 shows a comparison of the different types of moving averages applied to a daily chart. While each of these moving averages uses the same 20-period input value of closing prices, they follow the price action much differently. Each of these averages may be useful given the right situation, with the DEMA leading the pack as the fastest to respond to price moves.

While moving averages provide the basis for many other types of indicators, they have several trading applications by themselves. Applying multiple moving averages to a price chart can be used to provide a reference for trending activity. Many traders use moving average crossovers as signals to enter or exit a trade. As with any technical indicator, traders must use proper settings (such as look back periods) for the specific markets in which they are used. An example of a moving average crossover system is shown on the chart in Figure 5.18. Typically, when the smaller period moving average (20-period DEMA) crosses above the larger (50-period DEMA), a buying opportunity exists. Conversely, as the smaller moving average crosses below the larger, an opportunity for selling exists.

FIGURE 5.17

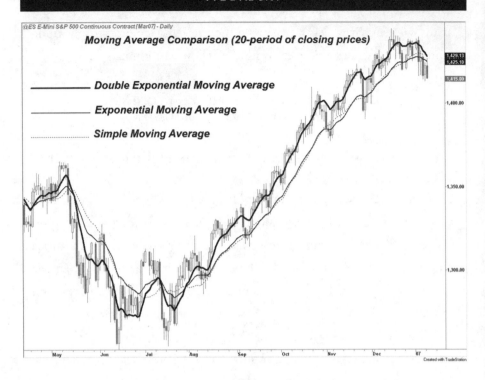

A COMPARISON OF THREE DIFFERENT TYPES OF MOVING AVERAGES: SMA, EMA, AND DEMA. (CREATED WITH TRADESTATION)

PRICE BANDS

Price bands form a channel that is projected onto a price chart, creating upper and lower lines. This type of technical indicator can help traders find short-term trading opportunities in choppy markets, since prices often bounce back and forth within this channel. As price crosses outside of the price bands, it can signal an opportunity to buy or sell in anticipation of a reversal. Price bands are constructed by adding and subtracting a distance from a moving average. This distance often considers volatility. In

FIGURE 5.18

A MOVING AVERAGE CROSSOVER SYSTEM USING TWO DEMAS OF DIFFERENT LENGTHS. THE ARROWS REPRESENT CROSSES OF THESE AVERAGES THAT OFTEN LEAD TO THE DEVELOPMENT OF A TREND. (CREATED WITH TRADESTATION)

other words, as larger price swings occur, the distance between the bands becomes greater and, conversely, the bands will constrict during times of consolidation. This concept is shown in Figure 5.19; the arrows represent areas where price has violated the upper or lower band of the Adaptive Price Zone (APZ). The APZ is based on a double smoothed exponential moving average and is calculated using the following formula:

$$\text{APZ Upper Price Band} = B * \text{DEMA of (highs} - \text{lows)} + \text{DEMA}$$
$$\text{APZ Lower Price Band} = \text{DEMA} - B * \text{DEMA of (highs} - \text{lows)}$$
$$B = \text{Band Distance}$$

Applying the APZ to a chart shows that the majority of price action tends to stay within the upper and lower bands of the zone. When price deviates significantly from its average and crosses out of the zone, there is an almost magnetic attraction back towards the statistical average. This

FIGURE 5.19

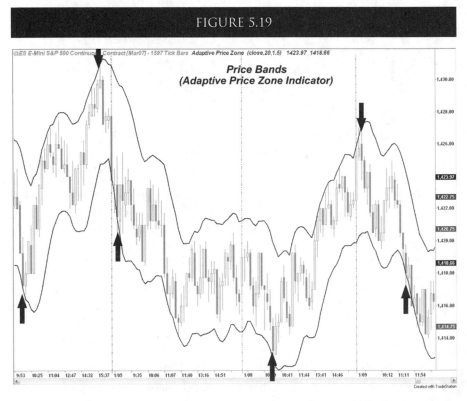

PRICE BANDS APPLIED TO A 1597-TICK CHART OF THE E-MINI S&P. THE ARROWS REPRESENT POINTS WHERE PRICE HAS MOVED ABOVE THE UPPER CHANNEL OR BELOW THE LOWER CHANNEL. (CREATED WITH TRADESTATION)

statistical "pull" forms the basis of the APZ's logic. It is important to note that this pull only becomes significant in markets that are not actively trending.

OSCILLATORS

Oscillator is a general term for technical indicators that bounce between two extreme values. This type of indicator is displayed separately from the underlying price chart. Oscillators can point out areas where

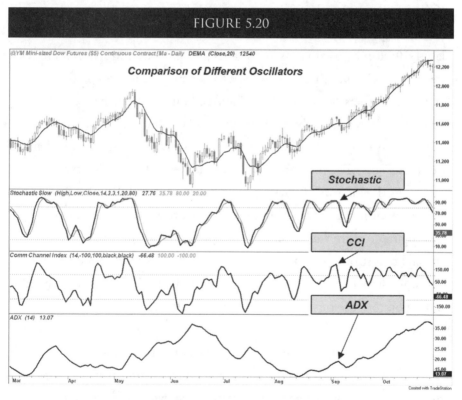

A COMPARISON OF DIFFERENT OSCILLATORS (STOCHASTIC, CCI, AND ADX) SHOWS HOW THEY REACT DIFFERENTLY TO PRICE MOVEMENTS. (CREATED WITH TRADESTATION)

turning points are likely to occur, and can be seen in Figure 5.20. As the value of an oscillator approaches a level close to its upper extreme, the value is referred to as becoming overbought. Values that approach the lower extreme are called oversold.

While moving averages are important tools used in spotting trends, oscillators are most useful in markets where a trading range has been established. Oscillators can help locate turning points and estimate when price may be forming a new trend. While there are many types of oscillators, the average directional index (ADX), stochastic and commodity channel index (CCI) oscillators are three of the most useful.

The ADX oscillator, originally developed by J. Welles Wilder in the late 1970s, can be used to assess the strength of a trend. Much like a moving average, this indicator uses a look back period to determine the speed at which it reacts to the market. The ADX can fluctuate between 0 and 100, although readings above 60 are uncommon. Indicator readings below 25 show a weak trend, while levels above 40 indicate a strong trend has occurred. The ADX may be most useful, however, to identify changes in trends. As the indicator values move from below 25 to above, for instance, it may confirm that price is breaking out of a range and a trend could be developing. An even more important application of the ADX is to spot the end of a strong price move. As the ADX returns from higher levels to below 45, it signifies the end of a short-term trend. This is often a good indication to close out a trade if you have been lucky enough to ride the initial trend. This often provides a method of getting out of a trade near the high or low of the price move (the maximum profit potential).

A stochastic oscillator measures momentum by comparing the current price of a trading instrument to its price range over a specified look back period. Developed by George C. Lane in the late 1950s, this indicator has become a popular trading tool. The stochastic looks inside candle bars to determine whether prices are closing nearer their highs or their lows, and can be seen in Figure 5.21. As price closes near the high of the candle bar, it indicates an up-trending market, while prices closing near the low show a downtrend. The main value is known as %K and is the faster of the two lines comprising the stochastic oscillator. A simple moving average is used to smooth the value of %K to produce the slower of the two lines, called %D. Both lines can be displayed on the indicator. In addition, horizontal lines are often used to illustrate upper and lower thresholds where price is considered overbought or oversold, respectively. The basic formula for a stochastic oscillator is as follows:

$$\%K = 100 \times [(C - L_N) / (H_N - L_N)]$$
$$C = \text{THE MOST RECENT CLOSING PRICE}$$

$$N = \text{LOOK BACK PERIOD}$$
$$L_N = \text{THE LOW OF THE N PREVIOUS PRICE BARS}$$
$$H_N = \text{THE HIGHEST PRICE TRADED DURING THE SAME}$$
$$N \text{ PERIOD.}$$

One effective method of applying stochastics to an intraday market is to use two separate stochastics of different periods on the same chart. This provides a short-term (13-, 5-period) and long-term (60-, 20-period) view of price oscillation. As both of these indicators reach an overbought or oversold area (above 70 or below 30, respectively) and begin to change direction, this indicates that price may be ready to reverse. Once in overbought or oversold territory, a short-term stochastic cross of one of these thresholds provides a good trade entry opportunity, as shown in Figure 5.21.

The CCI oscillator, created by Donald Lambert in 1980, was originally developed to identify cyclical turns in commodities. The CCI provides a method of gauging momentum by measuring the position of price in

FIGURE 5.21

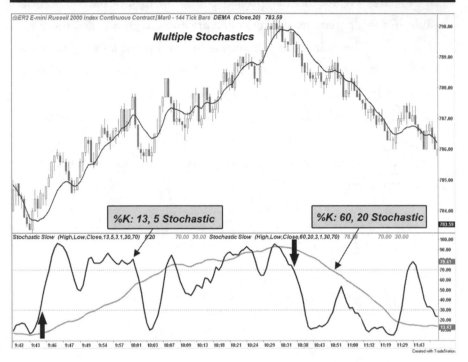

A MULTIPLE STOCHASTIC MAY LEAD TO POWERFUL PRICE MOVES. THE
ARROWS SHOW THE SHORT-TERM STOCHASTIC CROSSING A THRESHOLD LINE
WHILE THE LONGER-TERM STOCHASTIC TURNS AWAY FROM OVERBOUGHT
OR OVERSOLD TERRITORY. (CREATED WITH TRADESTATION)

relation to its moving average. Essentially, the CCI takes the wavy moving average line on a price chart, straightens it out, and plots the closing price relative to this line. While this indicator often zigzags around zero, values greater than 100 are considered overbought and values less than –100 are thought to be oversold. The steps for calculating the indicator are as follows:

1. Calculate the last period's **Typical Price (TP)** = (high + low + close) / 3.

2. Calculate a 14-period **simple moving average (SMA) of TP.**

3. Calculate the **Mean Deviation** by calculating the absolute value of the difference between the last period's SMA and the TP for each of the past look back periods. Add all of these absolute values together and divide by the look back period to find the Mean Deviation.

4. The final step is to apply the TP, the SMA, the Mean Deviation, and a Constant (.015) to the following formula:

$$CCI = (TP - SMA) / [(0.015) \times (\text{MEAN DEVIATION})]$$

The CCI has become a popular technical indicator among traders, and some have found unique ways of trading with this oscillator. The CCI tends to react quickly to price moves, as seen by its often-jagged shape. One method of applying the CCI involves a longer-term CCI (50-period) applied to a daily chart, as illustrated in Figure 5.22. In this instance, the direction of the CCI can be used to establish the formation of a new trend. When the CCI value is above zero it shows strength that can lead to a new uptrend, while CCI values below zero may illustrate a new downtrend. Once a new trend has been established, price will often pull back towards the zero-line creating an opportunity to buy or sell in anticipation of a continuing trend.

CUSTOM INDICATORS

Custom indicators can take many forms and must be programmed for or imported into a market analysis platform. These indicators may com-

FIGURE 5.22

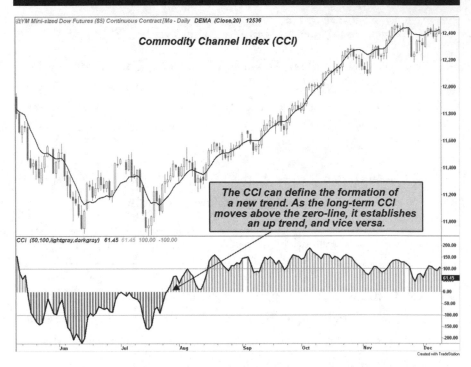

@YM Mini-sized Dow Futures ($5) Continuous Contract[Ma - Daily DEMA (Close,20) 12536

Commodity Channel Index (CCI)

The CCI can define the formation of a new trend. As the long-term CCI moves above the zero-line, it establishes an up trend, and vice versa.

CCI (50,100,lightgray,darkgray) 61.45 61.45 100.00 -100.00

THE CCI CAN DEFINE THE FORMATION OF A NEW TREND; AS THE
CCI MOVES ABOVE THE ZERO-LINE, IT ESTABLISHES AN UPTREND, AND
VICE VERSA. (CREATED WITH TRADESTATION)

pare different data functions, look for unique market conditions, or com-
bine several different conditions into trading signals. This type of technical
indicator allows traders to identify specific market conditions, instead of
being limited to preprogrammed indicators that are included in charting
platforms. Custom indicators can be purchased from independent developers or developed and programmed on your own. Custom indicators
can also provide a method of quickly checking the validity of a trading

FIGURE 5.23

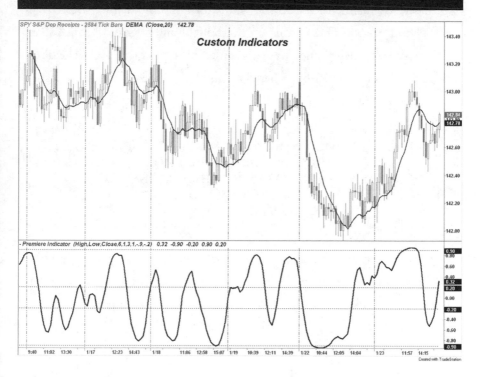

THIS CUSTOM INDICATOR, CALLED PREMIERE STOCHASTIC, PROVIDES
AN EXTREMELY FAST REACTION TO PRICE SWINGS. (CREATED WITH TRADESTATION)

idea. Building a trading plan using a custom indicator can streamline the development process since it is relatively easy to convert most custom indicators into a testable trading system.

The boundaries in designing custom indicators are limitless. Figure 5.23 shows a useful custom indicator that provides a double exponentially smoothed stochastic that is normalized on a scale from -1 to 1. The Premiere Stochastic indicator can be applied to any charting interval providing an extremely fast reaction to price swings. Unlike a traditional stochastic oscillator, there are four individual threshold lines located at +/- 0.9 and +/- 0.2. These create an overbought and oversold "zone" that can be used to determine the early onset of a price reversal. The Premiere Stochastic calculation is based on the %K of the 8-period stochastic as follows:

PREMIERE STOCHASTIC = (EXPONENTIAL VALUE (S) – 1) /
(EXPONENTIAL VALUE (S) + 1)
S = 5 PERIOD DOUBLE SMOOTHED EXPONENTIAL
EMA ((%K – 50) * .1)
%K = 8- PERIOD STOCHASTIC

Premiere indicator readings above 0.2 represent strong price moves favoring long positions, while readings below –0.2 show weakness. The TradeStation code for this indicator is included in Appendix B.

DATA INDICATORS

Data indicators can be used to gauge the current strength or weakness in the markets. Unlike the other technical indicators mentioned in this chapter, data indicators are not based on the price activity of just one trading instrument or symbol. A data indicator is a separate index of short-term trading data that is collected from the major stock indices. Similar to using the net change of the Dow Jones Industrial Average or the Nasdaq Composite as mentioned in Chapter 3—Getting to Know the Modern Markets, market indicators offer statistics about the current condition of the overall market.

FIGURE 5.24

Data Indicator	High Reversal Probability	Extremely Bearish	Bearish	Neutral	Bullish	Extremely Bullish	High Reversal Probability
TRIN - NYSE Traders Index (Actual Value)	1.30 or Higher	1.30 to 1.15	1.15 to 1.00	1.00 to 0.85	0.85 to 0.70	0.70 to 0.55	0.55 or Lower
TICK - NYSE Tick Index (Actual Value)	-1000 or Lower	-600 to -1000	-300 to -600	300 to -300	300 to 600	600 to 1000	1000 or Higher
TIKQ - Nasdaq Tick Index (Actual Value)	-600 or Lower	-475 to -600	-300 to -475	300 to -300	300 to 475	475 to 600	600 or Higher
TIKI - Dow Jones Tick Index (Actual Value)	-25 or Lower	-20 to -25	-12 to -20	12 to -12	12 to 20	20 to 25	25 or Higher

DATA INDICATORS THAT CAN BE USED TO GAUGE THE INTRADAY MARKET.

For day traders in particular, getting to know the behavior of these data indicators both individually and as a collective can provide a good reference for favorable market activity. Since traders can easily reach information overload by looking at too much data, data indicators should only be used in the background. Traders only need to glance at them to observe the overall market direction. Figure 5.24 lists four of the most important data indicators used to monitor the intraday direction of the US equities markets along with some guidelines on how to evaluate each. It should be noted that none of these indicators is predictive, but rather a reaction to what has already happened in the market.

TICK

The TICK stands for the NYSE Tick Index and can be a powerful gauge of intraday market activity. The TICK measures the difference in stocks currently trading positively on an uptick and stocks currently trading negatively on a downtick. An uptick occurs whenever a transaction goes from a lower price value to a higher one, and vice versa for a downtick. The TICK is an extremely fast indicator that can instantly determine whether the broad market is predominantly buying or selling.

Figure 5.25 shows a chart of the TICK. TICK readings between +/- 300 generally represent a neutral market (shown by the shaded area on the chart). Since normal price fluctuations between the bid and the ask price create upticks and downticks without any significant increase or decrease in a stock's value, it is not until the TICK reads +/- 600 that a significant market move has occurred. Values in the extreme levels of the index (+/- 1000) show an overbought or oversold market and often signal reversals.

While the TICK monitors the Big Board stocks, there are several other "tick" indicators that monitor other important stock indices. These include the "TIKQ" that represents the Nasdaq composite Tick Index, and

FIGURE 5.25

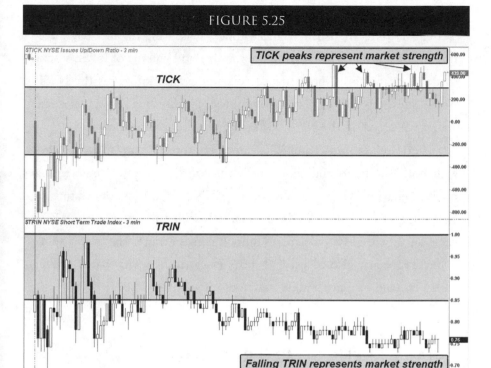

THE NYSE TICK INDEX AND THE NYSE TRIN INDEX APPLIED TO A
3-MINUTE CHART. THE SHADED AREAS REPRESENT NEUTRAL MARKET
ACTIVITY. (CREATED WITH TRADESTATION)

the "TIKI" that represents the Dow Jones Tick Index. These data indicators can provide an important snapshot of their respective markets. Each
tick indicator has a different relative value since each is based on the number of stocks in its particular index. A TIKI reading of −30, for instance,
would mean that all 30 stocks in the Dow Jones Industrial Average were
on a downtick, and would be an extremely bearish signal.

TRIN

The TRIN is the NYSE Trader's Index, measuring the intraday direction of the market by comparing the number and volume of NYSE stocks that are advancing to those that are declining. Also known as the NYSE Arms Index, the TRIN can be a helpful tool for assessing market strength, and, while based on the NYSE, often represents the broad market.

The TRIN, seen in Figure 5.25, can be interpreted many different ways with both the trend and the actual value of the indicator representing market behavior. When the value of the TRIN is increasing, or creating an uptrend, there is an increase in the market's selling pressure; as the TRIN value steadily decreases, it signifies more buying pressure. The overall value of the TRIN may also be used to show a bearish bias with values greater than 1.00, and becomes bullish as values move below –0.08.

CHART SETUPS FOR TRADING

So far in this chapter we have discussed some important components for technical analysis. Now it is time to put it all together and make sense of it. At this point, you may be wondering which components are critical to setting up basic charts for market analysis. Keep in mind that this is an ongoing process and you may find that you are frequently adding and removing indicators throughout your research. Below are some guidelines to setting up an effective charting workspace:

- Use contrasting colors to make charts and quotes stand out

- Place indicators in the same location, using the same color on all charts

- Use the same (neutral) background color for all active charts of the same symbol

- Use multiple monitors (at least two); one for order entry and the rest for charts

- Use bold fonts whenever possible

- Don't overload your screen with information (more than five open windows on the same screen gets confusing)

- Keep chart indicators to a minimum (don't put unnecessary indicators on your charts)

- Once you have a chart setup that you are happy with, save it and take a screenshot for backup purposes (setting up a desktop can be time consuming)

DAILY CHART SETUP

On a daily price chart, each candle bar represents one trading day. For most short-term traders, this points out key price levels that should be noted for more detailed analysis. It is often helpful to have several longer-term moving averages on the chart, such as 20-, 50-, and 200-period SMAs. These averages often provide areas of support or resistance that are commonly used by longer-term investors as well. A volume graph is another useful addition to this chart since daily price bars do not reflect the amount of daily trading activity that has taken place. This helps gauge the amount of buying or selling occurring within a price move, as greater volume often leads to moves that are more dynamic.

One way to interpret this information is if the SMAs stack up (in order of size) and volume is above its average, a trend has been established. The example in Figure 5.26 shows in mid-June the 20-period SMA was below the 50 SMA, which was below the 200 SMA. Once the volume exceeded the daily average, this confirmed a bearish market phase. Alternatively, in mid-October the 20 SMA was above the 50 SMA, which was above the 200

FIGURE 5.26

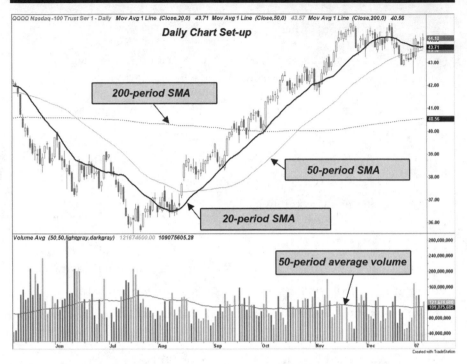

A DAILY CHART OF THE QQQQs ALONG WITH A VOLUME CHART
AND KEY MOVING AVERAGES. THE LINE ON THE VOLUME CHART REPRESENTS A
MOVING AVERAGE OF VOLUME. (CREATED WITH TRADESTATION)

SMA during higher than average volume. This confirmed an uptrend in the market. While this provides a very basic method of analyzing the daily market, it can become a starting point for more innovative methods.

PRICE QUOTES

Knowing the current price of other trading instruments, indices, and data indicators can be an important method for gauging the strength of the overall market, and is shown in Figure 5.27. A market analysis work-

FIGURE 5.27

Symbol	Description	Last	Trade Size	Bid Size	Bid	Ask	Ask Size	Net Chg
E-Minis								
@ES	**E-Mini S&P 500 Continuous Contract [Mar07]**	**1420.50**	1	361	1420.25	1420.50	145	0.00
@NQ	E-Mini Nasdaq 100 Continuous Contract [Mar07]	1809.00	1	8	1809.00	1809.50	43	-1.50
@ER2	E-mini Russell 2000 Index Continuous Contract [Mar07]	782.30	8	2	782.20	782.40	1	-1.00
@YM	Mini-sized Dow Futures ($5) Continuous Contract [Mar07]	12485	1	3	12485	12487	6	2
ETF's								
SPY	**S&P Dep Receipts**	141.05	2,000	100	141.04	141.05	24500	-0.14
QQQQ	Nasdaq -100 Trust Ser 1	44.10	200	300	44.10	44.11	20400	0.22
IWM	iShares Russell 2000 Index Tr	77.10	1,000	2500	77.06	77.12	1500	0.10
DIA	Diamonds Trust, Series 1	124.02	100	1000	123.80	124.15	100	-0.12

Futures / ETF's

Symbol	Description	Last	Net Chg
Market Indicators			
$COMPX	Nasdaq Composite Index	2443.83	5.63
$INDU	Dow Jones Industrial Average	12416.60	-6.89
$INX(D)	S&P 500 Index	1412.11	-0.73
$TICK	NYSE Issues Up/Down Ratio	560.00	173.00
$TIKI	DJIA Issues Up/Down Ratio	-6.00	0.00
$TIKQ	Nasdaq Issues Up/Down Ratio	409.00	-590.00
$TRIN	NYSE Short Term Trade Index	1.57	0.62
$VXB.X(D)	CBOE VIX Futures Underlying	119.10	-0.90

Indicies

A QUOTE SCREEN SHOWING KEY MARKET INDICES AND PRICE INFORMATION FROM WITHIN THE SECTOR. (CREATED WITH TRADESTATION) space should have a quote screen above the price charts with information on other stock, futures or forex prices from within the sector. A sector is simply a group that shares the same industry or market. Since sectors often move together, these intra-market relationships can help point out price moves that may affect the instruments or symbols you are trading. Spotting inefficiencies in other markets, such as very large bid sizes for instance, may create opportunities in the markets you are following.

INTRADAY CHART SETUP

While setting up intraday chart intervals has already been discussed, technical indicators that are applied to intraday charts need to react very quickly. In general, traders should avoid using intraday indicators with large look back periods, and should find technical indicators that respond with little or no lag. The chart in Figure 5.28 includes several technical indicators that are well suited for a fast-paced intraday market. These include the DEMA, stochastic, and the ADX.

FIGURE 5.28

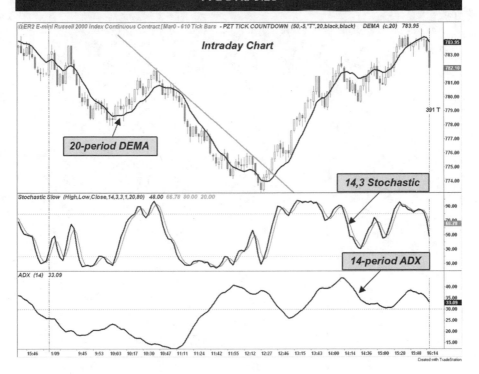

An intraday chart of the E-mini Russell 2000 showing several helpful technical indicators. (Created with TradeStation)

CHAPTER 6
PLACING TRADES

TRADE DYNAMICS

This chapter will explore the important aspects of placing trade orders and using multiple order types. Whenever possible, we'll use examples that show how these orders will look to a screen-based trader. A trade order is the specific instruction that is sent to a broker to enter or exit a trade. Traders often underestimate the importance of using proper trade orders. At first, placing trades may seem remarkably simple: when entry conditions are met, you push the buy button and, conversely, when exit conditions have been met, you push the sell button. This is called trading naked and, while it is possible to trade in this simplified manner, it is not very efficient. Trading naked requires constantly monitoring the market, and opens traders to the risks of missing important trade signals and trading without a protective stop loss.

Another important reason to avoid naked trades is what is known as slippage. Slippage refers to the difference between the price you expect and the price you actually get in a transaction. Since trade orders are filled in the order in which they are received, naked traders are often the last to place their orders and are subject to a greater amount of slippage. Over time, slippage can significantly erode trading profits, and traders should seek to minimize this factor in their trading plans.

In a sharp contrast to naked trading, most professional traders thoroughly plan their trade orders before entering into a position. Examples of this type of order planning can be seen later in this chapter. Modern trading technology allows for a multitude of order types and automation tools that can help traders place trades according to their trading plans, quickly and accurately. Employing the powerful tools that today's brokers and trading software developers offer can help minimize trading errors and reduce slippage. Just knowing when to trade is not enough; successful traders must also know how to trade.

To begin with, trades can be established in two different directions, depending on the anticipation of a rising or falling market. These are known as long and short trades.

LONG TRADES

Long trades are the classic method of buying and selling with the intention of profiting from a rising market. Long trades can be conducted through all brokers and do not necessarily require a margin account (as long as there is enough money in the account to fund the complete transaction). Shown on the daily chart of the QQQQs in Figure 6.1, a long trade begins with buying shares of at a price of 39.50 on September 12th. Once the value of the ETF increases to 43.00 per share, the position is closed by selling on November 7th. Even a small position size, 100 shares for instance, would show a $350 profit from this trade.

POSITION P/L FOR LONG TRADE = (EXIT PRICE
– ENTRY PRICE) * POINT VALUE * POSITION SIZE
= (43.00 – 39.50) * $1 * 100 = $350

Point value defines the dollar value for each point fluctuation of the symbol ($1 for stocks/ETFs; varies by contract for futures and forex).

It should be noted that for a trader to enter this position without the use of margin, it would require at least $3,950 (entry price value * posi-

FIGURE 6.1

A COMPARISON OF A LONG TRADE AND A SHORT TRADE.

tion size) to fund the trade. Had this trade gone the other way and the QQQQs had fallen in price, the trader would be responsible for funding the position loss as well as the initial purchase price.

SHORT TRADES

Short trades, otherwise known as selling short or going short, attempt to profit from the falling price of a market. This is accomplished by borrowing and then selling a stock, futures contract, or foreign currency from a broker. Once price has reached the target level, traders buy back the shares or contracts, called buying to cover. Buying to cover allows traders to replace what was originally borrowed from a broker. The difference in value between the initial sale and the replacement cost is what becomes the profit (or loss) from a short trade.

As a conceptual example, imagine a friend has purchased a new car. After he tells you the price he just paid, you find a dealer who is offering the same new car, but for a significantly lower price (well below the market). Instead of accepting that it is too late to get this deal, you see an opportunity, and ask to borrow your friend's car for the day. You then find a buyer and sell the car at the same price your friend paid for the car. Using the money from this sale, you buy a replacement car from the bargain dealer (at a much lower price than your friend originally paid). At the end of the day, you return a car to your friend, and you make a profit from the short sale. This represents the relationship of your broker (your friend with the car), a falling market (the bargain dealer), and the potential of a short trade (your profit from the transaction).

Trading short positions is an important facet of active trading, and allows traders to take advantage of moves in both up or down markets. While a bit more complex than the standard long trade, it is valuable for traders to be able to profit in both directions. Many traders find that, over time, they are equally comfortable placing short trades as they are long. In many cases, short trades offer faster, more dynamic price drops as market fear, or panic, creates unique trading opportunities.

Short trades, especially in volatile stocks, involve some risks of which traders should be aware. The ultimate risk involved with a long trade (the theoretical worst-case scenario) is that the company could go bankrupt, and the stock would lose its entire value. In this case, the total value of the investment (stock price * position size) would be lost. While this is a worrisome concept, the theoretical risk of a short trade is unlimited. The price of a stock may only fall a finite amount (to zero), but its value may continue to increase indefinitely. Since a short trade begins with a debt that must be eventually repaid, a trader's risk to cover this debt in a short trade is theoretically unlimited. Using proper trading techniques, such as trading with a stop loss, allows traders to manage the risks of a short trade.

Short trading requires a margin account with a broker since the broker must allow you to borrow in order to make this type of transaction. In addition, not all stocks may be available to use for a short trade since your broker must hold shares of these stocks in order for traders to borrow them. In general, ETFs, futures, and forex are the easiest instruments for short trading, as described in Chapter 3—Getting to Know the Modern Markets.

Figure 6.1 shows an example of a successful short trade on the QQQQs where a trade was initiated by selling short on May 11th at a price of 41.25. Then, on July 12th, the trade was closed by buying to cover at a price of 37.00. Using a 100-share example, this trade would have generated a $425 profit.

POSITION P/L FOR SHORT TRADE = (ENTRY PRICE
– EXIT PRICE) * POINT VALUE * POSITION SIZE = (41.25
– 37.00) * $1 * 100 = $425

FIGURE 6.2

AN ORDER ENTRY BAR USED TO PLACE TRADES.

ORDER TYPES

Once a trading account has been established, buying or selling stocks, futures contracts, or foreign currency can be as straightforward as the click of a mouse. Figure 6.2 shows an example of an order entry window for a direct access trading account, displaying a variety of trading options. From a trader's perspective, making a successful trade entails placing the trade order with a broker (clicking buy or sell), getting a confirmation of the trade order, and receiving the final price for the fill. A fill is the completed trade transaction that refers to the action of satisfying the trade order. Just placing a trade order does not guarantee that it will be filled, or if it will be filled at the intended price. This is why it is vital for traders to understand how to correctly place and manage their buy and sell orders.

Before a trade order can be placed, traders must submit the following information:

- Symbol that is being traded

- Position size of the trade

- Duration of the trade order

- Special routing instructions

- Type of trade order

The trade symbol represents the abbreviation for the instrument that is being traded. As described in Chapter 3—Getting to Know the Modern Markets, each trading instrument has a specific symbol that needs to be correctly entered into the order execution software. This symbol defines what is being bought or sold.

The position size or quantity of the trade refers to how many units a trader is buying or selling. Short-term traders often refer to the size of a trade in lots. A lot will vary between markets and refers to a standard minimum position size that a trader would wish to trade. One lot typically represents 100 shares of a stock or ETF, one futures contract, or $10,000 in foreign currency. In addition, forex brokers often use this lot as a standard to define the size of a trade.

The duration of a trade order defines how long an order will remain active in the market (sometimes referred to as time-in-force). Trade orders that will expire at the end of the current trading day are defined as "day" orders. In some cases, traders may wish for an order to remain in the market longer than the current day, or until they decide to remove it. This is known as a "GTC" or good-till-canceled duration and can be useful for trades that span multiple days. Traders should research the types of trade durations that are available, as they will vary from broker to broker.

Routing instructions refers to the ability to choose which exchange can fill an order. While this is not applicable to forex or futures, it can be an important option for stock traders. A typical Level 2 stock screen will show the market participants who are buying and selling. Knowing this information, traders can choose a specific electronic communication network (ECN) to trade with. In addition, many brokers offer an "intelligent" or "smart" order routing system that helps traders find the ECNs that have the greatest liquidity, a good choice if this feature is offered by your broker.

Order types come in three varieties: market, limit, and stop orders.

MARKET ORDERS

A market order is the most basic type of trade order and instructs the broker to buy or sell at the best price currently available. The advantage to using market orders is that a trader is guaranteed to get the trade filled. In other words, if a trader absolutely needs to get into or out of a trade, a market order is the most reliable method of accomplishing this. The down side of using a market order is that this type of order closes the door to any bargaining that could occur to get a better price, and often leads to greater slippage.

It is essential that traders understand when to use a market order. As a guideline, market orders should only be used to enter into a trade when there is good liquidity in the market. Otherwise, the slippage or inability to close out a trade could lead to significant losses. Figure 6.3 illustrates a Level 2 screen of the stock AZZ Incorporated that shows small trading volume with a relatively high, $0.10 bid-ask spread. If a trader were to place a market order to go long 500 shares of this stock, he may be in immediate trouble. While there are 500 shares currently available (in the ask column), only 300 shares are available at the inside ask price, while the rest are for sale at a higher price. Thus, the average price that it would cost to buy 500 shares would rise to 50.73.

AVERAGE PRICE = ((50.71 * 300) + (50.75 * 200)) / 500 = 50.73

At this point, the trader has taken a short-term loss on the transaction. In addition, the average price the stock could be sold for (the bid price) is

FIGURE 6.3

Symbol	Bid Tick	Bid	Ask	Last	Trd Size	Net Chg	Vol Tot
AZZ	⇑	50.61	50.71	50.61	100	-1.45	22,500

ID	Bid	Size	Time	ID	Ask	Size	Time
NYSE	50.61	100	10:31:32 AM	NYSE	50.71	300	10:31:31 AM
NASD	50.60	300	10:31:28 AM	ARCX#	50.75	100	10:30:38 AM
ARCX#	0.02	100	10:31:31 AM	NASD	50.75	100	10:31:28 AM

A LEVEL 2 SCREEN SHOWING THE RISKS OF USING A
MARKET ORDER TO ENTER A TRADE.

50.60, resulting in an immediate $0.13 loss per share. Furthermore, there are currently not enough buyers to sell back all 500 shares. [Note: the ARCX# bid of 0.02 is just a placeholder and does not really represent 100 shares of stock at 0.02.] The value of this stock must increase by at least $0.13, under increased market participation (more bids lined up to buy back the shares), before this trade could break even (not lose money).

Traders should not be overly anxious to enter trades, and should understand what price they can expect from a market order, based on the depth of the market. Figure 6.4 shows a price ladder display for an E-mini S&P futures contract. This type of display can be used for order entry. Traders can click on the proper cell to buy or sell at the amount specified in the price column. In this market, the bid-ask spread is .25, the smallest fluctuation, or tick size, possible for this market. [Note: each tick is represented by a 0.25 change in the E-mini S&P price column, but has a value to a trader of $12.50.] In other words, this is the smallest spread that can exist in this market and makes it a good candidate for entering a trade using a market order. If a trader wishes to buy one contract using a market order, they should expect to buy at a price of 1444.50, or the inside ask. Based on this market, traders could expect to sell (or sell short) one contract at a price of 1444.25. Another benefit to a trader in this market is the amount of contracts available to be bought and sold. In this case, there are 921 contracts available in the first two ask levels and 290 contracts in the first two bid levels. [Note: E-mini contracts are typically sold in single units (not 100s), and a single contract could be conceptually comparable to 100 stock shares. Thus, a 5-contract E-mini trade would be roughly similar to trading 500 shares of a stock or ETF.]

Traders should expect a market order to be filled at the ask price when buying, and at the bid price when selling. This defines what is meant by the "market price." When trades are filled at a price worse than the inside

FIGURE 6.4

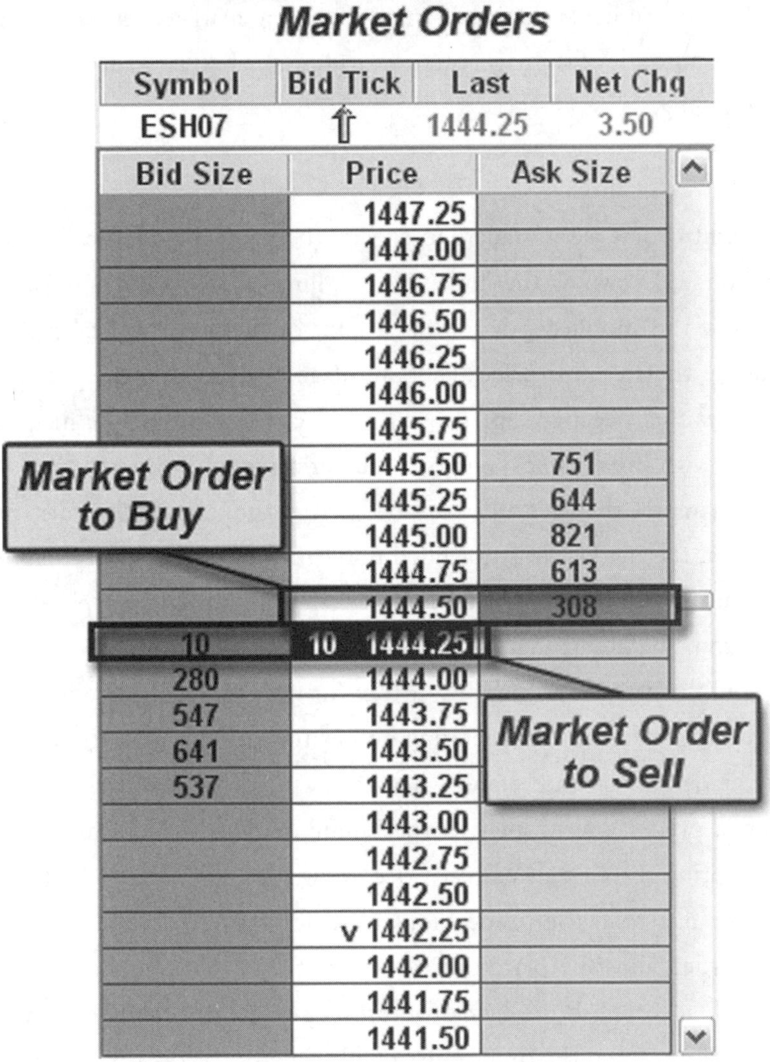

Market Orders

Symbol	Bid Tick	Last	Net Chg
ESH07	⇑	1444.25	3.50

Bid Size	Price	Ask Size
	1447.25	
	1447.00	
	1446.75	
	1446.50	
	1446.25	
	1446.00	
	1445.75	
	1445.50	751
	1445.25	644
	1445.00	821
	1444.75	613
	1444.50	308
10	10 1444.25	
280	1444.00	
547	1443.75	
641	1443.50	
537	1443.25	
	1443.00	
	1442.75	
	1442.50	
	v 1442.25	
	1442.00	
	1441.75	
	1441.50	

Market Order to Buy

Market Order to Sell

THE LOCATION OF MARKET ORDERS SHOWN ON A PRICE LADDER DISPLAY.

bid or ask, this is known as trade slippage. For instance, if a market order to buy was filled at 1445.00 (instead of 1444.50), this would represent two-ticks of slippage. As stated in Chapter 3—Getting to Know the Modern Markets, instruments that trade in all-electronic markets generally provide the least amount of slippage, often providing the best candidates for short-term trading.

LIMIT ORDERS

Limit orders allow traders to specify the price they are willing to get for a trade, known as the limit price. A limit order to buy will occur at or below the specified price, while a limit order to sell will take place at or above the specified price. The advantage of using a limit order is that it ensures that negative slippage will not occur, and provides a method to bargain with the market. The down side of using limit orders is that there is no guarantee that the order will be filled. Although a limit order can be placed in the market, it is not filled until price reaches the specified level. This means that a trader could miss a trading opportunity if price moves away from the limit order before it can be filled.

Limit orders are an important tool for traders, often providing an excellent means of precisely entering and exiting a trade. As with any order type, traders must understand when to use this type of order. Figure 6.5 shows a price ladder display of the E-mini S&P. In this example, instead of accepting the current market price, we want to try to get a better price (buy for less than the inside bid, or sell for more than the inside ask). Limit orders must be placed on the correct side of the market to ensure they will accomplish the task of improving price. In other words, to buy using a limit order, the order must be placed at or below the current market bid of 1444.25; to sell using a limit order, the price must be at or above the current market ask of 1444.50.

FIGURE 6.5

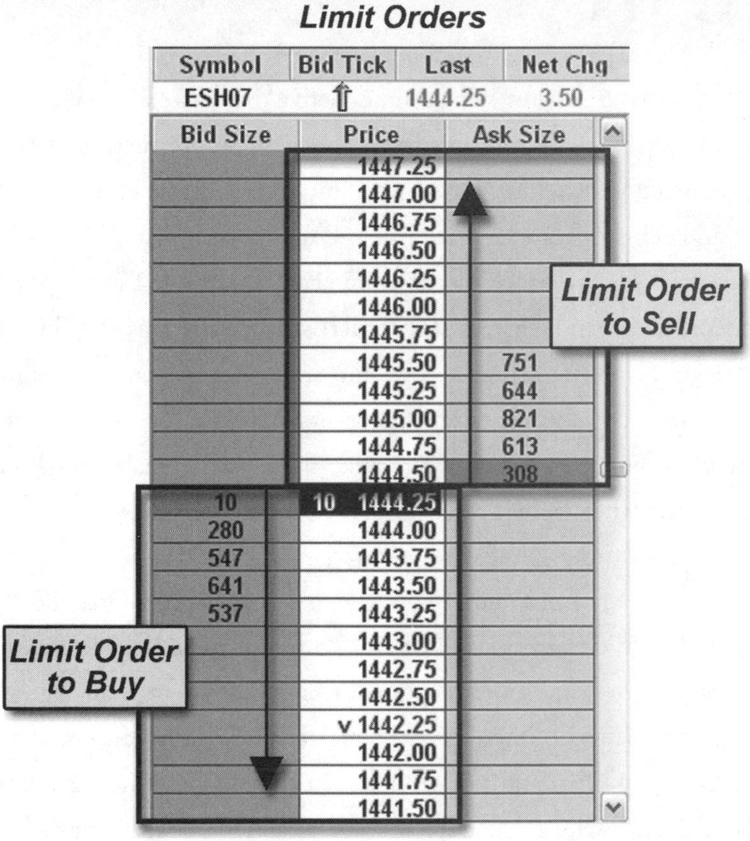

Limit Orders

Symbol	Bid Tick	Last	Net Chg
ESH07	⇑	1444.25	3.50

Bid Size	Price	Ask Size	
	1447.25		
	1447.00		
	1446.75		
	1446.50		
	1446.25		
	1446.00		
	1445.75		
	1445.50	751	
	1445.25	644	
	1445.00	821	
	1444.75	613	
	1444.50	308	
10	10 1444.25		
280	1444.00		
547	1443.75		
641	1443.50		
537	1443.25		
	1443.00		
	1442.75		
	1442.50		
	v 1442.25		
	1442.00		
	1441.75		
	1441.50		

Limit Order to Sell

Limit Order to Buy

THE LOCATION OF LIMIT ORDERS SHOWN ON A PRICE LADDER DISPLAY.

To enter a limit order for a long trade, we must first determine a level for the limit order. Let's say we want to go long with one contract if price drops to 1443.50. The next step is to enter this price level and submit the order (click the "buy" button). We would then see the number in the bid column at the 1443.50 price level change to 642, reflecting our order to buy at this price level. If price pulls back, we will get our buy order filled at exactly 1443.50 and enter into a long trade.

STOP ORDER

A stop order to buy or sell becomes active only after a specified price level has been reached (known as the stop level). Stop orders work in the opposite direction of a limit order, with buy stop orders placed above the market and sell stop orders placed below the market. Once a stop level has been reached, the order will be immediately converted into a market or limit order. In this sense, a stop order is not really an order in itself, but a trigger for either a market or limit order. Accordingly, stop orders are further defined as stop-market or stop-limit orders. The most common and useful is the stop-market order, since these are normally filled more reliably. Often, when traders refer simply to a stop order, they are referring to a stop-market order.

Traders that are not familiar with the use of stop orders may be wondering, "Why would anyone want to pay a worse price than the current market value?" In some instances, trading requires us to draw a line in the sand and challenge price to reach that level in order to demonstrate a significant level of strength or weakness in the market. Once this line is crossed, it provides the catalyst to enter or exit a trade. Traders may choose key support and resistance levels, for example, as described in Chapter 5—Charting the Market, to establish the levels of their stop orders. In essence, stop orders allow traders to confirm the market is headed in a particular direction before entering a position.

Figure 6.6 shows an example of the placement for stop orders. Possibly the most common use of a stop order is to set a risk limit for a trade, or a stop loss. As an example, if we were to enter a long position at 1444.50, we could use a stop order to define the maximum amount that

FIGURE 6.6

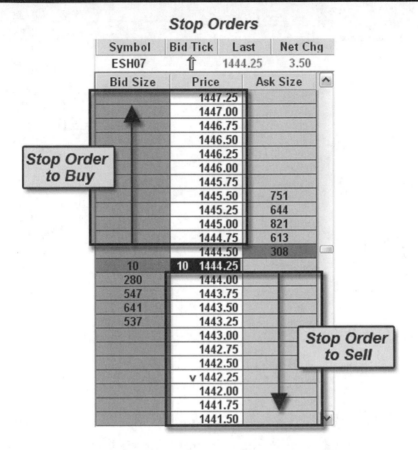

Stop Orders

Symbol	Bid Tick	Last	Net Chg
ESH07	⇑	1444.25	3.50

Bid Size	Price	Ask Size	^
	1447.25		
	1447.00		
	1446.75		
	1446.50		
	1446.25		
	1446.00		
	1445.75		
	1445.50	751	
	1445.25	644	
	1445.00	821	
	1444.75	613	
	1444.50	308	
10	10 1444.25		
280	1444.00		
547	1443.75		
641	1443.50		
537	1443.25		
	1443.00		
	1442.75		
	1442.50		
	v 1442.25		
	1442.00		
	1441.75		
	1441.50		v

Stop Order to Buy

Stop Order to Sell

THE LOCATION OF STOP ORDERS SHOWN ON A PRICE LADDER DISPLAY.

we were willing to risk on this trade as $150. This could be accomplished by setting a stop order to sell at a level of 1441.50. If price goes against us by 12 ticks [Note: E-mini S&P values, 12 ticks * $12.50 per tick = $150] we would exit the position with a $150 loss (less slippage and commission).

FIGURE 6.7

ESH07 E-Mini S&P 500 Mar 2007 - 3 min - PZT VSTOPS (21,4,black,black,black)   1438.31

Trailing Stop

Trailing Stop Exit

Trailing Stop Levels

Entry

Created with TradeStation

A TRAILING STOP APPLIED TO A LONG TRADE ON AN
INTRADAY CHART OF THE E-MINI S&P.

Another important application of a stop order is called a trailing stop. A trailing stop is a dynamic stop order that follows price trends in an attempt to lock in profits. A trailing stop will incrementally increase in a long trade to follow the rising market, and will decrease in a short trade to follow the declining price. Traders must define the magnitude of the price move, as either a percentage or a dollar amount, which defines the distance between the stop level and the current price. Figure 6.7 shows an example of a trailing stop applied to a long trade of the E-mini S&P. In this example, the stop level is shown with black dashed lines. The long trade is eventually closed out as price falls back and triggers the stop order to sell. Trailing stops have become a popular order type offered by most brokers, and will appear as an option in the order entry software.

TRADE EXAMPLES

The following examples are intended to demonstrate the application of multiple order types. While each example illustrates important trade management concepts, traders should first develop a clear, comprehensive trading plan before placing actual trades. Therefore, it is assumed in the following examples that a trading plan defining these specific trade entries and exits has already been developed and tested, verifying the effectiveness of these trades (discussed in Chapter 7—Developing a Trading Plan, and Chapter 8—Evaluation and Comparing Trading Plans).

It should also be noted that each example illustrates an ideal, winning trade. This is not always the case. The fact is that losing trades (trades that reach a predetermined stop loss) are much easier to manage than winning trades. Once a stop loss has been reached, traders should simply cancel all open orders and look for other trading opportunities, as defined by their trading plans. As mentioned earlier in this book, it is impossible to trade without losing.

Each of the following examples is applied to the E-mini Russell 2000 March 2007 futures contract (symbol: ER2H07). Keep in mind that the price on the charts does not equate to a per-share value but an index value specific to this contract. For the "Mini Russell," each point is worth $100 per contract, and the minimum price fluctuation, or tick value, is 0.10 of a point, which relates to a value of $10 per contract. For instance, a price move from 750.00 to 780.50 is worth $3,050 per contract to a trader. A more detailed description of popular E-mini index futures contracts can be found in Chapter 3—Getting to Know the Modern Markets.

TRADE EXAMPLE 1: BRACKET

In the first example, (Figure 6.8), a long trade will be entered using a stop order, and will then be managed using a combination of stop and limit orders, known as a bracket. The setup for this trade involves spotting an area of prior resistance, which occurred when price reached the swing high of 750.00 on September 28. This provides a point to place a buy

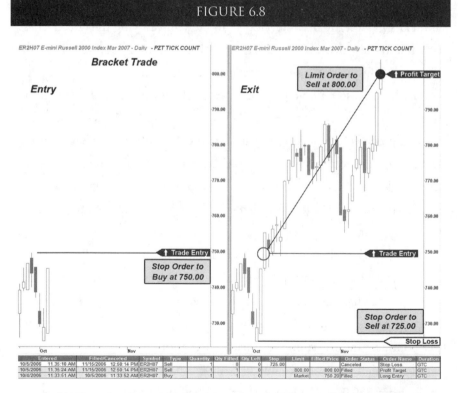

FIGURE 6.8

AN EXAMPLE OF A BRACKET TRADE ON THE E-MINI RUSSELL 2000.

stop order in anticipation of a rising market. The logic is that if price can push up to 750.00, it may continue higher. Using a stop order means that the order will automatically become active if price reaches the designated stop level. On October 4, we place the stop order to buy one contract at a price of 750.00. The next day we get the confirmation that the order has been filled at a price of 750.20 ($20 of slippage on one contract) as price surges upward.

Now that we are in a long position, our trading plan has defined the placement of the two sell orders to exit the position, depending on which way the market moves: a profit target and a stop loss. The stop loss is placed at an area of prior support below the current price, and the profit target is set for a +R advantage of two, well above the current price. The profit target is established by entering a limit order to sell at 800.00, and the stop loss is placed as a stop order to sell at 725.00. The combination of these two sell orders is called a bracket since they bracket, or surround, the trade entry price. At this point, price will either reach our profit target or fall back to the stop loss. Either way, we have the correct orders in the market to exit the position as soon as one of these events occurs. On November 15, price reaches the profit target and the limit order is filled at exactly 800.00. At this point, it is important to cancel the open stop order and completely flatten the position (otherwise, an unintended position could be initiated).

TRADE EXAMPLE 2: STOP-AND-REVERSE

This trade example (Figure 6.9) uses a reversal logic that switches positions between long and short trades, keeping a trader constantly in the market. The logic behind this method of trading is that the market must go either up or down, and a stop-and-reverse system attempts to catch strong trends since a trader will constantly be in the market. This trade is initiated on November 17 when a limit order to buy one contract at 780.00 is placed. At this point, the current price is well above the limit price. As outlined in our trading plan, if price pulls back to an area of previous resistance around 780.00 (remember, prior resistance often acts as support), it will provide the catalyst to take the long trade. On November 27, the limit order is filled and we open the long trade. Our stop loss is set 10 points below the entry price with a stop order to sell at 770.00. Similar to the previous example, we will place a simultaneous order for a profit target. This time, however, if price reaches our profit target we will not just sell, but we

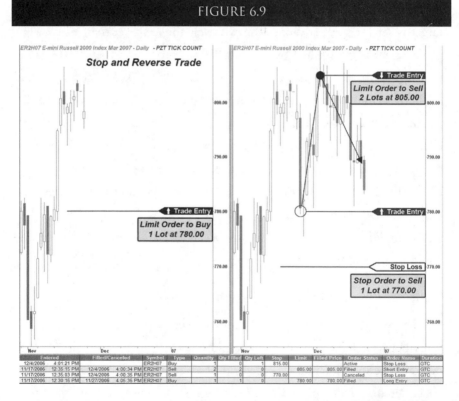

FIGURE 6.9

An example of stop-and-reverse trade on the E-mini Russell 2000.

will also reverse the position and enter a short trade. To accomplish this, we will submit a limit order to sell two contracts at 805.00 (one contract to close the long trade, and one contract to enter the short trade).

Six days after our entry, price jumps up to the limit price and is filled on December 4. We have successfully reversed our original trade and are now in a short trade. At this point, we must cancel the remaining stop order to sell and place another set of stop loss and profit target orders for our trade exits.

TRADE EXAMPLE 3: MULTIPLE PROFIT TARGETS

The next example (Figure 6.10) demonstrates a money management strategy that buys into a long position and aims to split the position and sell at two separate profit targets. In addition, a protective stop loss is put into place that will move up to a breakeven level (back to the original entry price) once the first half of the position reaches the initial profit target.

In the example, we enter a long trade using a market order to buy on October 9, getting immediately filled for two contracts at a price of 755.00. Now that we are in the market, we enter a stop order to sell two contracts at 725.00 for our initial stop loss. We then enter two separate orders to sell at different profit targets: a limit order to sell one contract at 780.00 and another limit order to sell one contract at 795.00. The trade quickly moves in our direction and, in a little over a week, we reach our first profit target; and, our first limit order is filled on October 16 at 780.00. Now, we want to protect our profits and prevent this trade from becoming a loser. Since we already have a nice profit, we move our stop loss for our remaining contract up to breakeven. To do this, we cancel the stop order for two contracts at 725.00, and enter a new stop order for one contract at 755.00. Even if the trade turns and goes against us, we are still guaranteed a profitable trade; however, we will give this trade a chance to become even more profitable. Over the next couple of weeks the market turns down and almost stops out at the breakeven level before moving back up to reach our second profit target on November 14. We then cancel the outstanding stop order to avoid entering an unintended position.

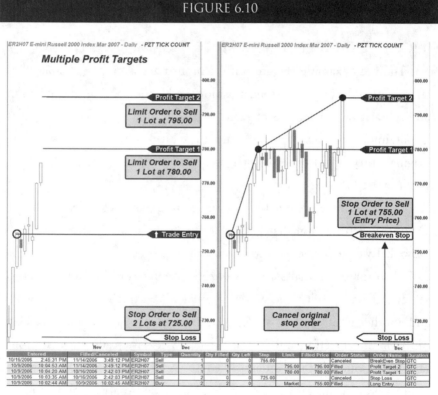

FIGURE 6.10

Entered		Filled/Canceled		Symbol	Type	Quantity	Qty Filled	Qty Left	Stop	Limit	Filled Price	Order Status	Order Name	Duration
10/16/2006	2:45:31 PM	11/14/2006	3:49:12 PM	ER2H07	Sell	1	0	0	755.00			Canceled	BreakEven Stop	GTC
10/9/2006	10:04:53 AM	11/14/2006	3:49:12 PM	ER2H07	Sell	1	1	0		795.00	795.00	Filled	Profit Target 2	GTC
10/9/2006	10:04:20 AM	10/16/2006	2:42:03 PM	ER2H07	Sell	1	1	0		780.00	780.00	Filled	Profit Target 1	GTC
10/9/2006	10:03:35 AM	10/16/2006	2:42:03 PM	ER2H07	Sell	2	0	0	725.00			Canceled	Stop Loss	GTC
10/9/2006	10:02:44 AM	10/9/2006	10:02:45 AM	ER2H07	Buy	2	2	0		Market	755.00	Filled	Long Entry	GTC

AN EXAMPLE OF A MULTIPLE PROFIT TARGET TRADE ON
THE E-MINI RUSSELL 2000.

Trade Automation

As demonstrated in the previous examples, traders often incorporate advanced order, position sizing, and money management strategies into their trading plans. In addition, traders will often trade several different instruments simultaneously, known as a trading portfolio. As the level of complexity of a trading plan increases, so does the potential for error in placing, canceling, and managing multiple trade orders. Trade automation is an important tool that allows traders to maintain their focus on the markets, instead of just watching trade orders. Currently, there are three different levels of trade automation available to retail traders: conditional trade orders, front-end software, and system trading.

Conditional Trade Orders

The most basic form of trade automation is known as a conditional trade order, and is available through many brokers. Unlike the basic market, limit, or stop orders, conditional trade orders will automatically be submitted or canceled only if specified criteria are met. Conditional trade orders must be specified before placing a trade, and are entered directly through the order entry software, as seen in Figure 6.11. The two most common conditional trade orders are the order cancels order (OCO) and the order sends order (OSO).

An OCO enables traders to place several orders; when one is filled, the remaining orders in the group are canceled. This type of order can be useful for both trade entries and exits, and examples of possible OCO applications are shown in Figure 6.12. Possibly the most popular application of an OCO is the bracket order, as shown in Figure 6.8. An OCO bracket order can simplify the process of placing simultaneous stop and limit orders in the market. With this type of an order, once either of these levels is reached, the outstanding order is automatically canceled. This type of

FIGURE 6.11

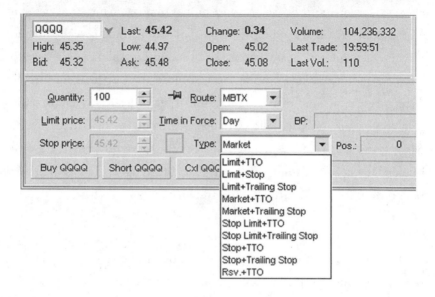

THIS ENTRY ORDER SCREEN FROM MB TRADING NAVIGATOR SHOWS A
VARIETY OF PROPRIETARY ORDER TYPES. IN THIS CASE, CONDITIONAL
ORDERS INCLUDE "TTO" (THRESHOLD TRIGGERED ORDER) AS AN OCO
ORDER, AND A "+" DENOTES A TYPE OF OSO ORDER.

OCO bracket order minimizes the order entry workload by allowing a trader to place a single OCO order, instead of three individual orders (a stop order, a limit order, and an order cancellation).

An OSO order is used to further automate the management of a trade by sending orders into the market following an entry order's fill. This order is often used in conjunction with an OCO, and can significantly streamline the process of placing protective stops and target limit orders. For instance, an OSO order can be set to automatically trigger a bracket order as soon as either a long or a short trade is entered.

FIGURE 6.12

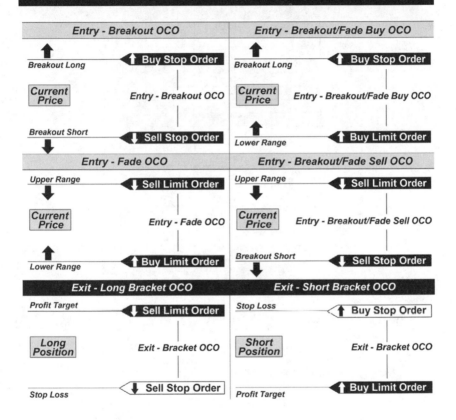

EXAMPLES OF POSSIBLE OCO APPLICATIONS.

FIGURE 6.13

HOLD	BUY	PRICE	SELL	
		1446.75		1 ✕
		1446.50		
		1446.25		
		1446.00		
		1445.75		1 ✕
		1445.50		
		1445.25		
		1445.00		
		1444.75		1 ✕
		1444.50	564	
		1444.25	111	
		1444.00	189	
		1443.75	35	
	20	(2)1443.50		
	69	1443.25		
	95	1443.00		
	323	1442.75		
	463	1442.50		
		1442.25		
		1442.00		
		1441.75		
		1441.50		
		1441.25		3s ✕
	BID	-0.25	BID	

| < | REV | 3 | CLOSE | C | ✕ |

Instrument:	ES 03-07 ▼	Order qty:	3 ◆
Account:	▼	TIF:	Day ▼
Strategy:	*Active Strategy 4 - Custom ▼		

Strategy parameters (ticks)

	○ 1 Target	○ 2 Target	● 3 Target
Qty:	1 ◆	1 ◆	1 ◆
Stop loss:	10 ◆	10 ◆	10 ◆
Profit target:	4 ◆	8 ◆	12 ◆
Stop strategy:	<Custom ▼	<None> ▼	<None> ▼

This front-end software from NinjaTrader shows a price ladder screen with an active position strategy. The dark gray cells with numbers and Xs along the right side show the active orders.

FRONT-END SOFTWARE

The next level of trade automation requires the use of an additional trading program, known as front-end software, which interfaces with a broker's order entry software. Front-end software, as seen in Figure 6.13, is used to automate more complex trade management and can be particularly helpful to day traders. Most front-ends use a price ladder, and traders can place or change an order by simply clicking and dragging the order from one of these cells. As the position size changes, the front-end recalculates all associated orders and cancels any outstanding orders.

The advantage to using front-end software is its ability to automate complex exit strategies that may include multiple profit targets, multi-level stop orders, or pyramiding (adding shares or contracts to a winning position). This tool can significantly speed up the order placement process, and it allows the trader to "fire-and-forget" to a certain extent, as the front-end can manage multiple trades with multiple conditions. Front-end software typically does not require complex program writing or coding to create exit strategies. Even intricate exit strategies can be set up using a relatively straightforward interface with a series of drop down lists and check boxes.

For newer traders, front-ends have a couple significant advantages. The first benefit is that most developers that sell (or lease) front-end software offer an accompanying trading simulator. This simulator functions identically to the actual software and allows traders to get familiar with the functions and capabilities of the software before beginning live trading. Many front-end simulators even attempt to simulate the delays and uncertainty associated with getting orders filled in volatile markets. The second advantage of using a front-end to manage trades is that it offers complete consistency in how traders exit their positions. This can really help traders fight the urge to deviate from their trading plans.

System Trading

The next degree of automation is fully automated trading or system trading. System trading allows traders to develop specific rules that establish both trade entries and exits. Similar to front-end software, system trading requires software that is linked to a broker. Trade entry and exit rules can vary from simple criteria, such as moving average crossovers or indicator values, to complex strategies that must be custom programmed.

Most traders who employ system trading, however, choose to program their own strategies or work closely with a programmer. This requires learning the proprietary programming language of the trading platform as well as thoroughly understanding the technical market theories that are to

FIGURE 6.14

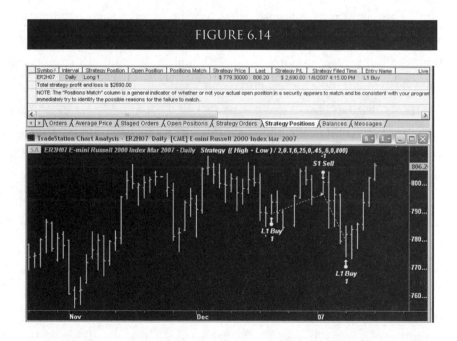

THIS TRADESTATION CHART SHOWS AN AUTOMATED TRADING STRATEGY
APPLIED TO THE MARCH 2007 E-MINI RUSSELL 2000 CONTRACT.

be implemented within the strategy. Once developed, a strategy is applied to a specific chart where it can be monitored in real-time as trades are automatically triggered and sent to the market, as seen in Figure 6.14. The trade entries and exits appear as arrows overlaid on the price chart.

Possibly the biggest advantage of system trading is the ability to take some of the emotion away from trading. Since these systems can trade completely mechanically based on the predetermined rules of a trading plan, dealing with losses or second-guessing a trade entry will not affect system performance. Additionally, trades can be automatically executed with extremely fast reaction times.

The various benefits of trade automation make it a helpful tool for traders, but it is important to remember that certain aspects of automation can fail. For instance, the downside of managing trades through front-end software is that the software must be running constantly with a live data feed in order to function properly. Even fully automated systems still re-quire monitoring since these systems can only react to the data that they receive. If the system receives incorrect market data or loses a connection to the data server, the trader must recognize the error and manually fix the problem. If left unnoticed, a trade could be left naked in the market.

CHAPTER 7
DEVELOPING A TRADING PLAN

THE IMPORTANCE OF USING A TRADING PLAN

Throughout this book, the trading plan development and implementation has been established as a necessary tool for successful trading. Not to overstate this point, but we are not aware of any traders who have become consistently profitable without using a well-researched trading plan. This chapter will discuss the elements involved in constructing a trading plan as well as several basic examples.

In Chapter 2–The Business of Trading, we defined the two distinct roles of a complete trader as a strategist and a market trader. Developing a trading plan defines the most important role of the strategist. Putting together a trading plan is a creative process wherein we apply our collective research to establish a set of definitive trading rules. These research concepts include risk management, intra-market relationships, technical analysis, and trade order dynamics. In other words, our individual research will provide the building blocks for establishing the rules of our trading plan. This is the point where we must roll up our sleeves and define the details of our business.

Trading plans must be somewhat dynamic. As traders gain more trading experience and greater skill, their plans should evolve as well. Very few experienced traders continue to use exactly the same trading plan as when they began trading. One of the key decisions a strategist should make is when and why to revise a trading plan. These criteria should be considered part of the overall trading plan and should be put into place before actual trading occurs.

It is important to mention that the greatest advantage to using a trading plan is the consistency that it offers. Consistently following the rules of an effective trading plan will allow a trading business to make money over time. Remember, we cannot win every trade, and we should not focus on the results of only our most recent trades, but instead in consistent trading over time. A trading plan should not change after each trade. In fact, changing a trading plan too often will create an overly flexible plan that will equate to not having a plan at all. A trader must strike a balance between deciding when to change the plan, and allowing enough trades for a trading plan to have the chance to demonstrate profitability.

Building a successful trading plan is a process, as illustrated in Figure 7.1. This process allows traders to develop and test their trading plans through a logical and systematic progression. The initial step is to define the trading plan objectives and establish a set of trading rules. A trading plan must be written, and should include the following components:

- Timeframe or conditions under which to reevaluate the
  trading plan

- Market(s) to which it will be applied

- Primary chart interval that will be used to make trading decisions

- Indicators and settings that will be applied to the chart

- Positions size that will be used, including when to increase/decrease size

- Entry Rules

- Exit Rules

The process of developing a trading plan is similar to hiring a new employee. In order to consider this trading plan for employment, it must prove that it has the performance record, character, and skill to benefit

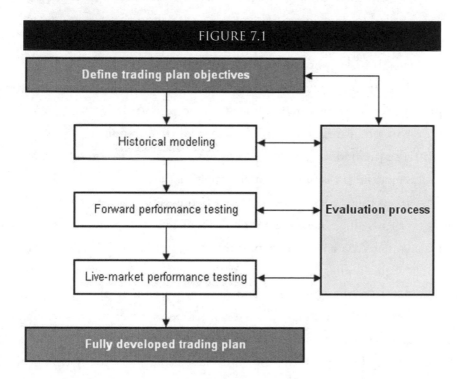

FIGURE 7.1

THE PROCESS FOR DEVELOPING A TRADING PLAN.

your trading business. The steps to evaluating a trading plan include historical modeling (reviewing resumes), forward performance testing (checking references), and live-market performance testing (the interview). It is only after a trading plan has successfully gone through this process that it has proven it is ready for employment in the market. Additionally, criteria must be set to determine when a trading plan needs additional development (training) or when it may need to be taken out of the market completely (fired).

Once the rules of a trading plan are defined, it can be tested on historical data. This process, referred to as historical modeling, or backtesting, can help prove the validity of the plan. It is essential to use enough data that the historical modeling becomes statistically significant. Analyzing just a few trades does not offer the type of confirmation that we are looking for. In general, the more trades that are involved in the historical model, the better. It is also possible to revise the plan at this point, as this process often leads to important research that can improve the performance of the plan. Traders must be careful, though, not to reconstruct a plan that will only work on historical data (this is known as over-optimizing).

Once the trading plan has shown positive, satisfactory results in historical modeling, it is time to practice applying the plan to the real market. This step is called forward performance testing, and is sometimes referred to as paper trading. Since there is no real trading at this point, we are only placing trades via an order entry simulator (described in Chapter 4—The Tools of the Trade), or on paper. At this point, the trading plan can no longer benefit from hindsight, and must prove itself in the real market environment. This testing will take some time in order to gain enough trading experience to become significant. A minimum of ten trades is recommended before making any initial judgments about the system. Forward performance testing is a vital step in the trading plan development process, and traders should look for good correlation between this and the historical modeling. If it is determined that the trading plan is performing as expected, it is time to begin live-market performance testing.

At this point, traders must put real money on the line to test the system. Live-market performance testing should only be conducted with a minimum position size. Remember, we have not yet completed the development process and are still testing. Large losses at this point can cause a significant setback to the overall business. While this step will feel exactly like real market trading, it is intended as a bridge to get the trading plan closer to being fully applied to the market. The focus of this phase is to establish a correlation between the live-market trading results and the previous development steps. Live-market testing will often provide feedback that will lead to future revisions of a trading plan. In some cases, traders may find that they do not yet have the market trading skill or mindset to follow the trading plan. This may require tailoring the plan to make it more tradable for the individual market trader.

Once a trading plan has gone through this rigorous process with positive results, it is ready to be fully applied to the market (traded for real). Traders should not rush through the testing process or try to take short cuts. Any setbacks along the development process require traders to go back to the initial phase, and continue through each step. These setbacks should not be considered failures, for each time a trader goes through the process of testing a trading plan, he or she becomes a more experienced and savvy trader.

A key part of this process is having the tools to evaluate a trading plan. This is accomplished by analyzing and comparing statistical results, or performance reports, from each phase of testing. Examining these reports and explaining key performance metrics will be described in Chapter 8—Evaluating and Comparing Trading Plans.

Asset Allocation and Position Sizing

A discussion of position sizing and asset allocation would not be complete without mentioning the Turtles. The Turtles have become somewhat of a legend in the trading world, with their almost mythical success story inspiring many new traders. The Turtles were actually the result of a study by famous commodities trader Richard Dennis and his long-time friend William Eckhardt. The two set out to determine if great traders were born or made, and advertised for trading apprentices. Out of 1,000 applicants, 10 people were chosen and an additional three added, whom Mr. Dennis had already known. This group was known as the Turtles.

This team of prospective traders attended a two-week training session at the end of December 1983, and began trading small accounts at the beginning of the next month. Mr. Dennis funded the Turtles with larger accounts, ranging from $500,000 to $2,000,000 the following month. Over the next four years, the Turtles earned an average annual compound rate of return of 80%. Mr. Dennis felt as though he had proven that trading could be taught: with a simple trading plan, people with little or no trading experience could become excellent traders.

Fundamental to the Turtles' success was their approach to position sizing and asset allocation. They believed in trading a fixed percentage of their account, which increases asset allocation as equity increases, and decreases asset allocation as equity decreases. After each trade, funds were reallocated based on the results of that trade. In addition, the Turtles would not risk more than two percent of capital on any trade, a percentage that is still accepted as the industry standard.

Another important element in the Turtles' trading plan was a volatility-based constant percentage risk position-sizing algorithm. It normalized the dollar volatility of a position by adjusting the position size based on the dollar volatility of the market. In other words, more contracts were held in markets that had lower volatility, and fewer contracts were held in markets that had higher volatility. The result was that a given position would tend to move up or down the same amount (in dollar terms) when compared to positions in other markets, regardless of the volatility of the particular market. Therefore, individual trades in different markets had the same chance for a particular dollar loss or a particular dollar gain. This improved the effectiveness of diversification.

Through the Turtles' consistent trading plan, they objectively answered the questions of what to trade and how much to trade.

LEVERAGE AND MARGIN

Deciding precisely how much to trade is a key aspect of a trading business that allows traders to control risk and maximize profits. The amount of margin, or leverage, that a trader chooses to use determines how much he or she can buy or sell at any given time. Traders must decide how to use this powerful tool most effectively without creating a high probability of ruin for their trading businesses.

It is recommended that traders begin trading only with a small percentage of the amount of money that is available in their accounts. Traders should start small and increase their position sizes as their profits and trading skills grow. Newer traders that are too anxious to trade larger positions (using the entire value of their accounts and/or large amounts of leverage) almost always fail. Margin and leveraging should be applied with extreme caution.

A trader can determine, for example, the maximum number of shares of QQQQs (trading at $44.20 per share) they could afford to buy with a $60,000 trading account, by dividing the account size by the current value of the stock.

> **MAX POSITION SIZE (STOCKS) = ACCOUNT SIZE / STOCK VALUE**
> **= $60,000 / $44.20 = 1,357 SHARES**

A standard overnight margin account allows 2:1 leverage for stocks, and would give this trader the buying power to purchase twice as many shares than the account size could otherwise afford. This brings the maximum marginable position size up to 2,714 shares (Max Position Size * Margin Rate). It is advised that traders should never trade at maximum margin levels.

A more responsible method to determine a position size is to trade a percentage of the overall marginable value of an account, instead of the complete account value. For example, a trader may choose to base the position size on 30% of the margin account value:

> **MAX% POSITION SIZE (STOCKS) = (ACCOUNT SIZE ***
> **MARGIN RATE * TRADING PERCENTAGE) / STOCK VALUE =**
> **($60,000 * 2 * 0.3) / $44.20 = 814 SHARES**

This amount is typically rounded down to the nearest 100 shares to allow for easier order entry and trade management. Accordingly, the above example would relate to 800 shares of the QQQQs.

It should be noted that the futures and forex markets require a necessary amount of margin and this should be factored into any type of position sizing. For instance, trading 30% of a maximum position in the E-mini Russell 2000 futures contract (initial margin of $3,500 per contract) with a $60,000 futures account could be calculated as follows:

> MAX% POSITION SIZE (FUTURES) = (ACCOUNT SIZE *
> TRADING PERCENTAGE) / INITIAL CONTRACT MARGIN = ($60,000
> * 0.3) / $3,500 = 5 CONTRACTS

As stated above, deciding how to establish a position size is a critical factor in building a trading plan. Two methods are commonly used by traders: constant position sizing and fixed percentage position sizing. Constant position sizing uses the same amount of shares, contracts or currency in every trade, while fixed percentage position sizing varies the position size as the value of the account changes.

FIGURE 7.2

Equity Curve - Emini Russell 2000 Futures (12/31/01 - 01/02/07)
Initial Account Value: $60,000 / Sample Trading Plan: Counter Trend w/ Fixed +R Adv. 2

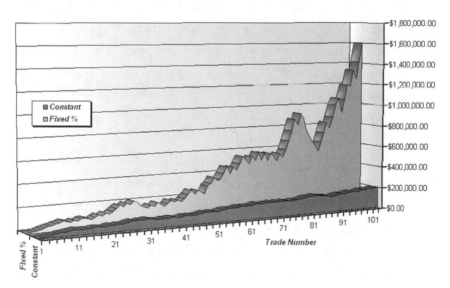

A COMPARISON OF CONSTANT POSITION SIZING AND FIXED PERCENTAGE POSITION SIZING MODELS. MAYBE THE TURTLES WERE ON TO SOMETHING!

A comparison of these two position sizing methods can be seen in Figure 7.2. The equity curve for each of these position sizing models is displayed using a sample trading plan applied to 6 years of historical data from the E-mini Russell 2000 futures contract. An initial account balance of $60,000 was used to construct these equity curves. While the constant position size model would have traded with a consistent five contracts, the fixed percentage model began with five contracts and increased the position size as the account grew. This progressive method of fixed percentage position sizing is one of the key concepts contributing to the effectiveness of the Turtles' trading plan. This essentially allows traders to compound their trading profits and risk more only after they have made more. The previous equations for max% position size can be used to calculate a position size based on the current account value, and should be calculated following every trade.

While fixed percentage position sizing clearly has the advantage, constant position sizing is still useful to traders. This method can work well for traders who are just getting started, or trading smaller accounts. Constant position sizing should also be used during the testing and evaluation of a trading plan.

INSTRUMENTS TO TRADE

Another aspect of a successful trading plan is deciding which instruments, or symbols, to trade. Choosing these instruments requires research, and traders often find that, after a period of observation, they will discover the instruments that are best suited to their trading styles and risk tolerances. Chapter 4—The Tools of the Trade introduces several trading instruments in the stock, futures, and forex markets that provide the liquidity and volatility that make good candidates for short-term trading.

In addition, trading instruments based on market indices provide a pre-established level of diversification.

A recommended practice is to develop a trading plan that will be used with just one instrument, and then diversify (add instruments) as a trading account and market trading skill increase. This can allow traders to focus their research on effectively testing and executing a trading plan, instead of constantly scanning for possible instruments to trade. This is not to say that diversification and testing across a portfolio of trading instruments is not important. In fact, many traders gain additional confidence if their trading plans test favorably in multiple markets.

Adding instruments to a trading plan requires the same intensive testing process that was used to establish the plan. In addition, traders should attempt to add instruments that trade in dissimilar, or non-correlated, markets. This provides the advantage of better diversification. A well-diversified trading portfolio can help reduce trading losses because individual losing trades can be offset by winning trades in other markets. In order to gain the most benefit from diversification, traders must choose to trade comparable position sizes. Establishing this type of portfolio diversification can become challenging, as traders must mix a cocktail of instruments to provide the best overall results. Similar to a well-mixed martini, a well-diversified trading portfolio must include the proper components, and in the correct proportions.

The Turtles offered a unique approach to mixing a portfolio cocktail by normalizing the instruments in their portfolio based on the volatility of the market. This approach can help traders decide which proportions to trade by establishing comparable position sizes (or trading units). While the Turtles applied this approach to large trading accounts, small investors can also use this technique to compare unit sizes between trading instruments. The first part in this approach is to establish the volatility using a concept known as average true range. Average true range (ATR), originally develop by Welles Wilder in the late 1970s, compares the trading range over a period of time. The following calculation is used to calculate an ATR of the past 20 periods:

AVERAGE TRUE RANGE = (PREVIOUS ATR * 19 * TR) / 20

TR = TRUE HIGH – TRUE LOW

TRUE HIGH = HIGHEST OF THE CURRENT HIGH OR PREVIOUS CLOSE

TRUE LOW = LOWEST OF THE CURRENT LOW OR PREVIOUS CLOSE

A trading unit can be established by dividing the risk capital by the 20-period ATR. In the following examples, a $60,000 trading account will be used with a 2% risk limit. Using these amounts, we can establish comparable trading units for several instruments using the calculation:

TRADING UNIT = (ACCOUNT SIZE * PERCENTAGE TO RISK) / (AVERAGE TRUE RANGE * DOLLAR VALUE OF POINT)

(ER2) E-MINI RUSSELL 2000 UNIT = ($60,000 *.02) / (10 * $100) = 1 CONTRACT

(YM) E-MINI DOW UNIT = ($60,000 *.02) / (87 * $5) = 2 CONTRACTS

(ES) E-MINI S&P UNIT = ($60,000 *.02) / (11 * $50) = 2 CONTRACTS

(NQ) E-MINI NASDAQ 100 UNIT = ($60,000 *.02) / (25 * $20) = 2 CONTRACTS

(EC) EURO FX FUTURES UNIT = ($60,000 *.02) / (.00957 * $125,000) = 1 CONTRACT

This normalization allows traders to establish a reference to use when creating a trading portfolio. For instance, the risk involved in trading one E-mini Russell 2000 contract using 2% of a $60K account is comparable to two E-mini S&P contracts.

CHART INTERVALS TO TRADE

While some may wonder why choosing a charting interval falls under the heading of asset allocation and position sizing, chart intervals are typically associated with a particular style of trading. The amount of price fluctuation per bar is much greater on longer-term charting intervals than on shorter intervals. Thus, a charting interval relates to position size since it defines a particular type of risk profile. This risk is typically adjusted by trading larger positions in shorter-term styles of trading, explaining the extremely low margin requirements available to day traders.

For a swing trader using a daily chart, risking $800 per contract may be an appropriate tactic. For a day trader using a 15-minute chart, however, this same level of risk might be spread into four contracts, each risking only $200. While both traders have the same amount of risk per trade, their styles of trading and corresponding chart intervals require different allocations.

There are no calculations or formulas to help determine which charting intervals are most useful for a particular style of trading. This will come down to personal preference and research. While traders may wish to incorporate multiple charting intervals into a trading plan, it is important to define a primary charting interval. This primary charting interval will be used to define the specific trade entry and exit rules that describe the type of trading strategy.

TRADE ENTRIES

The goal of establishing trade entry rules is to provide a consistent and decisive method of getting into the market. Traders may often find an inclination to be conservative or aggressive in their approach to trading. Being too conservative or too aggressive can have equally negative results. Conservative traders often look for multiple sources of confirmation, wanting to make sure they are placing the correct trade. This type of trader will often wait until the last possible opportunity to enter a trade and, as a result, is often too late to capture a move. An aggressive trader, on the other hand, will jump at the opportunity to get into a trade. This type of trader often tries to anticipate entry signals, entering the market frequently and sometimes without a real reason. Each trader should be aware of his or her inclination for trade entries and attempt to find a balanced entry method. A decisive entry includes two elements: trade triggers and filters.

TRADE TRIGGERS

A trade trigger is the line in the sand, so to speak, that defines precisely when a trade will be entered. While there may be several other conditions that will further define a trade entry, known as trade filters, the trade trigger tells traders exactly when to act. Once a trade trigger occurs, market traders do not have to think...they just react. A trade trigger allows for a fast and decisive trade entry. In many cases, having an immediate reaction to positive market conditions equates to greater profits. As mentioned above, traders who are slow to react often miss much of a price move.

There should be absolutely no ambiguity in a trade trigger. This means that trade triggers must be clearly defined within the trading plan. An example of a possible trade trigger would be: "Enter a long position once price breaks one tick above the high of the previous bar." This provides a market trader with the precise timing and location to enter a trade.

Trade triggers are often a specific trade order type, such as a stop or limit order, which will put traders into a position as soon as the predetermined stop or limit price occurs. They can also be the crossing of a price threshold (such as support and resistance levels), or an indicator value. Indicators can provide an objective means of trade entry since thresholds can easily be established. Traders should avoid using any generalities when defining their triggers. For instance, "Enter a long trade once the stochastic is oversold" should be further defined as "Enter a long trade once the 13, 5 stochastic crosses above a value of 20."

Another aspect of trade triggers is that they need to be simple. If there are too many trade triggers, or if they become overly complex, a trading plan will become more difficult to implement. This may lead to frequent trading errors and a less effective overall trading plan. Trade triggers should remain clear and obvious to a trader.

TRADE FILTERS

Trade filters define the setup conditions that will allow a trade to occur. An example of trade filters would be: "Price above its 50- and 200-period moving averages while making new 20-day highs." This example could define the setup for a long trade. Trade filters should not be confused with the trade trigger. Trade filters simply define the conditions for when the trade trigger is active. Trade filters can be thought of as the "safety" for the trade trigger. Once all of the conditions for the trade filters have been met, the safety is off and the trade trigger becomes active. Trade filters must occur before the trade trigger.

Unlike a trade trigger, trade filters may include a variety of factors. These can take into consideration the time of day, general market indices, multiple charting intervals, indicator values, and price relationships. As with any aspect of a trading plan, each of these factors must be clearly defined to avoid any ambiguity. Trade filters provide a method of sifting through numerous forms of market information to find the ideal, high probability trading opportunities.

As a general guideline, a trader should only use about four or five different filters in his or her initial trading plan. Too many filters can limit the "degrees of freedom" of a trading plan, and make it less effective in real trading. The goal of an effective trade filter is to define optimal market conditions or to create greater tradability. Too many filters may limit the ability of a trading plan to be robust and produce consistent trades.

TRADE EXITS

Trade exits are a critical aspect of a trading plan. While many traders put the majority of their research into trade entries, it is the exit plan that will define the ultimate success of a trade. Trade exits are often referred to as money management, since this is what trade exits really accomplish. Using the same entry method (trade filters and trigger), a trade could be either a winner or loser depending on when a trader chooses to exit the trade. Trade exits are an important and often overlooked component of a trading plan that require adequate research and testing—at least as much as trade entries.

Traders often elect to use multiple exits in a trading plan. Multiple exits help traders protect profits by cutting losses short and allowing winners to run. In addition, exits can allow a trade to reverse directions (change from a long to a short position, for instance) if there is a sudden change in the market environment.

STOP LOSS

The importance of a stop loss has been mentioned in earlier chapters. This type of trade exit allows traders to establish per trade risk limits, and is an essential element of a responsible trading plan. The fact is there is a limit to how much a trader can afford to lose before margin requirements are exceeded and they cannot continue to trade. We do not want to reach that level, ever.

Traders must decide how much they are willing to risk on any individual trade, and this should be a small percentage of an overall account value (the Turtles, for instance, used 2%). For newer traders, it is often easiest to

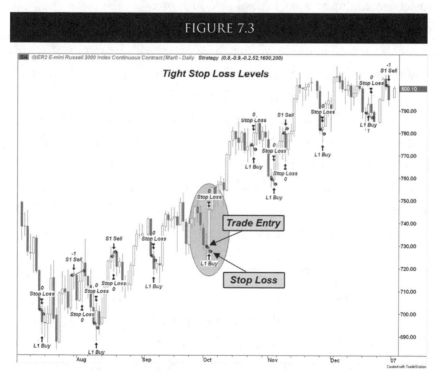

FIGURE 7.3

THIS CHART ILLUSTRATES THE NEGATIVE EFFECT OF SETTING STOP LOSS LEVELS TOO TIGHT. THE SAME CHART INTERVAL AND TRADING STRATEGY CAN BE SEEN IN FIGURE 7.8, BUT WITH MORE REALISTIC STOP LOSS LEVELS.

set a dollar amount as the stop loss. This allows consistency and a fast, reliable calculation of stop orders to a broker. It is important that traders do not let a stop loss pass by. Reaching a stop loss should not be considered a failed trade; it is simply a trade that got stopped out. A failed trade is one that does not follow the trading plan. Good market traders simply execute the trading plan exactly as it is written; any analyzing (or second-guessing) of the trading plan falls under the jurisdiction of the strategist.

It is important to develop realistic stop loss levels as part of a trading plan. Some traders feel overly confident when using a small stop loss, thinking that they are trading conservatively. The fact is, several small losses can add up to a big loss, as seen in Figure 7.3. The circled trade, in particular, represents a long trade that was quickly stopped out despite a significant price increase (favoring the long trade). The results of setting a stop loss level too small can provide the same negative outcome as setting a stop loss too large. When deciding on stop loss levels, it is important that they allow enough room for a trade to become profitable. Few trades will move immediately in the intended direction. More commonly, price will oscillate (possibly for a number of days) before making a more powerful move. Traders should understand the volatility of their intended markets to determine a reasonable stop loss level.

Once again, always trade with a stop loss.

PROFIT TARGET(S)

Profit targets define when an open trade will begin to take profits. A profit target is the most reliable means of achieving a profit goal, and is usually defined by a limit order. Unlike other exit methods, a profit target will close the trade as soon as price reaches the desired price level. In other words, we do not have to wait for price to fall back to exit the trade; it will happen immediately, even at the top of the price move, upon reaching the target price.

Profit targets should be defined prior to opening a trade and, like a stop loss, will depend on the volatility of the market. As a rule, the amount of a profit target (or average of multiple profit targets) must be higher than the amount of the stop loss. Maintaining a constant relationship between the level of the stop loss and the profit target(s) can help create a trading plan with a consistent +R advantage.

The down side of exiting a trade with a profit target is that it cannot follow the trend of the market. In many cases, a winning trade may exceed the profit target, continuing to produce a greater profit. Reaching a profit target will exit the trade at its predetermined level, regardless of the current strength of the market.

STOP EXITS

Stop exits include any type of exit that attempts to follow the movement of price. The goal of stop exits is to protect profits by moving the stop exit level in the direction of the market. This type of exit includes the breakeven and trailing stops described in Chapter 6—Placing Trades, as well as other stop methods that change with the volatility of the market.

Similar to a static stop loss, stop exits begin at a set distance from the entry price; however, stop exits move progressively towards the current price once a specific threshold is reached. Stop exits can be a good tool for following the price of a trending market while providing enough room for small price fluctuations. When using stop exits, price must fall back to a certain level in order to close the trade. This means that traders will never close a trade with a stop exit at the highest point of a price move. This type of exit is also prone to more slippage in live-market trading than may be illustrated in historical modeling.

Time Exits

Time exits will close a trade after a set amount of time or number of candlestick bars has passed. This type of a trade exit is used to establish the maximum time horizon in which a trade will take place. At the end of this time, the trade will be closed, with or without a profit. Time exits can be particularly useful to day traders who seek to close out all of their positions by the end of the trading day.

It should be noted that, in many cases, the overall style of trading could also be defined by the time exit. Day traders, for instance, must consistently exit all positions by the end of the day in order for this style of trading to be valid (otherwise, it would be considered swing trading). Day traders who ignore this time exit (deciding to hold onto a position overnight) may be violating their trading plans, and possibly changing the basic principles for their style of trading. This is similar to ignoring a stop loss, and can cause traders to lose control of their risk. It is important to obey the time exits of a trading plan, as this is a key tool for developing trading discipline.

Signal Exits

Signal exits refer to a condition occurring in the market that indicates when traders will exit, or flatten, their open positions. Signal exits are based on the adverse action of price, an indicator, or an outside market relationship. An example of a signal exit could be: "Close all long positions if the $TICK index rises above 1,200."

Signal exits can be a helpful tool that helps traders stay away from uncertain market conditions. Similar to a trade trigger, signal exits must be clearly defined and represent a point of immediate action.

STRATEGY TYPES

Unfortunately, there is no Swiss army knife of trading strategies that will work in every possible market condition. Traders must decide in which market conditions their trading plans will be designed to work best. Defining a strategy type helps traders develop a trading plan that will be effective at catching the right kind of market moves. This makes it possible to qualify the strategy, since either it has caught the correct market action or it has not. While there are many different strategy types, we will focus on the three basic models: trend following, counter trend, and pattern recognition.

Each of these strategy types focuses on different market conditions, and each has its advantages and disadvantages. Most importantly, traders can profit using any of these strategy types, provided they are designed properly and applied to the correct markets. Deciding what type of strategy to use comes down to personal preference. Most of us tend to have a natural inclination for a particular type of market action. For instance, some traders will see a powerful trend with skyrocketing prices and think, "It looks like it's time to sell," while others may think, "What an incredible opportunity to jump on for the ride!" Either of these concepts may work equally well if applied correctly.

Markets often go through phases or cycles of activity. These phases can range from slow moving, consolidating markets to fast-paced, trending ones. Each of these phases has only one thing in common: we are not certain when it will occur. Knowing this, we must accept that if our trading plan is designed to catch large trends, it may not show similar expectancy during non-trending or range bound market conditions. Conversely, trading plans that are designed to profit from quick turns in overbought/oversold market environments may miss the large trends.

Trying to create a trading plan that will work equally well in every market condition is almost impossible, and can significantly limit the effectiveness of the plan when optimal market conditions occur. Defining a strategy type requires a necessary compromise that traders must face in order to establish the goals of a trading plan. Traders that cannot accept this compromise often spend incredible amounts of time and money searching for the elusive "Holy Grail" of strategy types, only to find that it does not exist.

The following examples are meant to demonstrate different strategy types as well as the elements of trading plan design. These examples are not complete trading plans and are simply intended to act as a starting point from which traders may continue their own research. The EasyLanguage code for these strategies can be found in Appendix B.

TREND FOLLOWING

As the name implies, trend following strategies attempt to catch the largest price moves in a market. Trading plans that use trend following typically have a lower percentage of winning trades, offset by the size of the winning trades being much greater than the losing trades. In order for a trend following plan to be successful, it must catch every strong trend in a market. To accomplish this, trend followers are often continually in a trade (long or short), so they are guaranteed to be in the market when a strong trend develops. A common technical tool for trend following is a moving average or series of moving averages. This type of indicator can allow traders to spot a trending market based on the movement of price from its average.

The first trading plan example (Figure 7.4) uses a trend following strategy type applied to the Euro/US Dollar forex pair. The rules for this system can be seen in Figure 7.5. In general, because the forex markets will

FIGURE 7.4

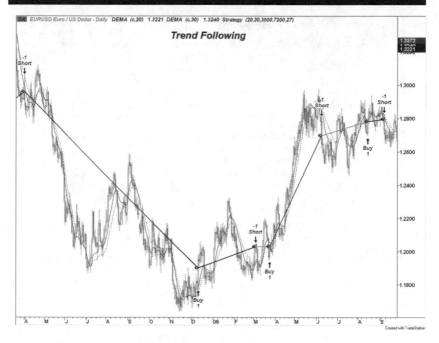

A TREND FOLLOWING STRATEGY APPLIED TO A DAILY CHART OF
THE EURO-DOLLAR FOREX PAIR.

often form strong, reliable trends, they make good candidates for trend following. This trading plan uses a daily chart and a constant, single lot size. A 20-period and 30- period DEMA is used to establish the direction of the market. If the shorter, 20-period DEMA rises above the 30, it indicates the setup for a bullish or long market, while the shorter average falling below the 30-period DEMA creates a setup for a short market. This is a stop-and-reverse system, meaning that trades will constantly be in the market unless the stop loss level is reached.

Since trend following is susceptible to frequent false signals during periods of choppy, non-trending markets, this trading plan uses a unique

FIGURE 7.5

Trading Plan Name		Trend Follower with unique entry	
Description			
Strategy Type	Trend Following	Target Market	EUR/USD
Chart Interval	Daily	Position Size	1 Lots
Entry Rules			
Trade Trigger	Long: High of the previous bar from the DEMA cross		
	Short: Low of the previous bar from the DEMA cross		
Filters	Long: 20-Period DEMA above 30-Period DEMA, candle bar closing below high of previous bar from the DEMA cross		
	Short: 20-Period DEMA below 30-Period DEMA, candle bar closing above low of previous bar from the DEMA cross		
Exit Rules			
Stop Loss	$2,400	Profit Target	none
Stop Exit	none	Time Exit	none
Reverse	on opposing signal	Signal Exit	none

A DESCRIPTION OF THE TREND FOLLOWER TRADING PLAN.

entry method to help define the start of a trend. These entry rules are detailed in Figure 7.6. Once the short-term and long-term DEMAs cross, the high or low of the previous day's price will be used as the trade trigger. For a long trade entry, once the 20-period DEMA crosses over the 30-period, the high of the previous bar is noted as the "trigger high". The next filter condition that must take place is a candlestick bar closing below this trigger high. This completes the filter setup, and a stop order to buy is placed at the trigger high level. Once price reaches this level, a long trade will be initiated. Reversing these signals and using a "trigger low" provides the entry rules for a short trade.

FIGURE 7.6

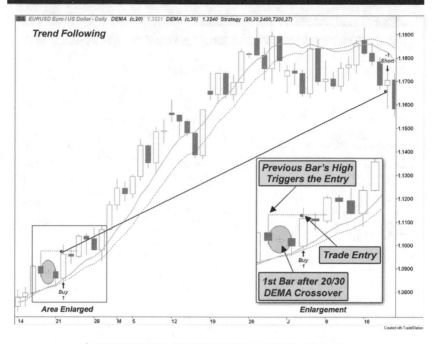

A DESCRIPTION OF THE ENTRY METHOD USED IN
TREND FOLLOWER TRADING PLAN.

The exit rules for this trading plan are quite simple since the majority of trades will exit on an opposing trade entry signal. This allows the trades to reverse direction and stay in the market to catch a newly developing trend. A protective stop loss exit is used to close out trades that have gone in the wrong direction. While this stop loss is quite large, most trades are exited long before the stop loss amount is reached. This allows for a much larger average winning trade than the average loser. A complete performance report for the historical modeling of this trading plan can be seen in Figure 7.7.

FIGURE 7.7

TradeStation Performance Summary			Collapse ⌃
All Trades			
Total Net Profit	$55,490.00	Profit Factor	4.01
Gross Profit	$73,940.00	Gross Loss	($18,450.00)
Open Position Profit/Loss	($1,130.00)		
Select Total Net Profit	$55,490.00	Select Profit Factor	4.01
Select Gross Profit	$73,940.00	Select Gross Loss	($18,450.00)
Adjusted Total Net Profit	$28,310.96	Adjusted Profit Factor	2.17
Adjusted Gross Profit	$52,595.36	Adjusted Gross Loss	($24,284.40)
Total Number of Trades	22	Percent Profitable	54.55%
Winning Trades	12	Losing Trades	10
Even Trades	0		
Avg. Trade Net Profit	$2,522.27	Ratio Avg. Win:Avg. Loss	3.34
Avg. Winning Trade	$6,161.67	Avg. Losing Trade	($1,845.00)
Largest Winning Trade	$13,300.00	Largest Losing Trade	($2,400.00)
Largest Winner as % of Gross Profit	17.99%	Largest Loser as % of Gross Loss	13.01%
Net Profit as % of Largest Loss	2312.08%		
Slct. Net Profit as % of Largest Loss	2312.08%	Adj. Net Profit as % of Largest Loss	1179.62%
Max. Consecutive Winning Trades	3	Max. Consecutive Losing Trades	3
Avg. Bars in Winning Trades	75.08	Avg. Bars in Losing Trades	25.90
Avg. Bars in Total Trades	52.73		
Max. Shares/Contracts Held	1	Account Size Required	$5,610.00

A HISTORICAL TESTING PERFORMANCE REPORT FOR THE TREND FOLLOWER TRADING PLAN DURING THE PERIOD OF 12/31/2001 TO 1/2/2007.

Trend following strategies work well for traders who like to catch the big moves and who don't mind sitting through long periods of regular market oscillations. Many enthusiastic trend followers use the expression, "The trend is your friend." Trend following requires an element of patience as markets are not always trending. Another factor that is critical to successful trend following is that traders must have the discipline to take every trade that meets their entry criteria since the overall success of trend following often comes from just a few trades that show extraordinarily large profits. Missing one of these large winning trades can have a significant negative impact on the results of the trading plan.

COUNTER TREND

Counter trend strategies rely on frequent market oscillations to make consistent gains. Each winning trade often reflects price moves that are many times smaller than the preceding trend. This type of logic anticipates the possibility of price reversing in the opposite direction. Technical indicators, such as trend lines and oscillators, are often used to help define market turns and establish areas of high probability reversals. In a counter trend trading plan, trades are much more frequent than with trend following. In addition, counter trend trading minimizes the amount of time open trades are in the market and may limit a trader's risk exposure.

FIGURE 7.8

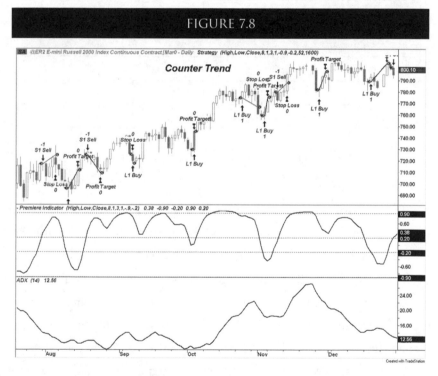

A COUNTER TREND SWING TRADING PLAN APPLIED TO A
DAILY CHART OF THE E-MINI RUSSELL 2000.

FIGURE 7.9

Trading Plan Name		Counter trend with fixed +R Adv. of 2	
Description			
Strategy Type	Counter Trend	Target Market	Emini Russell 2000
Chart Interval	Daily	Position Size	1 Contract
Entry Rules			
Trade Trigger	Long: (1) Premiere Stochastic crossing below 0.90, (2) Premiere Stochastic crossing below 0.20		
	Short: (1) Premiere Stochastic crossing above -0.90, (2) Premiere Stochastic crossing above -0.20		
Filters	Trades only taken when 14-Period ADX value is below 52		
Exit Rules			
Stop Loss	$800	Profit Target	$1,600
Stop Exit	none	Time Exit	none
Reverse	on opposing signal	Signal Exit	yes

A DESCRIPTION OF THE COUNTER TREND SWING TRADING PLAN.

The rules for a sample counter trend, swing trading plan can be seen in Figure 7.9. This plan uses the ADX and Premiere stochastic indicator that was introduced in Chapter 5—Charting the Market. A daily chart interval of the E-mini Russell 2000 futures contract will provide the target market. Frequent price swings are common in stock index futures, creating good markets for counter trend trading. The entry conditions for this trade plan require the 14-period ADX to be below 52. Since counter trend strategies trade in the opposite direction of the current trend, these trades are often stopped out if the trend becomes too strong. The ADX will help define

FIGURE 7.10

TradeStation Performance Summary			Collapse ☆
All Trades			
Total Net Profit	$49,740.00	Profit Factor	2.03
Gross Profit	$97,870.00	Gross Loss	($48,130.00)
Open Position Profit/Loss	$110.00		
Select Total Net Profit	$50,670.00	Select Profit Factor	2.07
Select Gross Profit	$97,870.00	Select Gross Loss	($47,200.00)
Adjusted Total Net Profit	$31,195.98	Adjusted Profit Factor	1.57
Adjusted Gross Profit	$85,539.54	Adjusted Gross Loss	($54,343.56)
Total Number of Trades	123	Percent Profitable	51.22%
Winning Trades	63	Losing Trades	60
Even Trades	0		
Avg. Trade Net Profit	$404.39	Ratio Avg. Win:Avg. Loss	1.94
Avg. Winning Trade	$1,553.49	Avg. Losing Trade	($802.17)
Largest Winning Trade	$2,050.00	Largest Losing Trade	($930.00)
Largest Winner as % of Gross Profit	2.09%	Largest Loser as % of Gross Loss	1.93%
Net Profit as % of Largest Loss	5348.39%		
Slct. Net Profit as % of Largest Loss	5448.39%	Adj. Net Profit as % of Largest Loss	3354.41%
Max. Consecutive Winning Trades	4	Max. Consecutive Losing Trades	7
Avg. Bars in Winning Trades	4.76	Avg. Bars in Losing Trades	3.15
Avg. Bars in Total Trades	3.98		
Max. Shares/Contracts Held	1	Account Size Required	$5,600.00

AN HISTORICAL TESTING PERFORMANCE REPORT FOR THE COUNTER TREND SWING TRADING PLAN DURING THE PERIOD OF 12/31/2001 TO 1/2/2007.

the strength of the trend; and if the trend is above a 14-period ADX level of 52, we will choose to stay out of the market.

The entry trigger for this plan requires the Premiere stochastic to cross below a level of 0.90 or 0.20 for a long position and above -0.90 or -0.20 for a short position. A trade will be entered with a market order on the open of the bar that follows the Premiere stochastic cross at any of these four levels. The logic for using these thresholds is that price will often retrace or reverse following a strong push. This counter trend entry attempts to identify these price pushes early and anticipate the change of price direction. Since we can profit from even a modest price move, an early entry will allow for the greatest chance of reaching our target.

The exit rules for this strategy involve an exit bracket (combination of stop and limit order) with an $800 stop loss and a single $1,600 profit target. The difference between the amount of the stop loss and profit target is set to a consistent +R advantage of 2, meaning the profit target is twice as much as the stop loss. Another possible exit would be an entry signal in the opposite direction. In this instance, the current trade would be immediately closed and another initiated in the opposite direction (stop-and-reverse).

The historical modeling results for this trading plan can be seen in Figure 7.10. Counter trend strategies offer an active style of trading that is appealing to many fast-paced traders. This type of trading will often trade against the dominant trend or will catch a new trend early, exiting after a small part of the move. Traders who use this type of strategy must maintain consistency in their money management. Since the success of this system depends on a constant +R advantage, missed stop losses or early profit taking can easily break down the profitability for this type of trading plan.

PATTERN RECOGNITION

Pattern recognition relies on regularly occurring price patterns for trade entry or exit rules. Individual markets often display a tendency to move in a particular direction following the formation of reoccurring price patterns. Candlestick charts may provide the best means for using this type of logic, since these charts make price patterns relatively easy to identify. Pattern recognition can be done visually or with the help of a computer. While there is a large variety of named price and candlestick

FIGURE 7.11

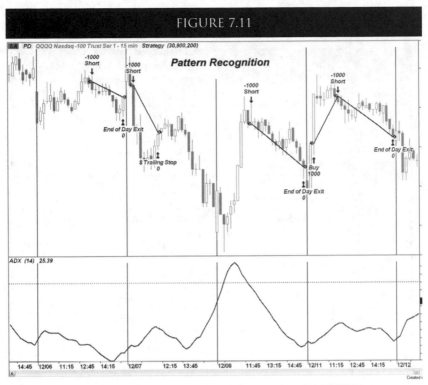

A PATTERN RECOGNITION DAY TRADING PLAN APPLIED
TO A 15-MINUTE CHART OF THE QQQQS.

patterns, traders must research which patterns work best in their intended markets and charting intervals.

The next sample trading plan (Figure 7.11) looks for bullish and bearish engulfing patterns to day trade the QQQQs using a 15-minute chart, and is described in Figure 7.12. Engulfing candlestick patterns (discussed in Chapter 5—Charting the Market) create a type of reversal pattern, often signaling the beginning of a new trend and a good point to enter a trade.

For this example, we will look for an established trend that can be defined by three candlestick bars, each with open and closing prices succes-

FIGURE 7.12

Trading Plan Name		Engulfing pattern with ADX filter	
Description			
Strategy Type	Pattern Recognition	Target Market	QQQQ
Chart Interval	15 - Minute	Position Size	1000 Shares
Entry Rules			
Trade Trigger	Long: Bullish engulfing pattern (up body of current candle bar engulfing the previous bar)		
	Short: Bearish engulfing pattern (down body of current candle bar engulfing the previous bar)		
Filters	Long: 14- Period ADX under 30 and a three bar downtrend (open and closing prices lower on each of the three bars)		
	Short: 14 - Period ADX under 30 and a three bar uptrend (open and closing prices higher on each of the three bars)		
Exit Rules			
Stop Loss	$200	Profit Target	$900
Stop Exit	Trailing stop at $200	Time Exit	End of day
Reverse	none	Signal Exit	yes

A DESCRIPTION OF THE ENGULFING PATTERN
RECOGNITION DAY TRADING PLAN.

sively lower for a long setup, or open and closing prices that are progres-
sively higher for a short setup. In addition to this price pattern filter, the
ADX will once again be used to stay away from excessively strong trends.
For this application, we will only consider a trade when the 14–period
ADX is lower than 30.

The trade trigger will be the bar that engulfs the previous bar. For
a long trade, the engulfing candlestick bar must be an up bar, and for a

FIGURE 7.13

TradeStation Performance Summary			Collapse ≈

All Trades

Total Net Profit	$7,850.00	Profit Factor	3.07
Gross Profit	$11,640.00	Gross Loss	($3,790.00)
Open Position Profit/Loss	$0.00		
Select Total Net Profit	$6,050.00	Select Profit Factor	2.60
Select Gross Profit	$9,840.00	Select Gross Loss	($3,790.00)
Adjusted Total Net Profit	$5,706.77	Adjusted Profit Factor	2.30
Adjusted Gross Profit	$10,111.59	Adjusted Gross Loss	($4,404.82)
Total Number of Trades	98	Percent Profitable	59.18%
Winning Trades	58	Losing Trades	38
Even Trades	2		
Avg. Trade Net Profit	$80.10	Ratio Avg. Win:Avg. Loss	2.01
Avg. Winning Trade	$200.69	Avg. Losing Trade	($99.74)
Largest Winning Trade	$900.00	Largest Losing Trade	($200.00)
Largest Winner as % of Gross Profit	7.73%	Largest Loser as % of Gross Loss	5.28%
Net Profit as % of Largest Loss	3925.00%		
Slct. Net Profit as % of Largest Loss	3025.00%	Adj. Net Profit as % of Largest Loss	2853.39%
Max. Consecutive Winning Trades	9	Max. Consecutive Losing Trades	6
Avg. Bars in Winning Trades	11.67	Avg. Bars in Losing Trades	4.13
Avg. Bars in Total Trades	8.63		
Max. Shares/Contracts Held	1000	Account Size Required	$1,420.00

AN HISTORICAL TESTING PERFORMANCE REPORT FOR THE
ENGULFING PATTERN RECOGNITION DAY TRADING PLAN DURING
THE PERIOD OF 1/3/2006 TO 1/3/2007.

short trade it must be a down bar. A market order will be used to enter the trade as soon as this engulfing bar is confirmed at the close of the 15-minute interval.

Since this is a day trading strategy, a mandatory time exit will close any open positions before the end of the trading day (4:00 EST). An initial stop loss will be set for $200 with an accompanying profit target at $900. A $200 trailing stop will be implemented that will move with price, maintaining a $200 gap between the stop level and the highest point of the price move during the life of the trade. In addition, this type of strategy can reverse positions if an opposing engulfing pattern occurs.

The performance of this trading plan can be seen in Figure 7.13, and depends heavily on its ability to follow a trend once in a position. The trailing stop allows this strategy to move with the trend and capture a potentially large move. Once the position has reached the $900 profit target, however, the probability of the trade falling back to its trailing stop level ($700 profit) becomes relatively high, and the position is closed with a profit that is 4.5 times higher than the initial risk.

Pattern recognition strategies are often a hybrid of trend following and counter trend strategies. They may attempt to catch a continuation of a trend or spot new market reversals. Traders should take the time to carefully define their patterns, as this form of trading can easily become subjective. While it is easy to spot patterns that would have led to powerful price moves in hindsight, traders should be able describe their patterns in a forward market as well.

CHAPTER 8
EVALUATING AND
COMPARING TRADING PLANS

In Chapter 1—The Fundamental Concepts of Trading, we introduced some important measures that could be used to determine the optimal amount of risk in a simple coin-tossing example. In this chapter, we will use those same concepts, and show how they can be applied to trading. While the math will be a little more complex and will require the use of a spreadsheet, the concept of objectively measuring trading risk and performance is very similar to the concepts demonstrated in the coin-tossing examples.

During this chapter, we will look at four important elements of assessing a trading plan:

1. Measuring key performance metrics that can be used to evaluate a trading plan.

2. Defining the amount of risk in a trading plan.

3. Establishing an optimal percentage of risk to use as a baseline for position sizing.

4. Applying methods that help a trading plan to perform as close as possible to historical modeling.

The overall goal of objectively measuring a trading plan is to improve on the plan. This may not just equate to making more money, but developing a plan that is more tradable or more consistent. In addition, every step in the development process of a trading plan requires an evaluation to ensure the system is on track and ready to move forward. Reliable testing will help traders develop and improve their plans in the shortest amount of time.

The easiest way to analyze a trading plan is to view the trade results in a backtesting program. This allows traders to instantly see performance reports from historical market data, such as those shown in Chapter 7—Developing a Trading Plan. Using a backtesting program also provides a method of quickly prototyping trading ideas, and allows for relatively accurate and objective testing. Traders that use backtesting software must make sure they have correctly programmed the rules of their strategies into the software and, in addition, should review each hypothetical trade on a chart to check for accuracy.

Backtesting software is not the only method of measuring a trading plan. Traders without automatic backtesting capabilities can still benefit from this important type of performance analysis. Long before backtesting software was available, traders developed tools and systems to manually test their trading plans on historical data. Traders can visually backtest the logic of a trading plan by reviewing historical charts and recording the

FIGURE 8.1

	A	B	C	D	E	F	G	H	I	J	K	L	M	N
1	Trade Entry	Trade Exit	Position Size	Long (1) / Short (-1)	Profit (Loss)	Winning Trades	Losing Trades	Running Total	DrawDown	R Advantage	Equity Multiplier		Full Point Value for Instrument	$100,000.00
2	0.8814	0.9845	1.00	1	$10,310.00	$10,310.00	---	$10,310.00	$0.00	4.2958	1.8592			
3	0.9845	1.0085	1.00	-1	($2,400.00)	---	($2,400.00)	$7,910.00	($2,400.00)	(1.0000)	1.4873			
4	0.9892	1.0132	1.00	-1	($2,400.00)	---	($2,400.00)	$5,510.00	($4,800.00)	(1.0000)	1.1899			
5	1.0117	1.0730	1.00	1	$6,130.00	$6,130.00	---	$11,640.00	$0.00	2.5542	1.7977			
6	1.0730	1.0970	1.00	1	($2,400.00)	---	($2,400.00)	$9,240.00	($2,400.00)	(1.0000)	1.4382			
7	1.0971	1.1657	1.00	1	$6,860.00	$6,860.00	---	$16,100.00	$0.00	2.8683	2.2603			
8	1.1657	1.1239	1.00	-1	$4,180.00	$4,180.00	---	$20,280.00	$0.00	1.7417	3.0476			
9	1.1239	1.2569	1.00	1	$13,300.00	$13,300.00	---	$33,580.00	$0.00	5.5417	6.4254			
10	1.2569	1.2809	1.00	1	($2,400.00)	---	($2,400.00)	$31,180.00	($2,400.00)	(1.0000)	5.1403			
11	1.2569	1.2001	1.00	-1	$5,680.00	$5,680.00	---	$36,860.00	$0.00	2.3667	7.5734			
12	1.2001	1.2230	1.00	1	$2,290.00	$2,290.00	---	$39,150.00	$0.00	0.9542	9.0187			
13	1.2230	1.2373	1.00	-1	($1,430.00)	---	($1,430.00)	$37,720.00	($1,430.00)	(0.5969)	7.9440			
14	1.2373	1.2133	1.00	1	($2,400.00)	---	($2,400.00)	$35,320.00	($3,830.00)	(1.0000)	6.3552			
15	1.2131	1.2309	1.00	-1	($1,780.00)	---	($1,780.00)	$33,540.00	($5,610.00)	(0.7417)	5.4125			
16	1.2309	1.2960	1.00	1	$6,510.00	$6,510.00	---	$40,050.00	$0.00	2.7125	8.3488			
17	1.2960	1.1902	1.00	-1	$10,580.00	$10,580.00	---	$50,630.00	$0.00	4.4083	15.7096			
18	1.1902	1.2030	1.00	1	$1,280.00	$1,280.00	---	$51,910.00	$0.00	0.5333	17.3853			
19	1.2030	1.2031	1.00	-1	($10.00)	---	($10.00)	$51,900.00	($10.00)	(0.0042)	17.3708			
20	1.2031	1.2699	1.00	1	$6,680.00	$6,680.00	---	$58,580.00	$0.00	2.7833	27.0405			
21	1.2699	1.2782	1.00	-1	($830.00)	---	($830.00)	$57,750.00	($830.00)	(0.3458)	25.1702			
22	1.2782	1.2796	1.00	1	$140.00	$140.00	---	$57,890.00	($690.00)	0.0583	25.4639			
23	1.2796	1.3036	1.00	-1	($2,400.00)	---	($2,400.00)	$55,490.00	($3,090.00)	(1.0000)	20.3711			

Performance Statistics

Maximum DrawDown	($5,610.00)
Total Net Profit	$55,490.00
Profit Factor	4.01
Percent Profitable	54.55%
Average Trade Net Profit	$2,522.27

Risk of Ruin Calculations

Initial Account Value	$30,000.00
Ruin % of Initial Account	0.50
Average Winning Percentage	20.54%
Average Loss Percentage	6.15%
Sum of Possible Outcomes	0.0841
Square of the Sum of Squares	0.1573
Z	0.7673
Risk of Ruin	2.25%

Optimal Risk Percentage

Maximum Risk Percentage	0.20
Theoretical Account Growth	$763,916.82

A PERFORMANCE ANALYSIS SPREADSHEET SHOWING THE RESULTS FROM THE TREND FOLLOWING SAMPLE PLAN THAT WAS INTRODUCED IN CHAPTER 7–DEVELOPING A TRADING PLAN. ONCE TRADE DATA IS ENTERED INTO SECTION A, THE SPREADSHEET WILL CALCULATE THE REST OF THE KEY PERFORMANCE MEASURES.

exact trade entry and exit points into a spreadsheet, as seen in Figure 8.1. This method, while more time consuming, often helps traders develop a feel for the implementation of their trading rules. For this process to be effective, traders must be careful not to use any hindsight in deciding which trades would or would not have been taken. A recommended practice is to use a piece of paper to cover all but the most recent bars on a chart and advance bar-by-bar until a trade entry or exit is located. Traders may also be able to accomplish this be scrolling a chart slowly across their monitors. The process of manually identifying trades must be objective, and if traders find themselves thinking things like, "I would have never taken that trade if I was really trading," they are not doing it correctly.

DEFINING IMPORTANT PERFORMANCE METRICS

There are a hundreds of different performance metrics or statistics that can be used to evaluate a trading plan. Traders often develop a preference for those metrics that are most valuable based on their particular trading style or business goals. We will look at several performance metrics that we consider the most important for assessing a variety of different trading plans.

While traders who use backtesting software will be able to get many of these performance metrics directly from within their programs, it is recommended to use the performance analysis spreadsheet described below, since it will be used to demonstrate other important concepts later in the chapter. The EasyLanguage code for importing trade data directly into a spreadsheet is provided in Appendix B.

Once traders have compiled a list of trades (the trade journal in Appendix C can be helpful for this purpose), the trades can be put into a spreadsheet for further analysis. The following spreadsheets were created using Microsoft Excel, and traders should familiarize themselves with this powerful tool. Traders can construct a performance analysis spreadsheet using the following procedure:

Section A–Individual Trade Data (Figure 8.1): For each trade, type the entry price, exit price, number of shares or contracts traded, and the trade direction (long "+1" or short "-1") into columns A, B, C, and D. Traders also must enter the full point value for the specific trading instrument ($100 for the E-mini Russell or $1 for the QQQQs, for instance) into cell N1. Please note that no data or formulas should be entered into the first row as this is reserved for the column labels. In addition, please note that the formulas reference an arbitrary number of rows as 122, which provides ample space to begin testing. If more than 122 trades are listed, all references to 122 will need to change to compensate for the increase in the number of listed trades.

Section B–Individual Trade Formulas (Figure 8.2): Enter the eight formulas in the second row of columns E through K, and drag them down to the last row in which a trade has been entered. (Column K has two formulas: the first formula is entered in cell K2 and is not dragged; the second formula is entered directly below in cell K3 and is dragged down to the last row in which a trade has been entered.) This data can be used to establish the per trade performance characteristics for the trading plan.

Section C–Performance Formulas (Figure 8.3): Add the initial account value, Ruin%, and Maximum Risk into cells N11, N12, and N21. Then, enter all of the formulas into the correct cells of column N. This section includes performance statistics, risk of ruin calculations, and an optimal risk percentage, allowing for an overall assessment of the trading plan.

FIGURE 8.2

	E	F	G	H	I	J	K
1	Profit (Loss)	Winning Trades	Losing Trades	Running Total	DrawDown	R Advantage	Equity Multiplier
2	=(B2-A2)*C2*D2*N$1	=IF(E2>0,E2,"---")	=IF(E2<0,E2,"---")	=SUM($E$2:E2)	=H2-MAX($H$2:H2)	= -E2/MIN(E$2:E$122)	=1+J2*N$21
3							=(1+J3*N$21)*K2
4							
5							
6							
7							
8							
9							
10							
11							
12							
13							
14							
15							
16							
17							

E2	▾	*fx*	= (B2 - A2) * C2 * D2 * N$1		I2	▾	*fx*	= H2 - MAX($H$2:H2)
F2	▾	*fx*	= IF(E2 > 0,E2,"---")		J2	▾	*fx*	= -E2/MIN(E$2:E$122)
G2	▾	*fx*	= IF(E2 < 0,E2,"---")		K2	▾	*fx*	= 1 + J2 * N$21
H2	▾	*fx*	= SUM($E$2:E2)		K3	▾	*fx*	= (1 + J3 * N$21) * K2

THE INDIVIDUAL TRADE FORMULAS USED IN SECTION B OF
THE PERFORMANCE ANALYSIS SPREADSHEET.

Once all of the data and formulas are entered, the spreadsheet is ready and can provide the necessary statistics to evaluate a trading plan. This spreadsheet should be saved as it can be used to compare multiple trading plans (without reentering all of the formulas) by simply changing the trade data in section A.

MAXIMUM DRAWDOWN

Maximum drawdown refers to the "worst case scenario" for a trading period. This measures the greatest difference, or loss, from a previous equity peak. This statistic can help measure the amount of risk and establish if a strategy is possible given the size of the trading account. In general, this number should be as small as possible. Trading plans that require large maximum drawdowns should be avoided.

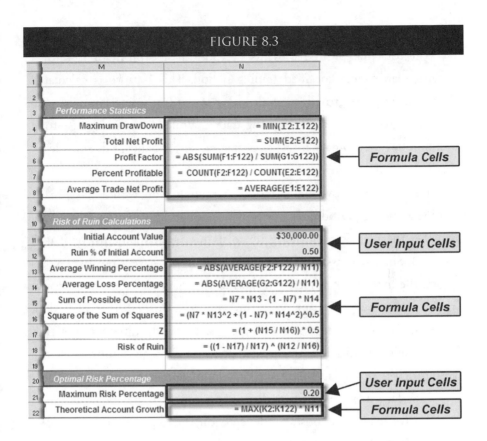

FIGURE 8.3

	M	N
1		
2		
3	*Performance Statistics*	
4	Maximum DrawDown	= MIN(I2:I122)
5	Total Net Profit	= SUM(E2:E122)
6	Profit Factor	= ABS(SUM(F1:F122) / SUM(G1:G122))
7	Percent Profitable	= COUNT(F2:F122) / COUNT(E2:E122)
8	Average Trade Net Profit	= AVERAGE(E1:E122)
9		
10	*Risk of Ruin Calculations*	
11	Initial Account Value	$30,000.00
12	Ruin % of Initial Account	0.50
13	Average Winning Percentage	= ABS(AVERAGE(F2:F122) / N11)
14	Average Loss Percentage	= ABS(AVERAGE(G2:G122) / N11)
15	Sum of Possible Outcomes	= N7 * N13 - (1 - N7) * N14
16	Square of the Sum of Squares	= (N7 * N13^2 + (1 - N7) * N14^2)^0.5
17	Z	= (1 + (N15 / N16)) * 0.5
18	Risk of Ruin	= ((1 - N17) / N17) ^ (N12 / N16)
19		
20	*Optimal Risk Percentage*	
21	Maximum Risk Percentage	0.20
22	Theoretical Account Growth	= MAX(K2:K122) * N11

Formula Cells (rows 4–8)
User Input Cells (rows 11–12)
Formula Cells (rows 13–18)
User Input Cells (row 20)
Formula Cells (row 22)

THE PERFORMANCE FORMULAS USED IN SECTION C OF THE
PERFORMANCE ANALYSIS SPREADSHEET.

As a basic rule, a trader should begin analysis of a trading plan by determining how much he or she can afford to risk. If the maximum drawdown for a trading plan exceeds this amount, the trader may not need to look any farther; the plan must be revised before it can advance to the next level. While this performance metric often appears at the bottom of performance reports in many software packages, it is among the most valuable. It is recommended that traders begin their analysis by looking at the maximum drawdown, as this determines the feasibility of a trading plan.

EVALUATING AND COMPARING TRADING PLANS 215

TOTAL NET PROFIT

The total net profit represents the bottom line profit or loss for a trading plan over a specified trading period. This statistic is calculated by subtracting the gross loss of all losing trades (including commissions) from the gross profit of all winning trades. While many traders use total net profit as the primary measure of trading performance, this statistic by itself can be deceptive.

Just knowing how much money a trading plan would have made during a trading period does not provide enough information to measure whether the plan is performing up to its historical standards, or if it is efficient. Since it is assumed that trading plans will have a positive expectancy, the more time a trading plan is in the market, the more it should theoretically make. By comparing the same plan during different trading periods, therefore, traders could expect significantly different total net profit results. In addition, this metric does not allow us to normalize the results of a trading plan based on the amount of risk that is incurred.

Let's face it, we all want to know how much money a trading plan could have made...our business depends on this type of projection. We must be careful, however, not to get blinded by this number, and we must continue to look at the overall statistics for a trading plan. Total net profit alone does not allow traders to adequately compare or track the performance of a trading plan.

PROFIT FACTOR

The profit factor can be thought of as the R advantage for the complete trading plan. While the R advantage is only used to measure the risk ratio of individual trades, the profit factor is defined as the gross profit divided by the gross loss (including commission) for the entire trading period. This performance metric relates the amount of profit per unit of risk, with values greater than one showing a profitable trading plan.

In theory, this number should be as high as possible. In reality, extremely high profit factors rarely correlate to actual trading performance. Most successful trading plans may have anywhere between a 1.5 and 5.0 profit factor. One method of comparing profit factors is by looking for consistency over time, regardless of the trading period.

PERCENT PROFITABLE

The percent profitable is also known as the probability of winning. This statistic is calculated by dividing the number of winning trades by the total number of trades for a given trading period. The percentage of profitable trades depends entirely on the type of strategy employed in a trading plan.

Typically, trading plans will have between a 40 and 60 percentage of winning trades. Trend following strategies tend to have lower values, while trading plans using counter trend or shorter-term styles of trading tend to be higher. In addition, trading plans that rely on values greater than 80% are rarely reliable in live trading. Traders do not necessarily need a high percentage of profitable trades to create a successful trading plan. A more important goal of using this metric is to find a consistent percent profitable during each level of development, and in live trading.

AVERAGE TRADE NET PROFIT

The average trade net profit is the expectancy of a trading plan. This metric represents the average amount of money that was won or lost per trade, and is calculated by dividing the total net profit by the total number of trades. This metric provides a useful indication about the future performance of a trading plan. This calculation is significantly affected by the position size, since larger position sizes will magnify the average winning and losing trade amounts. For this reason, it is recommended to initially test a trading plan using a constant, minimal position size. This will allow a more accurate comparison that can be used to gauge the efficiency of the plan. In other words, traders should avoid increasing position size to improve this statistic.

Another factor that should be taken into account is how close this average relates to the biggest trades. Occasionally, historical modeling results may be skewed by a single trade that creates a profit (or loss) many times greater than a typical trade. This type of trade, know as an outlier, may create unrealistic results by over-inflating the average trade net profit. In this case, it may be best to remove the outlier, especially if the success of the trading plan is based on this single trade. Trading plans that rely on one or two abnormally large trades over a trading period are often closer to gambling that realistic trading.

Risk Measurements

For every success story like the Turtles, there are even more tales of trading disaster due to improper risk management. Such is the case with a hedge fund trader for Amaranth Advisors who lost over $4 billion in the course of one week during the fall of 2006. Hedge funds, which are aggressively-traded portfolios catering to high net worth investors, attempt to generate unusually high returns by employing many of the same tactics used by active traders. This includes short trades, trading a wide variety of alternative markets, and applying trading leverage, or margin.

As mentioned earlier in this book, leverage must be used responsibly; otherwise, traders risk very high losses. For the Amaranth trader whose account had previously been up roughly $2 billion earlier in the year, a 5-to-1 leveraged trade in the gas futures market spelled disaster. Looking back on this incident, traders should be wondering, "What type of risk management was he using?" This catastrophic loss points out the importance of measuring and assessing risk in a trading plan. While this trader may have generated impressive returns in the past, he ignored the excessively high risk of ruin that his trading tactics were creating. Even worse, he dismissed the primary goal of successful trading: to always protect your trading capital

RISK OF RUIN

Previously, we defined the risk of ruin as the probability of losing everything. At this point, we must redefine the risk of ruin for an individual trading plan. The reality is that most traders would not risk bringing a trading account all the way down to zero, nor is this even possible given minimum margin requirements. Thus, we must define a percentage of an account to consider as the point of ruin, or bankruptcy.

It is important to acknowledge that the risk of ruin is most critical during the early stages of trading. When traders first begin, they often have the least amount of money to lose since they have not yet begun making trading profits to grow their accounts. A string of losses at the beginning of a trading business can be much more significant than later on. For this reason, traders must approach the initial stages of their trading businesses very carefully.

The risk of ruin calculation section of the performance analysis spreadsheet, shown in Figure 8.4, defines the elements used for this measurement. Traders must enter their starting account balances and the ruin percentage in order to define an ultimate risk level. For this example, we have used 21 trades from the counter trend swing trading plan that was introduced in

FIGURE 8.4

Full Point Value for Instrument	$100.00

Performance Statistics	
Maximum DrawDown	($1,600.00)
Total Net Profit	$14,400.00
Profit Factor	3.25
Percent Profitable	61.90%
Average Trade Net Profit	$685.71

Risk of Ruin Calculations	
Initial Account Value	$15,000.00
Ruin % of Initial Account	0.50
Average Winning Percentage	10.67%
Average Loss Percentage	5.33%
Sum of Possible Outcomes	0.0457
Square of the Sum of Squares	0.0901
Z	0.7535
Risk of Ruin	0.20%

Optimal Risk Percentage	
Maximum Risk Percentage	0.43
Theoretical Account Growth	$533,059.80

Trade Entry	Trade Exit	Position Size	Long (1) / Short (-1)	Profit (Loss)	Winning Trades	Losing Trades	Running Total	DrawDown	R Advantage	Equity Multiplier
768.60	784.60	1.00	1	$1,600.00	$1,600.00	---	$1,600.00	$0.00	2.0000	1.8571
778.70	770.70	1.00	1	($800.00)	---	($800.00)	$800.00	($800.00)	(1.0000)	1.0612
764.10	780.10	1.00	1	$1,600.00	$1,600.00	---	$2,400.00	$0.00	2.0000	1.9708
800.50	784.50	1.00	-1	$1,600.00	$1,600.00	---	$4,000.00	$0.00	2.0000	3.6601
779.70	795.70	1.00	1	$1,600.00	$1,600.00	---	$5,600.00	$0.00	2.0000	6.7974
757.60	749.60	1.00	1	($800.00)	---	($800.00)	$4,800.00	($800.00)	(1.0000)	3.8842
746.20	730.20	1.00	-1	$1,600.00	$1,600.00	---	$6,400.00	$0.00	2.0000	7.2136
756.70	740.70	1.00	-1	$1,600.00	$1,600.00	---	$8,000.00	$0.00	2.0000	13.3966
725.50	717.50	1.00	1	($800.00)	---	($800.00)	$7,200.00	($800.00)	(1.0000)	7.6552
717.80	701.80	1.00	-1	$1,600.00	$1,600.00	---	$8,800.00	$0.00	2.0000	14.2168
701.60	693.60	1.00	1	($800.00)	---	($800.00)	$8,000.00	($800.00)	(1.0000)	8.1239
716.80	724.80	1.00	-1	($800.00)	---	($800.00)	$7,200.00	($1,600.00)	(1.0000)	4.6422
695.60	711.60	1.00	1	$1,600.00	$1,600.00	---	$8,800.00	$0.00	2.0000	8.6213
725.10	709.10	1.00	-1	$1,600.00	$1,600.00	---	$10,400.00	$0.00	2.0000	16.0110
725.40	717.40	1.00	1	($800.00)	---	($800.00)	$9,600.00	($800.00)	(1.0000)	9.1491
729.50	745.50	1.00	1	$1,600.00	$1,600.00	---	$11,200.00	$0.00	2.0000	16.9912
774.70	766.70	1.00	1	($800.00)	---	($800.00)	$10,400.00	($800.00)	(1.0000)	9.7093
759.30	775.30	1.00	1	$1,600.00	$1,600.00	---	$12,000.00	$0.00	2.0000	18.0315
779.90	787.90	1.00	1	($800.00)	---	($800.00)	$11,200.00	($800.00)	(1.0000)	10.3037
781.70	797.70	1.00	1	$1,600.00	$1,600.00	---	$12,800.00	$0.00	2.0000	19.1355
789.00	805.00	1.00	1	$1,600.00	$1,600.00	---	$14,400.00	$0.00	2.0000	35.5373

A PERFORMANCE ANALYSIS SPREADSHEET SHOWING THE RESULTS FROM 21 TRADES IN THE COUNTER TREND SWING TRADING SAMPLE PLAN.

Chapter 7—Developing a Trading Plan. We have chosen a $15,000 trading account and are willing to risk 50% of this amount, or $7,500. In other words, if the value of this account falls below $7,500, all trading will cease, and we will have reached the point of ruin. This trading plan shows strong historical performance characteristics while trading a single E-mini Russell 2000 futures contract. As a result, we have a very reasonable 0.2% risk of ruin probability.

The user-defined ruin% (cell N12 in our spreadsheet example) should not be confused with the percentage of the overall account that we are trading. The ruin% simply defines how much of the initial account will be considered in the risk of ruin calculation. A larger ruin% will equate to a smaller risk of ruin because we now have more money that can be lost before we reach the point of ruin. For instance, changing the ruin% to .70 would mean that we would have a larger, $10,500 amount to risk, and would decrease the risk of ruin to only .02%. For the most part, these numbers should remain constant as traders begin the development of a trading plan.

The purpose of this statistic is to objectively measure the risk in any possible trading plan or position sizing methodology. As traders increase their position sizes, for example, the risk of ruin will also change to reflect additional risk. If, for instance, we were to use our original ruin% of .5 and trade a constant position size of 10 contracts instead of one (changing the value of every cell in column D to 10 or -10), we would increase the probability of ruin to 54%. This would tell us that if we began trading 10 contracts, the chances of losing $7,500 would be greater than the odds of a fair coin toss. (The only way traders could trade 10 contracts using a $15K account is with day trading margin rates). It can also be noted that the maximum drawdown for trading 10 contracts in this sample trading plan is -$16,000; more than the entire value of the account. Trading at this level is not realistic, and most responsible traders would not even consider such terrible odds.

OPTIMAL RISK PERCENTAGE

The optimal risk percentage is simply the mathematical optimization of trading risk...it should not be used as a recommendation for how much to risk in actual trading! In fact, trading at optimal risk percentages could lead traders to take on high levels of risk with excessively large probabilities of ruin. Traders should only use the optimal risk percentage as a reference to understand the possibility of geometric account growth for a particular trading plan.

In Chapter 7—Developing a Trading Plan, the importance of fixed percentage position sizing was discussed as a method of controlling risk and maximizing profits. Using this concept, we can look at the performance analysis spreadsheet to explore the possibility of different per-trade risk percentages. The sample trades in Figure 8.4 will once again be used to demonstrate these calculations. An initial maximum risk percentage value must be entered into cell N21 to represent an arbitrary risk level, and will be changed later on (this percentage must be entered as a decimal). The theoretical account growth represents the possible total net profit of the trading plan had it used this maximum risk percentage.

To optimize this theoretical account growth, we can use the chart in Figure 8.5 that was created by varying the maximum risk percentage and recording the corresponding theoretical account growth values from the spreadsheet (this may also be accomplished using the Solver Add-In feature in MS Excel). In this case, a 0.43 maximum risk percentage will optimize the account at an impressive $533,038.26. The darker grey bar behind the curve represents the initial account value.

Traders should not assume that they could turn a $15K account into $533K just by increasing their trade risk to 43%. This could only happen if all 21 trading conditions lead to exactly the same profits and in the same sequence all over again (without consideration of margin requirements). This is simply not a reality of actual trading. Instead, we have established the upper limit to the maximum risk percentage for each trade. Knowing this limit, traders can now determine a much lower risk percentage that offers a more reasonable risk of ruin while maintaining decent profit potential.

FIGURE 8.5

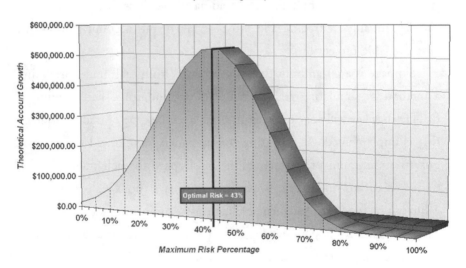

Optimal Risk for 21 Trade Sample Plan: Counter Trend Swing
(+R Advantage of 2)

A CURVE REPRESENTING THE RELATIONSHIP BETWEEN
THEORETICAL ACCOUNT GROWTH AND MAXIMUM RISK PERCENTAGE.

It should be noted that the calculations associated with optimal risk in the performance analysis spreadsheet are only projections, while all of the other statistics relate to the actual performance of the trade data. For instance, changing the maximum risk percentage will not affect the risk of ruin or any other trade metrics, with the exception of the theoretical account growth value and the equity multiplier column. While we feel it is important to understand the implications of optimal risk—that there is a point where more risk does not equate to greater profits—trading at optimal risk levels is not practical because of the corresponding high risk of ruin levels.

SLIPPAGE AND COMMISSION

Slippage and commissions are important factors that will have a negative effect on the profitability of a trading plan. These factors are an unavoidable reality of trading and must be taken into account in order to create reliable projections.

Slippage is a set amount that is subtracted from each trade, providing a method of simulating real market trading conditions. The amount of real-life slippage will vary between markets and the type of trading strategy that is implemented. As a starting point, traders should add at least one tick (the minimum price fluctuation) of slippage to each trade. Once a trading plan has undergone live-market testing, a more realistic slippage value can be used in subsequent evaluations. Commission rates are easy to calculate because they are readily available from a broker and are simply subtracted from every trade.

Slippage and commissions will have a much larger effect on shorter-term styles of trading due to the greater frequency of trades. Day trading plans, for instance, can see a significant eroding of profits due to this factor. For these traders, it is especially important to test a system using realistic slippage and commission values. Traders who wish to add slippage and commission to the results of the performance analysis spreadsheet can change the formula in cell E2 and drag it down to the bottom of the sheet:

CELL E2 (AND DRAG DOWN): = (B2-A2)*C2*D2*N$1-30

This formula will now subtract $30 from every trade to account for slippage and commission. Traders may change the "30" in the formula to another number that reflects values more appropriate for an individual market, position size, or trading plan.

OPTIMIZING AND OVER-OPTIMIZING (CURVE FITTING)

Optimizing refers to the process of modifying values within a trading plan with the goal of achieving better performance. Once traders develop the tools to assess a trading plan, it is possible to change part of the plan, such as the length of a moving average or ADX value, to create better historical results. Optimizing can help tune a trading plan to a specific market by definitively answering the question, "Which value would have worked best?"

Traders often find that they can make significant improvements to the performance of a trading plan through careful optimizing. For example, the Counter Trend swing trading plan uses a 14-period ADX value of 52 as a filter. This value was chosen as the result of testing an entire range

FIGURE 8.6

ADXValue (^ Counter)	Test	All: Net Profit	All: ProfitFactor ▼	All: % Profitable	All: Avg Trade	All: Max Intraday Drawdown	All: Gross Profit	All: Gross Loss	All: Total Trades
52	12	49,740.00	2.03	51.22	404.39	-5,710.00	97,870.00	-48,130.00	123
48	10	47,470.00	2.01	50.83	395.58	-5,710.00	94,670.00	-47,200.00	120
68	20	48,590.00	1.98	50.79	385.63	-5,710.00	98,320.00	-49,730.00	126
70	21	48,590.00	1.98	50.79	385.63	-5,710.00	98,320.00	-49,730.00	126
46	9	45,870.00	1.97	50.42	385.46	-5,710.00	93,070.00	-47,200.00	119
66	19	48,140.00	1.97	50.40	385.12	-5,710.00	97,870.00	-49,730.00	125
58	15	48,140.00	1.97	50.40	385.12	-5,710.00	97,870.00	-49,730.00	125
56	14	48,140.00	1.97	50.40	385.12	-5,710.00	97,870.00	-49,730.00	125
62	17	48,140.00	1.97	50.40	385.12	-5,710.00	97,870.00	-49,730.00	125
60	16	48,140.00	1.97	50.40	385.12	-5,710.00	97,870.00	-49,730.00	125
54	13	48,140.00	1.97	50.40	385.12	-5,710.00	97,870.00	-49,730.00	125
64	18	48,140.00	1.97	50.40	385.12	-5,710.00	97,870.00	-49,730.00	125
50	11	46,540.00	1.97	50.41	384.63	-5,710.00	94,670.00	-48,130.00	121
30	1	32,340.00	1.96	50.00	385.00	-4,910.00	65,940.00	-33,600.00	84
44	8	44,510.00	1.94	50.00	377.20	-5,710.00	91,710.00	-47,200.00	118
42	7	42,110.00	1.91	49.57	366.17	-5,710.00	88,510.00	-46,400.00	115
40	6	39,790.00	1.86	48.67	352.12	-5,710.00	86,190.00	-46,400.00	113
38	5	38,740.00	1.83	48.21	345.89	-5,710.00	85,140.00	-46,400.00	112
36	4	37,940.00	1.83	48.18	344.91	-5,710.00	83,540.00	-45,600.00	110
32	2	33,140.00	1.81	47.96	338.16	-5,710.00	73,940.00	-40,800.00	98
34	3	34,740.00	1.79	47.62	330.86	-5,710.00	78,740.00	-44,000.00	105

AN OPTIMIZATION REPORT SHOWING THE PERFORMANCE
METRICS FOR THE POSSIBLE ADX VALUES THAT COULD HAVE BEEN USED
IN THE COUNTER TREND SWING TRADING PLAN.

of 14-period ADX values between 30 and 70, as seen in the optimization report in Figure 8.6. This report, available in backtesting software, allows a quick comparison of the effect that different values would have on the plan. From this report, we find the ADX value of 52 to show the best overall performance metrics for the 123 trades that were tested. Thus, this optimized value was chosen for our sample trading plan.

While most trading plans will benefit from some level of optimizing, traders must be careful of the risk of over-optimization. Over-optimizing refers to excessive curve fitting that produces a trading plan that is unreliable in actual trading. An over-optimized plan will often show outstanding performance statistics, but will only work on the historical data on which it was tested. Fortunately, there are some indications that a plan has been over-optimized during the development phases of a trading plan, including:

1. Performance metrics that are "too good to be true," such as profit factors in the double digits or the percentage of profitable trades above 80%.

2. Performance metrics that are based on very few trades.

3. A lack of correlation between in-sample and out-of-sample trading periods (described below).

The bottom line is that traders must be aware of the risk of over-optimization when using this form of historical modeling. Optimizing can become an addicting part of trading plan development. Traders must keep in mind that too much optimizing will decrease the effectiveness of a trading plan in real trading.

USING IN-SAMPLE AND OUT-OF-SAMPLE HISTORICAL DATA

Most traders are familiar with the phrase, "Past performance is not indicative of future results." It is important to emphasize that although historical modeling is an important component in measuring the potential of a trading plan, it does not guarantee the same results in real trading. Much like developing a trading plan to begin with, effectively testing and optimizing a trading plan takes skill and practice. Inadequate historical modeling can lead to incorrect assumptions about the legitimacy of the trading plan. In addition, historical modeling is only the first step in building a complete trading plan.

One of the most critical factors in evaluating a trading plan is having enough reliable data for the results to be statistically significant. Keep in mind that the basic concepts used to measure trading performance, such as probability and the law of averages, are only valid when applied to enough trades. While we have not included the number of trades as a performance metric, it is a significant aspect of dependable testing. Ideally, traders should look for as many trades as possible for testing purposes. In general, more trades often equate to a higher probability that a trading plan will live up to its historical expectations. Performance statistics that are based on very few trades are simply not reliable.

Assuming there are enough trades, one method that can be used to improve the likelihood of a trading plan performing as expected is to set up in-sample and out-of-sample trading periods. While this creates an additional step in the process of historical modeling, it can significantly improve the performance of a trading plan as it is moved forward through each phase of development and traded in a live market.

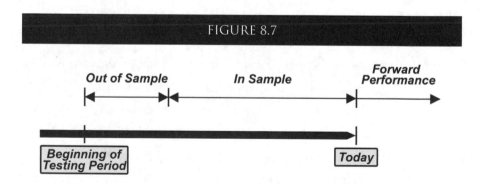

FIGURE 8.7

A TIMELINE REPRESENTING THE PROPORTIONS OF IN
SAMPLE AND OUT OF SAMPLE TRADE DATA.

An example of this type of testing involves breaking the historical testing period into thirds and assigning two-thirds of this time as in-sample trade data and the remaining third as out-of-sample trade data, as seen in Figure 8.7. Once these sample periods have been established, traders should only use the in-sample data for the initial testing and development of their trading plan. The out-of-sample data should be set aside and not used for anything other than to confirm the validity of the trading plan (absolutely no optimizations using this data set).

Once a trading plan has been developed using in-sample trade data, it is ready to be applied to the out-of-sample trades. Comparing the performance statistics from the data used to develop the system to out-of sample data will show how close a trading plan is to being ready for real trading. Closer correlation between in-sample and out-of-sample data provides a much greater probability of positive results during forward performance testing and live trading. It should be noted, however, that as soon as out-of-sample data is used in a comparison, it is no longer truly out-of-sample. Each additional test with out-of-sample data decreases its value; therefore, the data should be used as infrequently as possible.

Once a trading plan has successfully passed through the phase of historical modeling, the next phase of forward performance testing, or paper trading, provides additional out-of-sample testing. Close correlation between the real-time results and the historical results provides even greater confidence that the system will perform as expected during live trading.

FORWARD PERFORMANCE TESTING (PAPER TRADING)

Forward performance testing involves a simulation of actual trading. This process is often referred to as paper trading since no real trading occurs and any profit or loss will only be on paper. This portion of trading plan development requires traders to practice all of the elements used during live trading, without actually placing real trades. This type of practice can help traders establish a solid trading routine and develop the skills that are necessary for successfully implementing their trading plans. The goal is that forward performance testing will relate to better live trading performance. Perfect practice makes perfect performance.

Traders should make their forward performance testing as realistic as possible. More realistic simulated trading will create a much easier transition into live market trading. When done properly, forward performance testing acts as a bridge between the historical testing and the actual implementation of a trading plan.

The problem with forward performance testing is that traders often take it too lightly. Creating a trading atmosphere with absolutely no stress or accountability will decrease the usefulness for this type of testing. While it can be difficult to simulate the pressures of trading with real money, traders should do their best to create a realistic trading environment. When done correctly, forward performance testing can significantly help traders begin to build the confidence and discipline required for successful live trading.

Two methods should be used to create more realistic forward performance testing. The first is to document all simulated trades in a trading journal, and the second is to maintain a running total of simulated trading results. Keep in mind that this is practice for becoming an effective "market trader" and traders should mimic all of the steps that will be used in live trading.

Writing trades down in a trading journal will provide a record that can be evaluated and compared with the performance of historical modeling. In many cases, reviewing the simulated trades in a trading journal will point out areas where traders can improve their ability to precisely follow their trading plans.

Many brokers offer a simulated account that can be used to gain familiarity with their order entry software. Using a simulated trading account can really add to the experience of forward performance testing. When setting up a sample account, traders should use a realistic value to mimic the size of their real trading accounts. While it is often an option, traders should avoid resetting this account, even if it has been significantly depleted. As much as possible, this account should be treated like an actual trading account. Even without a simulated account, traders should maintain a running total of simulated trading performance.

CHAPTER 9
LIVE TRADING

I have to admit, when I first told my father that I was going to start trading as a business, he smirked and said, "Oh, you're getting into gambling." In my naivety, I viewed trading as a calculated business that relied on research, statistics, and technical analysis to make educated predictions about future market direction. "Dad, the trading that I will be doing is not gambling at all," I asserted. At first, the comparison really bothered me. Was I really trying to support my family by gambling?

I have now come to realize that the gambling analogy is more accurate than I could have imagined. Much like the uncertainty in a deck of cards, live trading also carries a high degree of unpredictability; no one knows for certain what the market will do next. The truth is that someone always makes money in gambling (usually the casino!) What we are trying to do as traders is stack the odds in our favor by using a positive, consistent approach: we want to be the house.

In the simplest sense, when we place a trade it will either reach our profit goals or get stopped out. Either way, it does not really matter; it is not the individual trade that is important, but the outcome of trading over time. Experienced traders know this and do not get frustrated with losing trades, nor do they get overly excited about their winners. Through their research and experience, they know that following their trading plans allows for the greatest odds of success in a somewhat random market.

Live trading can be stressful at first because we are betting real money on the success of a trading plan. As mentioned earlier, good trading is simply reacting to and following a trading plan. It is important to understand that winning or losing in live trading is not something over which we have complete control. Just like the uncertainty of choosing the ace of hearts in a well-shuffled deck of cards, no one can always predict the moves of the market. Strictly adhering to a trading plan, however, will provide the greatest odds of success and can significantly reduce the stress of live trading.

Throughout this book, we have been working towards developing a profitable trading plan that will identify high probability market setups. This plan, along with live trading practice, will allow us to react quickly as we see positive market conditions unfold. Additionally, it will also allow us to react to non-favorable conditions so we can minimize our losses.

PREPARATION

Many of us can remember our high school coaches enthusiastically barking, "Remember the five Ps of winning: Prior Planning Prevents Poor Performance." This recommendation rings true in trading as well as sport.

Thorough preparation is an often overlooked but critical aspect of successful live trading. Over the course of time, things will go wrong in live trading, and not having a plan to deal with these situations can cost money and stress. Developing emergency protocols for live trading can help traders minimize losses and create a more relaxed trading atmosphere when problems do arise. More importantly, it can also help traders avoid these situations all together. This type of preparation can be as simple as scheduling regular computer maintenance or having a trading account number handy.

For example, consider the following scenarios:

1. Imagine that a trading plan signals an entry into a short position in a stock shortly after the open. Once the entry criteria have been met, the trader carefully places an order to sell short and quickly gets the confirmation that the order has been filled. The price starts to bounce around as market participation increases. The trader begins placing a protective stop loss order in the market. Suddenly, he notices that the price on his charts and quote screen is no longer updating. After the sobering realization that he has gotten disconnected from his data server, the trader quickly picks up the phone and pushes the speed dial button that is preprogrammed to call his broker. After another long pause, he realizes that it is not just the data server, but also the phone line that is not working. What should this trader do?

2. In another scenario, a trader has taken a long position in several index futures contracts over the past couple of days. The trade is only showing modest profits and the trading plan signals a time exit to close the trade. After submitting the order to close out the position, it is rejected and the trader resubmits the order. A small box appears on the bottom right corner of the monitor stating that the

broker's server is currently down and cannot process any new trade orders. A quick phone call to the trade desk confirms this and that no trading can take place. What should this trader do?

In both of these examples, traders were correctly following their trading plans. The problem was that an event occurred that fell outside the scope of the trading plan. While some would say that these events are out of a trader's control, responsible traders still must consider these possibilities. We will discuss various methods of trader preparation, and then come back to these scenarios.

BACKING UP EVERYTHING

Before live trading begins, traders should think about all of the critical tools on which they rely for trading. These should all be replaceable. In other words, traders should have a backup for all of the key tools in their trading arsenals. This includes both the data and hardware that is critical for the business. Since a computer is the primary trading tool, it is important to make regular backup disks and be able to reformat a computer from scratch if necessary. This includes all essential computer programs, operating systems, drivers, and data. Some traders even like to have trading software installed on a secondary notebook computer in case the main computer fails.

This does not mean that traders need to have an inventory of computer monitors, keyboards, or modems on hand just in case one gets broken. These items are easily replaceable, costing a day or two to replace. More important is making a backup of the complex items that may be more difficult to replace such as charting workspaces, research, or files containing an entire trading plan. Since many brokers now use electronic statements to record trading activity, these should also be backed up on a regular basis as well.

Traders should be familiar with checking and resetting Internet and telephone connections. Other backups include adding brokers to the speed dial of a main phone line and to a cell phone. Many traders like to have a second Internet connection or dial-up backup. In additional, cell phones should have a strong battery charge and be recharged, if necessary, at the end of every day. Traders may even consider using a secondary broker if they are planning on trading larger positions.

MAKING AN EMERGENCY LIST OF NUMBERS

Traders should have a list of emergency numbers and contact information nearby in case they need to call their brokers or service providers. If the conditions arise requiring phoning in a trade order, or reporting a service failure, something unexpected has already happened. At this point,

FIGURE 9.1

Important Numbers

	Service	Account #	Username	Password	Telephone #	
Broker 1	Tradestation	12345678	Trader	favorite song	800-837-8951	Futures Desk
					800-871-3563	Trade Desk
					800-292-3442	Technical Support
					800-871-3577	Customer Service
Broker 2	MB Trading	87654321	Trader	favorite place	866-628-3003	Futures Desk
					866-628-3002	Trade Desk
					866-628-3001	Technical Support
					866-628-3001	Customer Service
Charting	eSignal	999999	Trader	first pet's name	510-264-1700	Technical Support
					510-264-1700	Customer Service
ISP	Verizon	12121212	xyzxyz	abcabc	800-567-6789	Technical Support
					800-567-6789	Customer Service

AN EXAMPLE OF AN EMERGENCY CONTACT LIST

the goal is to fix the problem quickly and with the least amount of stress (and financial loss). While most brokers can take trade orders over the phone, traders must first prove who they are by stating their account numbers and answering security questions. This information should be readily available so that traders may prepare for these often-stressful situations.

It is highly recommended that traders compile a list of important phone numbers, usernames, and password hints (not the actual password, but a hint for remembering the password). This list, as seen in Figure 9.1, should be posted visibly near the trading desk. Traders will find this to be an indispensable tool during the early stages of live trading. A worksheet for creating a custom list of emergency numbers can be found in Appendix C.

CREATING A TROUBLESHOOTING LIST

A troubleshooting list allows traders to establish and follow a predetermined protocol in the event of a problem. The list helps traders take decisive action as soon as a problem is suspected. A well-defined list will also help traders establish consistency in troubleshooting which, in many cases, may mean not repeating prior mistakes. This list should be frequently updated as traders develop more experience (and experience more problems). The goal is to have the troubleshooting list as inclusive as possible, which requires thinking about potential problems before they occur, and including problems (and their solutions) that have already happened.

Although we would like to think that trading platforms are infallible, this is far from true, and it is to our advantage to plan for the inevitable failures. The best way to be prepared to fix a problem is to create a troubleshooting guide specific to the platform being used. This should be an easy-to-read list that gives a systematic solution to each problem. Giving it a permanent home on the workstation wall will ensure that it can be

FIGURE 9.2

I lost my internet connection	1. Check the phone line. If there is no dial tone and I am in a trade, use the cell phone to call my broker and close the trade. If there is a dial tone: 2. Check the connection status at my ISP's website (under favorites). Try to reconnect. If that doesn't work: 3. Manually disconnect the power from both the modem and the router. Wait 30 seconds and reconnect. Try again to reconnect at my ISP's website. If that doesn't work: 4. Close down all applications, and restart the computer. Try again to reconnect at my ISP's website. If that doesn't work: 5. Call my ISP to report the problem. 6. Open TS with backup ISP and confirm that I have no open positions.
I think I got a partial fill on an order	1. Check the bottom of the TS window. Open positions will read "0" if I am flat. Any number besides "0" means I still have an open position. 2. Click on the "Orders" tab in the TradeManager window. Check how many contracts were filled. (Filed orders will be highlighted in blue). 3. Outstanding orders will be white. 4. Manually close the rest of the position if necessary; see below ("I need to manually close a position")

AN EXAMPLE OF A TROUBLESHOOTING LIST FOR A
SPECIFIC TRADING PLATFORM.

found during stressful times. Color can be used to make the guide easier to read and follow. This guide should state the problem, and list the steps that need to be taken to fix it, as seen in Figure 9.2.

Now that we have covered some elements of live-trading preparation, it is time to revisit the scenarios introduced at the beginning of the chapter:

In Scenario #1, the trader has an open (naked) position in the market and has lost his telephone and Internet connections. This well-prepared trader simply takes out his (fully-charged) cell phone, presses the preprogrammed speed dial, and is connected to his broker. Using the list of emergency numbers located at his desk, he easily finds his account number and password hint to confirm the trade order, and that he is in an open position. Then, using his troubleshooting guidelines, the trader determines whether to close the position or place an exit order over the phone. The next step is to once again use the list of emergency numbers and locate the contact information for the telephone and Internet service providers to file a work order to fix the problems.

Scenario #2 involves an open long trade that cannot be closed due to a broker's server being down. While not common, this does happen on rare occasions. Since this breakdown is on the broker's end, there is nothing the trader can do from her computer...unless she has another trading account. Experienced traders often use a "backup broker" just for this type of collapse. An open position that cannot be closed can significantly damage a trading account, and the broker will not cover the loss. Using her troubleshooting guidelines, she will open a short trade for the same size with her backup broker. Since she is not able to close her original position, the short trade will offset any losses for the long position that she cannot close (this is known as hedging). While this is a fairly extreme and rare case, it highlights some of the considerations that traders may have to make to help control unexpected risks.

Staying Mentally Focused

Getting behind a trading desk can feel a bit like climbing into the cockpit of a fighter jet. Similar to modern jet combat, live trading relies on a high level of situational awareness in order to make fast, important decisions. Much like a novice pilot sitting behind the dials, switches, and controls of an aircraft for the first time, the sheer amount of information available to traders can be overwhelming. Taking a structured approach to learning which aspects in trading require the most attention and focus allows traders to gradually increase awareness and avoid distractions. This will ultimately allow traders to process information faster, and develop the reaction times necessary to do battle in today's markets.

Becoming a focused trader will have different implications depending on trading style, or specific trading plan. For day traders, this may mean carefully monitoring price fluctuations throughout the day, while swing traders may only have to check the intraday markets periodically. Position traders, alternatively, may not need intraday data at all, and will simply check the markets at the end of each trading day or week. For each style of trading, traders must be ready to place a trade order as soon as they encounter the conditions defined by their trading plans.

Since trading plans are developed and tested using idealized trading, no allowances have been made for missed trades or trades that fell outside of the plan. It is just as important that live trading maintain this same consistency. Traders must follow their trading plans exactly if they hope to gain the same expectancy from live trading. Following a trading plan perfectly takes practice, and requires staying mentally focused.

Live trading involves going from long, slow periods of inactivity to fast, dynamic cycles requiring instant action. Staying mentally focused during these slower times in the market will help traders stick to their plans

FIGURE 9.3

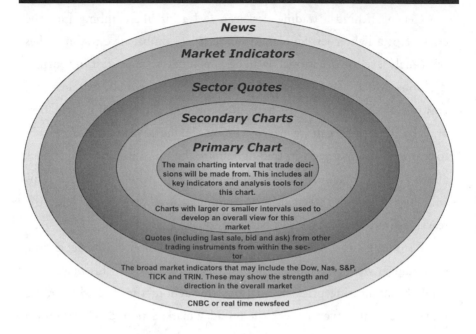

A CONCEPTUAL SCOPE FOR DEVELOPING MARKET AWARENESS.
A TRADER SHOULD MAINTAIN FOCUS ON HIS OR HER PRIMARY CHART,
AND EXPAND AWARENESS OUTWARD.

FIGURE 9.4

AN EXAMPLE OF A TRADER ALERT THAT CAN BE USED TO
HELP TRADERS MAINTAIN FOCUS.

and not miss trading opportunities. To maintain focus and avoid information overload, traders should prioritize which elements are most critical to successful live trading. Figure 9.3 provides a conceptual scope from which traders can prioritize market focus. Starting from the inside of this chart and expanding outward, traders can steadily increase their awareness of market dynamics as they become more familiar with this information.

Many traders find trader alerts to be a useful tool in helping to improve market focus. Trader alerts are audio or visual alerts that are set to activate when certain conditions in the market occur. Traders can customize these alerts within their market analysis platforms. A typical alert may sound an alarm if a filter condition for a trading plan is met. Once the condition occurs in the market, a bell may sound along with a pop-up window, as seen in Figure 9.4, alerting a trader to the potential trade.

Traders should also avoid distractions that may cause missed or incorrectly managed trades. Incoming phone calls, instant messages, or a noisy office space should all be avoided during active live-market trading. These distractions can contribute to trading errors.

It should be noted also, from a physical standpoint, that being well-rested and well-hydrated, making healthful food choices, and getting enough physical activity (exercise) can all contribute significantly to being able to maintain focus while trading.

Staying mentally focused on the market takes practice, and traders can measure this by tracking how well they are following their trading plans. This can be accomplished using a simple percentage scale to rate performance, with 100% representing perfect live trading. This rating is most important during the initial stages of live trading, and it can be included on the notes section of the trading journal.

USING A TRADING JOURNAL

A trading journal can help traders gain important feedback from live trading and forward testing performance. This type of trading diary, as seen in Figure 9.5, includes detailed information about individual trades that performance reports alone do not provide. A trading journal can be used for the following purposes:

1. To identify potential weaknesses in a trading plan.

2. To verify the individual trades in brokerage account statements.

3. To help determine areas where live trading performance can be improved.

Whenever live trading or forward performance testing (paper trading), traders should use a trading journal. The date, time, price, direction, reasons for the trade, and individual trade notes should be written down for each trade. In the simplest sense, this provides a record of trading activity that can be later used to evaluate the performance of the overall trading plan.

A trading journal can help traders find potential flaws in the plan that may only become obvious during live trading. For instance, traders may discover on days when there are Federal Reserve Meetings (commonly referred to as Fed Days), trades do not follow through or quickly turn into losers. This type of observation, recorded over time in a trading journal, can be later evaluated and, if confirmed, a Fed Day filter (for example) could be added to the trading plan. As another example, if a trader notes that nine out of ten losing trades were barely stopped out, it may be cause to evaluate the stop loss level in the trading plan. Conversely, if a trader notes that nine out of ten winning trades would have gone on to much greater profits, it may be cause to evaluate the profit target level(s) in the

FIGURE 9.5

Trading Journal

	Date	Symbol	Shares / Contracts	Reason for Trade	L / S	Entry Price	Exit Price	Profit (Loss)	Notes	
1	8-16-05	ER2U05	2	Strat V4.2	+1	660.40	660.80	① +14	Right on pivot	100%
2							660.40	+0	Breakeven stop 2nd contract	100%
3			2	Shrt V4.2	+1	658.30	659.70	② +14	Another move right to the pivot	100%
4							658.30	② +0	Breakeven stop 2nd contract	100%
5	8-17-05	ER2U05	2	Strat V4.2	-1	658.00	657.10	② +18	Sporadic data feed; closed position	80%
6	8-18-05	ER2U05	2	Strat V4.3	-1	652.30	650.90	① +13	Profit target w/ slippage	100%
7							652.30	-1	Breakeven stop w/ slippage	100%
8			2	Strat V4.2	+1	651.70	652.80	① +11	A little choppy	100%
9							654.20	① +35	Nice move on this 2nd contract	100%
10										

A TRADING JOURNAL USED TO RECORD LIVE TRADING DATA.

trading plan. And, as noted earlier with the Fed Days, outside factors, such as the release of economic data, can turn out to have a predictable effect on a trading plan. The goal for this type of analysis is to create a more profitable trading plan that is tuned to live trading experiences.

Another useful purpose of a trading journal is to confirm the trading activity from a brokerage statement. A brokerage statement, as seen in Figure 9.6, lists the trades that were taken during the month. Similar to balancing a checkbook, a trading journal can be used to confirm each trade transaction and verify that the broker has not made any errors. Entry and exit prices, profit and loss figures, and commissions and fees should be carefully checked each month. It should be noted that many brokers require notification within 24-48 hours of trading activity if there is an error in their records; for this reason, it is recommended that traders also check each daily electronic statement (if applicable) for accuracy.

FIGURE 9.6

MONTHLY COMMODITY STATEMENT

ACCOUNT NUMBER   999 99999
STATEMENT DATE   OCT 31, 2005

DATE	AT	LONG/BUY	SHORT/SELL	DESCRIPTION	EXCHANGE	PRICE/LEGEND	CC	DEBIT	CREDIT
* *YOUR ACTIVITY THIS MONTH* *
10/3/2005	F1	4	4	DEC 05 MINI RUSL	16	P&L	US		$430.00
10/3/2005	F1	4	4	DEC 05 MINI RUSL	16	FEE/COMM	US	$20.16	
10/4/2005	F1	2	2	DEC 05 MINI RUSL	16	P&L	US	$200.00	
10/4/2005	F1	2	2	DEC 05 MINI RUSL	16	FEE/COMM	US	$10.08	
10/5/2005	F1	4	4	DEC 05 MINI RUSL	16	P&L	US		$440.00
10/5/2005	F1	4	4	DEC 05 MINI RUSL	16	FEE/COMM	US	$20.16	
10/6/2005	F1	2	2	DEC 05 MINI RUSL	16	P&L	US		$200.00
10/6/2005	F1	2	2	DEC 05 MINI RUSL	16	FEE/COMM	US	$10.08	
10/10/2005	F1	4	4	DEC 05 MINI RUSL	16	P&L	US		$490.00

A MONTHLY BROKERAGE STATEMENT THAT IS OFTEN SENT ELECTRONICALLY.

Possibly the most critical reason for using a trading journal is to be able to assess live trading performance. Since traders are ultimately responsible for evaluating their roles as market traders, reviewing these journals can help spot aspects of live trading that require improvement. The individual trade notes section can be especially telling if it is filled out thoughtfully. It is important to note if the trading plan was not followed and, if not, to explain why. An amazing trading plan can still lead to great losses if it is not traded correctly. It is essential that traders are honest with themselves and that they identify problem areas in their live trading. There is great opportunity in the notes section of a trading journal; it is recommended that traders put solid effort into this aspect of the journal since it can provide useful information that is not available from other sources.

TRADE AUTOMATION

While trade automation has already been discussed in Chapter 6—Placing Trades, live trading with this technology involves some unique considerations. The theory behind automated trading makes it appear simple; just set up the software, program the rules, and watch it trade. The reality is that automated trading requires a much higher degree of sophistication in troubleshooting than other methods of trading. Trading platforms that support fully automated trading typically involve two components: the strategy that generates the "theoretical trades" and the order entry platform that turns them into real trades. Because of this integration, there are twice as many aspects to troubleshoot if an automated system fails during live trading.

Traders that employ this technology should also maintain a trading journal, making sure to note all of the system parameters and any anomalies that occur. Since troubleshooting an automated system often requires a phone call to tech support, having this information on hand is important. Traders who automate their trading plans must also anticipate an event where the strategy may get disconnected from the live trades. This will require an element of manual trade management that must be included in the troubleshooting list. As such, traders who automate their strategies should also be practiced in manual trading.

Automating a trading plan can be a good option for traders who are comfortable with computers and technology. With the ability to constantly monitor the markets, errors associated with staying mentally focused and precisely following the rules of a trading plan are minimized: there is less opportunity for "pilot error" when using trade automation. This technology often requires modifying strategies to meet the demands of live trading, however, and may require additional programming to more precisely define the entry or exit rules of the automated strategy based on live trading performance.

TRUSTING YOUR TRADING PLAN

Traders must learn to trust their trading plans if they hope to develop a profitable trading business. For many traders, the emotional aspects of live trading can be significantly underestimated. This is the leading cause for traders to disregard the rules of their trading plans. A big challenge in effective live trading is removing as much emotion as possible from trading. Our goal in live trading is to precisely follow our trading plan and become unemotional, mechanical market traders.

Imagine that a trader has just begun live trading and the first three trades have each resulted in a loss. While this trading plan has shown reasonable performance statistics throughout the prior development stages, should this be cause for concern? The fact is, three consecutive losers can be a rough way to start live trading, but it does not show any flaws in the logic of the overall trading plan at this point. There has not yet been enough trading activity to assess the real performance of this plan.

Aside from the loss of capital, a string of losing trades, or a drawdown, can have a considerable emotional impact on a trader. It is during these negative phases that traders have a tendency to question their trading plans. The risk of second-guessing, and not completely following a trading plan, is significant. Traders will not benefit from any previous research and will lose any type of expectancy. Even during a drawdown period, a trading plan can still be on target to reach its performance measures. In most cases, continuing to follow the trading plan will allow it to trade its way back to profitability.

Traders should not assume that there are flaws in their trading plans just because they show a short-term loss. As much as possible, traders should remind themselves that losing trades and drawdowns are a reality of the trading business. A trading account should be thought of as an inventory that will both decrease and grow over time: these are necessary and normal fluctuations. This account should not be thought of as money that is being lost, or which could be spent on other things. Traders that view their trading accounts simply as money often have a difficult time removing their emotions from trading and making objective decisions.

One method of overcoming the tendency to second-guess a trading plan is to develop a motivation system for correctly following a trading plan. Traders that provide themselves with incentives for good trading (meaning, following their trading plans) often perform more consistently. Traders that make mistakes might need to take out a piece of paper and write 100 times, "I will always follow my trading plan, I will always follow my trading plan, I will..." Just acknowledging this can help traders improve market trading performance.

Below is a list of reminders that may help traders control emotions and trust their trading plans. It is recommended to review this list regularly before trading:

- Trading is fun and challenging.

- Approach every trade as an opportunity to make money.

- Trade confidently: trust your trading plan.

- Stay relaxed: do not get frustrated about a loss (or several), do not get excited about a win (even a big win).

- Be prepared to lose on every trade: no single trade will break you; no single day will break you.

- Only closed trades equate to profits: do not dollar count the profit or loss of an open position.

- Trading errors will happen: learn from these mistakes.

- Focus on your plan: a trading plan cannot catch every move in the market; all you can do is follow your trading rules.

Another element that can increase a trader's confidence in his or her trading plan is to establish the criteria for reevaluation. This essentially places a limit on the amount of trading losses that can occur. This helps traders to understand when their trading is still within its statistical range or whether it is really off base. Establishing this principle, as well as measuring live trading performance, will be discussed in Chapter 10—Evaluating Live Performance.

CHAPTER 10
EVALUATING LIVE PERFORMANCE

The goal of evaluating any aspect of a trading plan is to minimize risk, create consistency, and generate greater profitability. Nowhere is this more important than in the evaluation of live trading. Measuring live trading performance allows a trader to determine how effective his or her trading plan really is and how to become a better market trader.

Until now, the performance of a trading plan has been primarily quantified using historical data. At this phase, live trading results are all that matter since this is what will generate the true profit or loss for the trading business. If the performance of live trading does not match the results of historical modeling, it may be necessary to revise the trading plan based on the live results. Tuning a trading plan to a live market may require making compromises that decrease historical performance. This is reasonable, since historical profits are not the same as real profits. The significance of historical performance has little value if live trading does not confirm these results.

In this chapter, we will look at some methods of evaluating live trading that can help traders:

1. Set goals to improve live trading performance.

2. Track how closely live trading compares with the historical testing that was used to create the trading plan.

3. Determine when to make revisions to a trading plan based on the results of live trading.

4. Decide when it is necessary to stop using a trading plan.

Measuring live performance is critical to successfully implementing a trading plan. Even a solid trading plan will fail if traders are unable to effectively trade it in a live market. As a result, traders may find it necessary to fine-tune their trading plans based on their experiences in live trading.

Reviewing Trading Journals

Trading journals provide a record of live trading which should be reviewed on a regular basis. For new traders, it is recommended to examine trading journals following each completed, round-turn trade. In addition, traders should set up a schedule to review their trading journals over a monthly or quarterly basis. This provides a larger, more statistically significant group of trades to analyze. In many cases there is a lot of information hidden in trading journals that will only become apparent over time.

The initial purpose of reviewing trading journals is to gain insight that will improve live trading. While the individual trade data such as date, time, and entry/exit points will allow traders to measure overall performance statistics, the notes that traders take during live trading can be equally valuable. These notes can help traders spot patterns in their live trading that may be causing trading errors. Once these trends are discovered, traders can take the necessary actions and set goals to fix these reoccurring errors.

Trading errors can take two distinct forms: intentional and unintentional. Intentional trading errors occur when a trader deliberately violates his or her trading plan. This is usually the result of the trader's emotions overriding the rules of the trading plan. Examples of intentional errors include closing a trade early, ignoring a stop loss, or entering trades that are not defined within the trading plan. These errors can be particularly destructive to a trading account since any type of risk management or expectancy is lost. Once a trader has spotted a pattern of intentional trading errors, they must acknowledge the mistakes and take immediate action to stop them. Traders must learn to avoid intentional trading errors, making this their primary market trading goals. As stated repeatedly, good trading is all about sticking to your trading plan.

Unintentional trading errors are "honest mistakes" that occur due to of a lack of trading experience or skill. This type of trading error may include placing incorrect order types (going long instead of short, for example), missing a trade signal, or using the wrong trading symbol. The level of skill that is involved when implementing a trading plan is often underestimated. Overly complex trading plans may need to be scaled back in order to create better results in live trading and minimize unintentional trading errors. As traders gain more experience and develop greater proficiency in their market trading, the occurrences of this type of trading error will become less frequent.

NUMBER CRUNCHING

Once traders have reviewed their trading journals, the next step is to employ the identical statistical performance measures that were used to originally develop their trading plans. This can be accomplished using the same performance analysis spreadsheet that was presented in Chapter 8—Evaluating and Comparing Trading Plans. Entering the trade data from live trading journals provides useful information about trading performance. Close correlation between the results of live trading and the historical data used to develop a trading plan can provide additional confidence in the rules of the trading plan.

Reviewing these performance metrics will help traders see the big picture in their live trading. Errors that have been made during live trading will often be magnified during this type of review. For instance, imagine that a trader decides to close profitable trades early in an attempt to protect profits. This trader may rationalize this as a way to increase the percentage of profitable trades (percentage profitable). When examined over time, however, closing trades early will also decrease the R advantage of these individual trades. This will also decrease the average trade net profit and possibly create a negative expectancy for the entire trading plan. Remember, trading plans must have a positive expectancy to make money over time. From this information, a trader can determine that taking profits too early will decrease overall profitability and that he should stick to the rules of the trading plan.

One method of comparing data is to use a side-by-side comparison of historical and live trading results, as seen in Figure 10.1. The results of this comparison show the historical performance on the left and live trading on the right. For this trading plan, the live trading results have exceeded historical expectations. While this is certainly a nice way to begin live trading, we must also consider the amount of trading that has taken place. Since only five trades have been used in this analysis of live trading, it does not hold much statistical significance just yet. Once we have taken and recorded more live trades, this type of comparison will become more reliable.

Because these statistics can be utilized to develop projections that can be used to determine position sizing, more live trades means greater confidence and potentially less risk. It is important to subtract commissions from both sets of data and apply realistic slippage to the historical data. This also contributes to a more realistic comparison.

Figure 10.2 shows another comparison of historical versus live trading results (with slippage and commissions factored in). While the individual performance statistics in these reports are only mediocre, the close correlation between data shows good reliability. In this example, there are

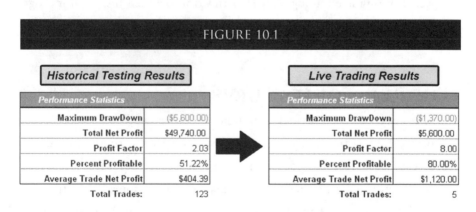

FIGURE 10.1

Historical Testing Results			Live Trading Results	
Performance Statistics			**Performance Statistics**	
Maximum DrawDown	($5,600.00)		Maximum DrawDown	($1,370.00)
Total Net Profit	$49,740.00		Total Net Profit	$5,600.00
Profit Factor	2.03		Profit Factor	8.00
Percent Profitable	51.22%		Percent Profitable	80.00%
Average Trade Net Profit	$404.39		Average Trade Net Profit	$1,120.00
Total Trades:	123		Total Trades:	5

A COMPARISON OF HISTORICAL DATA AND LIVE TRADING RESULTS
FOR A TRADING PLAN. THE SMALL AMOUNT OF LIVE TRADES MAKES
THIS COMPARISON UNRELIABLE.

FIGURE 10.2

Historical Testing Results		
Performance Statistics		
Maximum DrawDown	($6,000.00)
Total Net Profit	$9,600.00
Profit Factor	1.27
Percent Profitable	39.13%
Average Trade Net Profit	$104.34
Total Trades:	92

Live Trading Results		
Performance Statistics		
Maximum DrawDown	($2,960.00)
Total Net Profit	$6,480.00
Profit Factor	1.24
Percent Profitable	43.55%
Average Trade Net Profit	$104.52
Total Trades:	62

ANOTHER COMPARISON OF HISTORICAL DATA AND LIVE TRADING.
THE NUMBER OF TRADES AND CLOSE CORRELATION IN STATISTICS PROVIDE
CONFIDENCE IN THE LOGIC OF THE TRADING PLAN.

enough trades to gain greater confidence in the correlation of live trading data. Consistent performance statistics between historical and live trading is much more important than strong historical performance alone. In fact, the most important test of a trading plan is its ability to perform as expected during live trading. Closer correlation between historical testing and live trading relates to a more reliable trading plan.

THE REAL EQUITY CURVE

An equity curve provides a graphical representation of trading performance by charting the number of trades versus the running total of trading profits. This provides traders with another tool with which to evaluate performance. Using the performance analysis spreadsheet, traders can quickly create a chart that represents the equity curve for a trading plan, as demonstrated in Figure 10.3. The steps to creating an equity curve in Microsoft Excel are as follows:

1. Highlight all of the cells containing a value in column H under the heading "Running Total."

2. Go the "Insert" menu and choose Chart.

3. Select the Chart type: "Line" and click the Finish button.

Equity curves based on historical data alone do not provide much useful information about the real performance of a trading plan. For this purpose, a real equity curve should be used to determine if live trading is measuring up to its historical projection. A real equity curve is constructed by combining the data from live trading and from the development phases

FIGURE 10.3

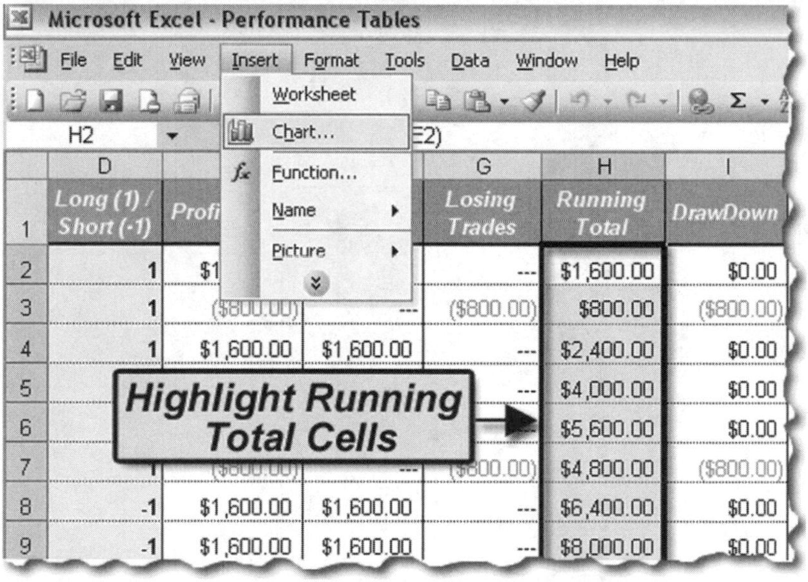

MICROSOFT EXCEL IS USED TO CHART AN EQUITY CURVE
FROM THE PERFORMANCE ANALYSIS SPREADSHEET.

FIGURE 10.4

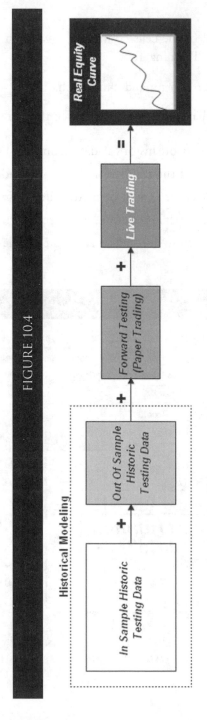

THE COMPOSITION OF A REAL EQUITY CURVE.

FIGURE 10.5

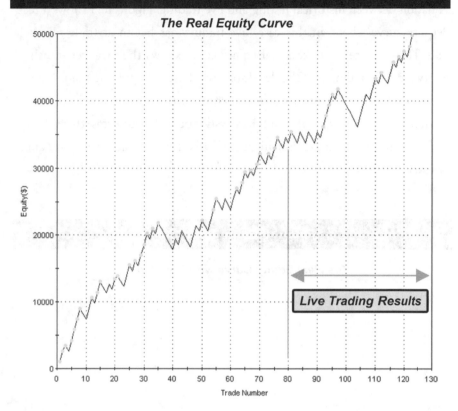

A REAL EQUITY CURVE SHOWING GOOD CORRELATION
BETWEEN HISTORICAL TESTING AND LIVE TRADING.

of a trading plan, as shown in Figure 10.4. A real equity curve can be calculated for a specific trading plan by copying and pasting all of the individual trade data (for both historical and live results) into one combined performance analysis spreadsheet. Following the steps mentioned above, a chart can be created representing the real equity curve for the trading plan. Alternatively, backtesting software often has the ability to plot a real equity curve based on all available trade data for a system.

A real equity curve can provide a method of easily spotting the correlation between historical testing and live trading. Figure 10.5 shows a real equity curve where, in this case, live trading has begun at trade number 80. The consistency of this real equity curve shows the ideal relationship between live trading and the development phases of a trading plan. Notice that the live trading equity acts as a continuation of the previous curve. Establishing this type of equity analysis not only confirms the validity of a trading plan's logic, but illustrates effective live trading performance as well.

FIGURE 10.6

The Real Equity Curve with Trendline

THE SHADED AREA IN THIS REAL EQUITY CURVE SHOWS HOW A POTENTIAL
SHIFT IN MARKET DYNAMICS CAN AFFECT A TRADING PLAN.

In most cases, the real equity curve will show some type of variation between the development phases and live trading. These variations may be in the slope of the curve, the size of the drawdown troughs, or the overall shape. As long as the trading plan is continuing to create new equity peaks at regular intervals (continuing to make money) without exceeding its historical maximum drawdown, live trading performance should be considered on target. It is only when the real equity curve shows an extreme change during live trading or plummets into a perpetual drawdown, that a trading plan or its implementation must be reconsidered.

While changes in a real equity curve are most common and significant during the early stages of live trading, they can occur at any time. Changes to the shape of a real equity curve can point out changes in a market environment that may require adjusting the trading plan. The fact is, markets will change over time and trading plans may need to be updated to fit the current market. Examining the real equity curve can provide an early warning to shifts in the market that may cause a profitable trading plan to become less effective.

Drawing a trendline along the most recent drawdown troughs of a real equity curve, as shown in Figure 10.6, provides an additional tool to help traders analyze their trading. This simple trendline acts as a reference for estimating trading potential, with breaks below this line illustrating a negative turn in live trading performance. In the case of this trading plan, the equity curve has shown a profitable upward slope and has just begun to show signs of weakening as represented by the shaded area. While this trading plan may pull its way out of the drawdown and continue to reach new equity peaks, traders may use this trendline break as a signal to review their recent trading.

When to Abandon a Trading Plan

Deciding when to stop using a trading plan can be a difficult decision. Given the time and effort that goes into development, abandoning a trading plan is an absolute last resort. Each trader must establish his or her own criteria for when to stop using a trading plan, and this should be included as part of the written trading plan. This is an important decision that every trader should make before beginning live trading. For the market trader, there should be no subjectivity in deciding when to stop trading.

There are several objective methods that traders can use as criteria for deciding when to abandon their plans. To begin with, comparing the performance statistics between live and historical trading data can provide an important starting point. The performance metric that is most useful for this purpose is the maximum drawdown. Since this number represents the worst-case scenario for the historical testing period, a drawdown during live trading that is greater than this amount can be a cause for concern. Traders can use a percentage of the maximum historical drawdown as a trigger to shut down a trading plan.

Another method of determining when to discard a trading plan is applying a trendline to the real equity curve as mentioned in the previous section. If the equity curve breaks well below the trendline in the early stages of live trading, it is a trigger to stop live trading. In Figure 10.7, the live trading results are clearly not performing up to expectations. In fact, traders would be advised to stop using this trading plan long before it sunk so far below the trendline and into such a large drawdown. This type of discrepancy between historical testing and live trading can be the result of an over-optimized trading plan.

While the prospect of abandoning a trading plan is not pleasant, it can provide an important learning experience. Just because a trading plan

FIGURE 10.7

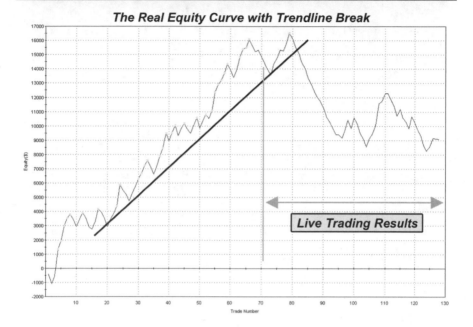

The Real Equity Curve with Trendline Break

THIS CHART SHOW HOW THE RESULTS OF LIVE TRADING CAN
FALL FAR BELOW THE HISTORICAL EXPECTATIONS.

has failed, does not mean that the entire trading business is a failure. Most importantly, traders should step back and learn why their plans failed. Once this is determined, traders will be better equipped to develop profitable, viable trading plans that fit the current market. The important point is recognizing when to abandon an unprofitable trading plan before it does unrecoverable damage to a trading account. Remember, our goal is to stay in the game as long as possible. Abandoning a trading plan should only be a setback in a trading business.

CHAPTER 11
RECORD KEEPING

The directive "stay organized" sounds like rather basic advice, but is an important part of the trading business. For instance, imagine the IRS showing up for an audit of your business. Would you have all of your paperwork in order, or would you have to scramble? Consolidating trading specific information and maintaining well-organized records can help traders stay prepared and minimize the stress of trading. As with any aspect of trading, good planning will help to create and maintain an organized, professional business.

Staying Organized

The Organized Market Trader

Staying organized in a trading business is multifaceted. Primarily, traders must be organized for actual trading. Trading desks (or workstations) must be in order with adequate office supplies kept handy. A missing calculator will probably never lead directly to a losing trade, but being disorganized, even on the office supply level, can lead to greater stress. Through organization we are trying to avoid stress and run more efficient businesses.

Traders should also keep a legal pad or other notepad of paper on the trading desk for note taking, observations, and keeping a record of any out-of-the-ordinary events. Each trading day should begin a new page in the pad, with the day's date clearly written at the top. While not a trading journal, this pad is useful for recording unusual market behavior, market affecting news events, or any technological issues confronted during the day. If, for example, a trader needs to call technical support for a problem with a trading platform, this is the place to take notes for future reference. In doing so, important information will be in one place rather than scattered around the office. These daily notes can also be valuable when developing or updating a troubleshooting list.

Traders need quick access to trading-specific support tools around the workstation. These include a reliable economic calendar, the important phone numbers list, and troubleshooting list (described in Chapter 9—Live Trading). Economic calendars help traders be better prepared for the quick market moves that often accompany key economic reports. Ideally, the economic calendar, important phone numbers list, and the troubleshooting list should hang next to the trading desk, close enough to be easily read while sitting at the desk and speaking on the phone. As a backup, these items should also be placed inside a three-ring binder and kept within reach of the trading desk (as described later in the chapter).

A trading journal is another component in trader organization that should always be present at the workstation. Previous chapters have discussed the merits of keeping a trading journal. A trading journal is a practical way for traders to keep track of trades in an orderly fashion (useful for balancing broker statements and during tax time), and also provides an organized method for reviewing past trades and notes. This is particularly valuable during trading plan evaluations and development.

THE ORGANIZED STRATEGIST

In addition to being well organized for actual trading, traders need to have a structured means of conducting research and development; this is, after all, what prepares us to trade. Imagine spending hours compiling a performance analysis spreadsheet, only to never find it again. Most of this work can be saved on a hard drive, and regular backup disks should be burned (made), labeled, and filed. For hard copies, it is recommended that traders use a filing cabinet or bookcase, or a portable file box at the very least, to organize this important paperwork that falls under the jurisdiction of the strategist. Hard copies provide an extra backup of important work.

A separate folder should be used for each trading plan or strategy. Any corresponding research and development materials should be in the file, such as performance statistics, optimization reports, mathematical equations, or pertinent magazine articles. If minor changes have been made to a trading plan, consider using the same trading plan name, and attaching a version number (similar to software versions) to the end:

Trend Follower V1.0

Trend Follower V1.1

Counter Trend Strat V1.4

Counter Trend Strat V1.5

As a business owner, regular reviews must be performed to determine the financial status of the business. Monthly profit and loss statements should be compiled, reflecting trades, commissions, platform fees, and other expenses. When reviewing these monthly reports, it is essential to remember that in trading (as with most businesses) the big picture is what counts: an unprofitable month does not automatically make an unprofitable year. Monthly reviews allow traders to gauge the progress of their businesses.

A lawyer or CPA can be consulted if a trader wishes to form a business entity, such as a Limited Liability Corporation (LLC). Many traders operate as sole proprietors of their trading businesses. Special consideration should be given to filing as a business entity if more than one person is involved in the trading business. A lawyer or CPA can explain the various business designations and recommend what will work best for a given situation.

CREATING A TRADING BINDER

It is possible to incorporate a trading journal and other important paperwork into a complete trading binder. Maintaining a trading binder is one method for organizing the important paperwork that is necessary to a trading business. A three-ring binder works well, with clearly labeled dividers in between each section. A three-hole-punch can be used to fit the pages neatly into the binder. A new binder should be started each year, and the old ones filed away for reference. The different sections include:

❖ Trading Plan

  • Written description of the trading plan's logic

- Hardcopy of programming/coding for the trading plan (if applicable)
- Past versions of trading plans

❖ Trader Resources

- Important phone numbers list
- Troubleshooting list
- Economic calendar
- List of market holidays

❖ Trading Journals

- Past journal pages (a paperclip on the current page makes it easy to find)
- Blank journal pages

❖ Brokerage Statements

- Separate section for each broker
- Statements should be balanced monthly

Compiling all of these materials into one binder allows for better organization. You may have noticed that some of the recommended materials in the trading binder, such as the important numbers list and troubleshooting list, should also be hanging next to a trading desk. This is done not so much out of redundancy as it is for convenience. Having a complete trading binder puts all of the important paperwork in one place, and it is handy for traveling or if a trader needs to leave the office in a hurry.

TAXES FOR TRADERS

By default, the IRS considers trading to be an investment activity. Traders are expected to follow the tax laws for investment activities unless they rise to the level of trading as a business (thereby achieving "trader tax status"). Active traders may choose the Mark-to-Market (MTM) election for tax purposes. This is the only designation for traders that allows deductions for trading-related expenses, such as platform fees or education. The IRS is rumored to be particular about who actually qualifies for the MTM status. In general, they expect to see that a trader has spent all day, every day, trading. If a trader elects the MTM status, all positions must be counted as closed out at the end of the year, whether or not they have actually been closed, and all related taxes become due.

The MTM election can be beneficial to securities traders, but in most cases is a detriment to futures or commodities traders who typically receive better tax treatment (due to lower tax rates) without the election. Reversing the MTM election can be challenging, and its pros and cons should be discussed with a tax professional prior to making the election. Additionally, the election must be made by April 15th for individuals and partnerships (March 15th for corporations) of the tax year in which a trader wishes to take the MTM status.

It is recommended that traders seek the advice and expertise of a Certified Public Accountant (CPA) or other tax specialist for handling yearly and any quarterly taxes. It is outside the scope of this book to provide any authoritative information regarding taxes. Trader tax laws are complicated, and vary greatly depending on what is traded and how often it is traded; different types of trading instruments are taxed differently. In addition, the laws do change, and new laws are created to encompass the latest trading instruments as they are introduced. It may be worth the effort to find a

CPA qualified to handle trader taxes (with a good understanding of the relevant tax laws) to achieve the greatest benefits at tax time. Traders can check with a CPA or other tax professional to see what deductions may be allowed for expenses such as:

- Office space

- Home office

- Start-up costs

- Trading platform expenses

- Utilities, such as cell phone, Internet, phone, cable

- Books, seminars, subscriptions

- Education

- Professional affiliation dues

- Travel expenses

- Consulting expenses

Ongoing effort is required throughout the year to be prepared to file a tax return. Electing the MTM status, for example, could save a trader thousands of dollars at tax time. Traders can best plan for tax time by consulting with a tax professional ahead of time and staying organized.

CHAPTER 12
TOP 10 RULES OF SUCCESSFUL TRADING

Rule #1: Always use a trading plan.

Rule #2: Treat trading like a business.

Rule #3: Use technology to your advantage.

Rule #4: Protect your trading capital.

Rule #5: Become a student of the markets.

Rule #6: Risk only what you can afford to lose.

Rule #7: Develop a trading methodology based on facts.

Rule #8: Always use a stop loss.

Rule #9: Know when to stop trading.

Rule #10: Keep trading in perspective.

Though a bit cliché, we thought it valuable to include a list of important trading rules. Each of the ten rules has been covered in the previous chapters of this book. Some of the rules are the same rules that traders may read in other books—and with good reason. The rules are well-known, tested methods of improving trading success. We don't think anyone would argue that protecting capital is essential to profitable trading. Other rules may make their debut in this book. These lesser-known rules are every bit as important as their big brothers.

Becoming a profitable trader takes time and planning. The previous chapters have introduced a host of concepts that can help traders minimize the time to reaching trading success. This chapter is somewhat of a recap of the key ideas that have been presented throughout this book. These ten rules are interrelated: one rule may require strict adherence to another rule in order to reach fruition. For example, Rule #4 (Protect your trading capital) requires traders to follow all the other rules to meet this challenge. Following these ten basic rules can help establish and maintain a consistently profitable trading business.

RULE #1: ALWAYS USE A TRADING PLAN.

There is a common axiom among professional traders: "Plan your trade, trade your plan." Using a trading plan allows traders to do this. The development phase of a trading plan can be challenging and time-consuming. Once completed, the next obstacle is adhering to the plan. Once traders have developed a solid trading plan, they must stick to it. Taking trades that fall outside of a trading plan, even if they turn out to be winners, is considered bad trading and destroys any expectancy in the plan. Without the consistency of a trading plan, traders cannot develop a baseline for making their trading more profitable.

This does not mean that a trading plan will never change. In fact, traders should establish regular intervals to perform "system maintenance" on their trading plans. Systems that perform beautifully in today's market are likely to become less effective eventually. Sometimes a minor adjustment is all that is needed to maintain a system's profitability.

RULE #2: TREAT TRADING LIKE A BUSINESS.

Approaching trading as a full-time or part-time business (not as a hobby or a job) is essential. As a hobby, trading can be very expensive; as a job, it can be frustrating since there is no such thing as a regular paycheck. Trading is a business—complete with expenses, losses, taxes, uncertainty, stress, and risk. Understanding that trading is a business, and planning for it as such, can prepare traders to overcome the inevitable hurtles along the way.

As with any successful business, traders much carefully develop their trading businesses using some form of strategic planning. In particular, it is important to thoroughly research, test, and effectively apply to the appropriate market(s) the trading methodology (the trading plan). Rules #1 and #2 go hand in hand.

RULE #3: USE TECHNOLOGY TO YOUR ADVANTAGE.

The technology available to today's traders is vast. Charting platforms provide an array of choices for viewing the markets. The ability to backtest a trading idea on historical data before risking real money is invaluable. High-speed Internet has dramatically improved the speed with which traders can enter and exit positions. These are just a few of the ways in which today's traders can take advantage of available technology.

Trading is a competitive endeavor, and it is safe to assume that the person sitting on the other side of a trade is taking full advantage of the available technology. It is wise to do the same.

RULE #4: PROTECT YOUR TRADING CAPITAL.

Saving enough money to open a reasonably funded trading account can take a considerable amount of time. It can be even more difficult the second time around. "Protect your trading capital" should never be confused with "Don't have any losing trades." We all know that would be impossible. Protecting your capital means doing everything possible to trade smart: use a plan, use a stop loss, risk only what you can afford to lose.

RULE #5: BECOME A STUDENT OF THE MARKETS.

There is so much to learn about the markets that it would be virtually impossible to learn it all before starting to trade. Therefore, it is important to remain vigilant about learning more each day. Hard research allows traders to learn the facts; focus and observation allow traders to absorb some of the nuances in the markets. It would be a mistake for a trader to ever assume that he or she knew "enough" about the markets and could therefore stop trying to learn new things.

World politics, world events, world economies, consumer sentiment, technology, trading instruments—all of these things are dynamic, and by default create a dynamic, ever-changing market environment. The more traders know about the past and current markets, the better prepared traders will be to tackle the future.

RULE #6: RISK ONLY WHAT YOU CAN AFFORD TO LOSE.

It is important that the money in your trading account is expendable. It may take time to save enough money to fund a brokerage account with "extra" money. You have to count on losing all the money in your trading account, and still being able to pay the bills. Before you begin trading, make sure that the money in the account is truly expendable. If it isn't, keep saving until it is.

If your trading account has been depleted, these rules still apply. You must wait until you have saved money that is not needed for paying the bills. It should go without saying that your trading account should never be money that is earmarked for, say, the mortgage or the kids' college funds. Losing money is stressful enough; it is even more so if it is money that should have never been risked to begin with.

RULE #7: DEVELOP A TRADING METHODOLOGY BASED ON FACTS.

Facts, not emotions or speculation, should be the driving force behind developing a trading plan. As such, traders should expect to spend a significant amount of time researching and developing their trading plans. It is important to be objective about the research, and to be wary of any fantastic claims of success in other people's trading systems that are prevalent over the Internet. Traders who acknowledge that the development process is challenging (but well worth the effort) typically have an easier time sorting through all the information that is available over the Internet. Traders that want to hurry up and make some money are usually more apt to fall for the "make millions" scams.

RULE #8: ALWAYS USE A STOP LOSS.

It is important to always trade with a stop loss. A stop loss limits the risk that a trader is exposed to for each trade. Setting a predetermined amount of risk on each trade can take some of the emotion out of trading—as long as traders stick to the stop loss. Letting a stop loss blow by is never a good idea, even if it leads to a winning trade. It is a bad precedent, and more than likely it will simply lead to greater losses. Remember this: exiting on a stop loss is good trading. We would all like to always exit with a profit, but that is not realistic. Since we know we are going to have losing trades, it makes sense to know how big those losing trades are going to be. If the trade goes against us that far, we close it. And then we move on to the next trade.

RULE #9: KNOW WHEN TO STOP TRADING.

There are two main reasons to stop trading. The first reason is that the trading plan is ineffective and losing more than anticipated in historical testing. Markets may have changed, interest in a particular trading instrument may have changed, or the trading plan simply is not performing up to expectations. It may be time to take a step back and reevaluate the trading plan. It is important to remain businesslike and unemotional during these potentially stressful times. An ineffective trading plan is a problem that needs to be solved; it does not necessarily mean the end of the business.

On the other hand, the second reason to stop trading is that the trader is ineffective: things like external stressors, bad health, and negativity can have a significant impact on trading performance. It is beneficial to both the trader and the business that any personal problems be recognized and dealt with as soon as possible. In such a stressful environment, recognizing that there is a problem can be challenging. If traders feel that they are not performing well, it is recommended that they take at least a long weekend away from trading. Stepping away from the situation can provide some clarity, and allow traders to make the necessary changes to improve trading performance.

RULE #10: KEEP TRADING IN PERSPECTIVE.

While it is important to remain focused each and every trading day, it is equally important to remain focused on the big picture. Since trading is a business, it is the cumulative profits that matter. A losing day is just that—a losing day. We all have losing days; it is an inescapable part of trading. Likewise, a winning day is just that—a winning day. Win or lose, it's just another day at the office. Keep the emotions to a minimum.

It is helpful to remember the glamorous, multi-million dollar traders are the exception, not the norm. Most traders who can survive the tough part of the learning curve can make a nice living trading. Most individual traders are not trading seven figure accounts every day, making millions of dollars a year. It is important during business planning that traders set realistic goals for their businesses.

Traders who have the patience and discipline to follow all of these rules will greatly increase their odds of success in the incredibly challenging and competitive trading arena.

APPENDIX A
SAMPLE TRADING PLAN

A SIMPLE TRADING PLAN by Raymond Deux,
President and CEO of NinjaTrader, LLC

Early in my trading career I learned that having a trading plan was vital if one wanted to be a successful trader. Having a trading plan does not mean that you will be successful but it does mean that you can hold yourself accountable for your actions. Primary components of my trading plan included:

- Key trade set ups

- Pre-defined trade management rules

KEY TRADE SET UPS

There are many different trade set ups that you will come to explore or develop on your own but what is important is that you limit the amount of trade set ups to a select few that you intimately understand and can execute without letting emotions negatively influence your actions. As part of the learning process, I tried many different trade set ups, indicators, and markets. It wasn't until I focused on trading a select few set ups that I began to make decisions with more clarity and confidence. As a new trader, your plan should only include one trade set up. Learn this well, and then add another one.

PRE-DEFINED TRADE MANAGEMENT RULES

It is critically important to have defined rules that dictate when and where you take profits or cut your losses. These rules and conditions form the basis for your trade management and ensure that you are able to control your emotions, which then promotes discipline and consistency in your trading. When trading intraday, having a trading platform that can execute these trade management strategies can give you a dramatic advantage and this is what motivated me to conceive the NinjaTrader trading application. Once I have identified a trade set up and have entered the market, NinjaTrader takes over and semi-automates my trade strategy by submitting my stop loss and profit target orders based on my pre-defined parameters.

I CAN NOW GO INTO A FIGHT WITH A SHARP KNIFE!

A trading plan provides me with a well defined plan of "action" and more importantly, a plan of "no action" when trading the markets. From my experience, when you act outside of your trading plan, you surely pay for it many times over. My key trade set ups tell me what to look for and my trade management rules manage my trades. I only focus on what is in my plan and I do it with a patient demeanor.

ONE OF MY FAVORITE TRADE SET UPS

One of my favorite trade set ups is a "Bull Flag" which is akin to a flag on a pole. It is an area of price consolidation right after an advance that implies buyers are taking a break before resuming their advance. Through my experience, I have found that the odds of the "Bull Flag" chart pattern following through and continuing an advance significantly increases if the pattern forms after the 1st measurable change in trend as detected by a downtrend line break. I only use the raw chart bars for this set up and no supplementary indicators. The set up includes the rules for trade entry and trade management directly from my trading plan.

The trade entry set up as show in Figure 1:

1. A clear downtrend

2. A trend line break to the upside

3. A bull flag continuation pattern

4. Go long above the high of the bar that breaks the flag to the upside

This set up is valid in any market on any time frame. Although this set up discussed in the long direction, it works equally well or better in the short direction.

Setting up the trade management rules in NinjaTrader as show in Figure 2 and Figure 3:

1. Set up a stop loss of 8 ticks

2. Set up a profit target of 24 ticks

3. *Set up a multi-step automatic trailing stop

This pre-defined trade management set up provides me with a 1:3 risk to reward ratio.

I like protect profits as the trade moves into profitable territory. The Ninja-Trader automatic trailing stop allows me to set an initial liberal trail stop that only activates at a predefined level of profit.

SUMMARY

Everyone's trading plan will be different since we all have different tolerances for risk and psychological states. What's important is that you have one, you manage it, and you work it and hold yourself accountable to it.

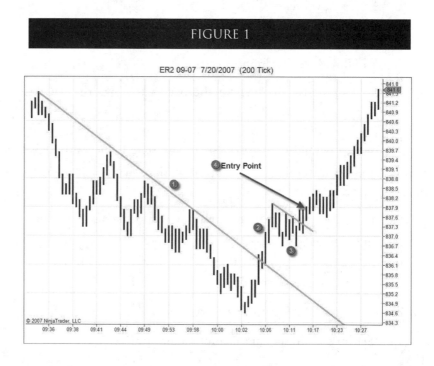

FIGURE 1

FIGURE 2

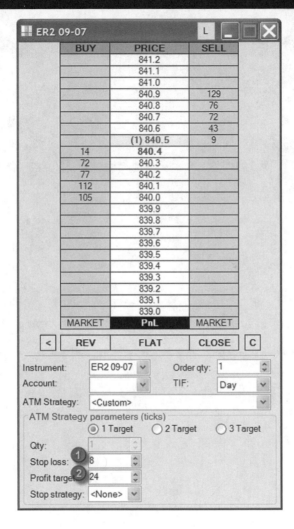

FIGURE 3

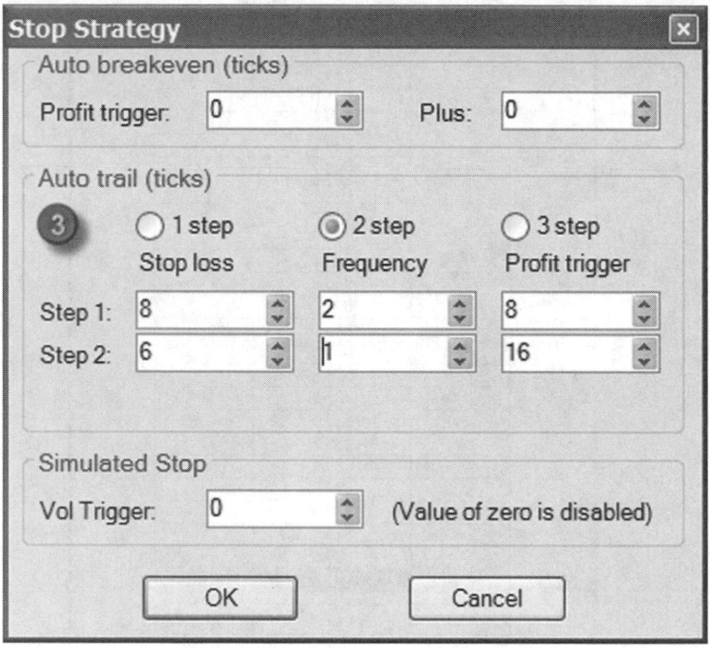

Stop Strategy [×]

Auto breakeven (ticks)

Profit trigger: 0   Plus: 0

Auto trail (ticks)

3   ○ 1 step   ◉ 2 step   ○ 3 step
     Stop loss   Frequency   Profit trigger

Step 1: 8   2   8
Step 2: 6   1   16

Simulated Stop

Vol Trigger: 0   (Value of zero is disabled)

OK   Cancel

EASYLANGUAGE CODE FOR SAMPLE INDICATORS AND STRATEGIES

FIB / PIVOT POINTS INDICATOR: CHAPTER 5

```
inputs:
    UseFibPivots(true),
    Color(red),
    PivotColor(blue);
arrays:
    pivotLevel[7](0),
    lineID[7](0),
    textID[7](0),
    textSTR[7]("");
variables:
```

```
        Pivot(0),

        R1(0),

        R2(0),

        R3(0),

        S1(0),

        S2(0),

        S3(0),

        count(0),

        PrevHigh(0),

        PrevLow(0),

        PrevOpen(0),

        PrevClosed(0);

If date <> date[1] then begin

    PrevHigh = highd(1);

    PrevLow = lowd(1);

    PrevOpen = opend(1);

    PrevClosed = closed(1);

    if UseFibPivots then begin

            Pivot = (PrevHigh + PrevLow + PrevClosed )/3;

            R1 = Pivot + (PrevHigh - PrevLow) * .382;

            S1 = Pivot - (PrevHigh - PrevLow) * .382;

            R2 = Pivot + (PrevHigh - PrevLow) * .618;

            S2 = Pivot - (PrevHigh - PrevLow) * .618;

            R3 = Pivot + (PrevHigh - PrevLow);

            S3 = Pivot - (PrevHigh - PrevLow);

    end

    else begin

            Pivot = (PrevHigh + PrevLow + PrevClosed )/3;

            R1 = 2 * Pivot - PrevLow;
```

```
        S1 = 2 * Pivot - PrevHigh;

        R2 = Pivot - S1 + R1;

        S2 = Pivot - R1 + S1;

        R3 = Pivot - S2 + R2;

        S3 = Pivot - R2 + S2;

end;

if bartype < 2 then begin

        PivotLevel[1] = R3;

        PivotLevel[2] = R2;

        PivotLevel[3] = R1;

        PivotLevel[4] = Pivot;

        PivotLevel[5] = S1;

        PivotLevel[6] = S2;

        PivotLevel[7] = S3;

        TextStr[1] = "R3";

        TextStr[2] = "R2";

        TextStr[3] = "R1";

        TextStr[4] = "Pivot";

        TextStr[5] = "S1";

        TextStr[6] = "S2";

        TextStr[7] = "S3";

        for count = 1 to 7 begin

                LineID[count] = tl_new(date, 0, PivotLevel[count], date, 2359, PivotLevel[count]);

                TextID[count] = text_new(date, time, PivotLevel[count], textStr[count]);

                text_setstyle(textID[count], 0, 1);

                text_setcolor(textID[count], Color);

                tl_setcolor(LineID[count], Color);

                if count = 4 then begin

                        tl_setcolor(LineID[count], PivotColor);
```

```
                    text_setcolor(textID[count], PivotColor);

        end;

        if date = currentdate then value1 = tl_setextright (lineID[count], true);

        commentary(textstr[count] + "- " + numtostr(pivotlevel[count],2) + newline);

    end;

end

else begin

    plot1(Pivot, "Pivot", PivotColor);

    plot2(R1, "R1", Color);

    plot3(S1, "S1", Color);

    plot4(R2, "R2", Color);

    plot5(S2, "S2", Color);

    plot6(R3, "R3", Color);

    plot7(S3, "S3", Color);

end;

end;
```

DOUBLE EXPONENTIAL MOVING AVERAGE INDICATOR: CHAPTER 5

```
inputs:

    Price(close),

    Period(20);

variables:

    X1(0),

    X2(0),

    DEMA(0);
```

```
X1 = xaverage(Price, Period);

X2 = xaverage( X1, Period);

DEMA = iff(currentbar <= 1, Price,  X1 * 2 - X2);

plot1(DEMA, "DEMA");
```

ADAPTIVE PRICE ZONE INDICATOR: CHAPTER 5

```
inputs:
    Price(Close),
    Period(20),
    BandPct(1.4);
variables:
    Length(0),
    DSPrice(0),
    DSRange(0),
    PctBand(0),
    UpBand(0),
    DnBand(0);
Length = iff(Period < 0, 1, squareroot(Period));
DSPrice = xaverage(xaverage( Price, Length ), Length);
DSRange = xaverage(xaverage( h - l, Length ), Length);
PctBand = BandPct * DSRange;
UpBand = DSPrice + PctBand;
DnBand = DSPrice - PctBand;
Plot1( UpBand, "UpBand" );
Plot2( DnBand, "DnBand" );
```

Premiere Stochastic Indicator: Chapter 5

inputs:

Line1(.9),

Line2(.2),

Period(25);

variables:

oFastK(0),

oFastD(0),

oSlowK(0),

oSlowD(0),

Length(0),

NormStoch(0),

SmoothStoch(0),

Premiere(0);

Value1 = Stochastic(h, l, c, 6, 1, 3, 1, oFastK, oFastD, oSlowK, oSlowD);

Length = iff(Period < 0, 1, squareroot(Period));

NormStoch = .1 * (oslowK - 50);

SmoothStoch = xaverage(xaverage(NormStoch, Length), Length);

Premiere = (expValue(1 * SmoothStoch) - 1) / (expValue(1 * SmoothStoch) + 1);

plot1(Premiere, "Premiere");

plot2(Line1, "1");

plot3(Line2, "2");

plot4(Line1 * -1, "3");

plot5(Line2 * -1, "4");

TICK INTERVAL COUNTDOWN METER INDICATOR: CHAPTER 5

```
inputs:
    DescripText("T"),
    Color(blue);
variables:
    SetPosition(0),
    LowestDispValue(0),
    HighestDispValue(0),
    TickReg(0),
    TxtStr(""),
    TxtID(-1);
if BarType = 0 then begin
    HighestDispValue = getAppInfo(aiHighestDispValue);
    LowestDispValue = getAppInfo(aiLowestDispValue);
    SetPosition = LowestDispValue + 0.01 * 50 * (HighestDispValue - LowestDispValue);
    if BarNumber = 1 then begin
        TxtID = text_new(date, time, close, "Start");
        text_SetStyle(TxtID, 0, 2);
        text_SetColor(TxtID, Color);
    end;
    if time <> time[1] or TickReg <= 0 then begin
        TickReg = BarInterval;
        text_SetStyle(TxtID, 0, 1);
        text_SetLocation( TxtID, Date, Calctime(time, 1), SetPosition);
    end;
    TickReg = TickReg - ticks;
```

```
TxtStr = numToStr(TickReg, 0) + " " + DescripText;

text_SetString(TxtID, TxtStr);
```
end;

TREND FOLLOWING POSITION TRADING STRATEGY: CHAPTER 7

```
inputs:

    StopLoss(2400),

    Length1(20),

    Length2(30);

variables:

    X1(0),

    X2(0),

    Y1(0),

    Y2(0),

    BuyPrice(0),

    SellPrice(0),

    DemaX(0),

    DemaY(0);

X1 = xaverage(c, Length1);

X2 = xaverage( X1, Length1);

DemaX = iff(currentbar <= 1, c, X1 * 2 - X2);

Y1 = xaverage(c, Length2);

Y2 = xaverage( Y1, Length2);

DemaY = iff(currentbar <= 1, c, Y1 * 2 - Y2);

if DemaX crosses over DemaY then BuyPrice = h[1];
```

```
if DemaX > DemaY and c < BuyPrice then buy next bar at BuyPrice stop;

if DemaX crosses under DemaY then SellPrice = l[1];

if DemaX < DemaY and c > SellPrice then sellshort next bar at SellPrice stop;

setstoploss(StopLoss);
```

COUNTER TREND SWING TRADING STRATEGY: CHAPTER 7

```
inputs:

    StopLoss(800),

    ProfitTarget(1600),

    ADXValue(52),

    Line1(-.9),

    Line2(-.2),

    StochLength(8),

    Period(25);

variables:

    oFastK(0),

    oFastD(0),

    oSlowK(0),

    oSlowD(0),

    Length(0),

    NormStoch(0),

    SmoothStoch(0),

    Premiere(0);

value1 = Stochastic( h, l, c, StochLength, 1, 3, 1, oFastK, oFastD, oSlowK, oSlowD);

Length = iff(Period < 0, 1, squareroot(Period));
```

NormStoch = .1 * (oslowK - 50);

SmoothStoch = xaverage(xaverage(NormStoch, Length), Length);

Premiere = (expValue(1 * SmoothStoch) - 1) / (expValue(1 * SmoothStoch) + 1);

if adx(14) < ADXValue then begin

    if Premiere crosses over Line1 or Premiere crosses over Line2

        then sellshort ("S1 Sell") next bar at market ;

    if Premiere crosses under Line1 * -1 or Premiere crosses under Line2 * -1

        then buy ("L1 Buy") next bar at market ;

end;

setstopcontract;

setstoploss(StopLoss);

setprofittarget(ProfitTarget);

PATTERN RECOGNITION DAY TRADING STRATEGY: CHAPTER 7

inputs:

    ProfitTarget(900),

    TrailingStop(200),

    PosittionSize(1000),

    ADXValue(30);

condition1 = c > o and c[1] < o[1] and c > o[1] and o <= c[1];

condition2 = o[3] > o[2] and o[2] > o[1] and c[3] > c[2] and c[2] > c[1];

condition3 = c < o and c[1] > o[1] and c < o[1] and o >= c[1];

condition4 = o[3] < o[2] and o[2] < o[1] and c[3] < c[2] and c[2] < c[1];

if adx(14) < ADXValue then begin

    if condition1 and condition2 then buy PosittionSize shares next bar at market;

```
    if condition3 and condition4 then sellshort PosittionSize shares next bar at market;

end;

setexitonclose;

setdollartrailing(TrailingStop);

setprofittarget(ProfitTarget);
```

TRADE IMPORT STRATEGY ADD-ON: CHAPTER 8

Please Note: This is not a complete strategy, and should be copied into the end of an existing strategy to import trade information for further analysis. This program will create a spreadsheet (.csv file) whose location may need to be further defined within this code.

```
variables: TradeNum(0);

TradeNum = totaltrades;

if TradeNum > TradeNum[1] then fileappend("C:\Documents and Settings\TradeList " +
    getsymbolname + ".csv", "," + numtostr(entryprice(1), 4) + "," + numtostr(exitprice(1), 4) + "," +
    numtostr(maxcontracts(1), 0) + "," + numtostr(marketposition(1), 0)+ Newline);
```

For a online version go to www.traderslibrary.com/TLEcorner

Appendix C
Trader Worksheets

Included in this Appendix are several worksheets meant to guide you in building a successful trading business. There is a sample trading strategy outline, a sample journal entry, an emergency contact list, and a reference of important market indicators. For printable versions of these worksheets, please visit www.traderslibrary.com/TLEcorner.

Trading Plan

System Name

Date

A trading plan is an essential part of a successful trading business. Please use this template as a quick reference for your specific trading plan. Remember, good trading is simply following your trading plan.

Description

System Type
(Such as trend following, support & resistance, volatility expansion)

Time Frame(s)
(Such as daily, 5-minute, 144 tick, 250 volume)

Trading Instruments
(Such as e-mini Russell 2000, GOOG daily stock scan)

Position Sizing
(Such as fixed number of contracts/shares, percent of account)

Entry Conditions - include trade triggers and filters

Exit Conditions - include stop loss, profit targets and money management

powerzonetrading.com

Trading Journal

	Date	Symbol	Shares / Contracts	Reason for Trade	L / S	Entry Price	Exit Price	Profit (Loss)	Notes
1									
2									
3									
4									
5									
6									
7									
8									
9									
10									
11									
12									
13									
14									
15									
16									
17									
18									
19									
20									

powerzonetrading.com

Important Numbers

Service	Account #	Username	Password	Telephone #
Broker 1				Futures Desk ___-___-___-___ / Trade Desk ___-___-___-___ / Technical Support ___-___-___-___ / Customer Service ___-___-___-___
Broker 2				Futures Desk ___-___-___-___ / Trade Desk ___-___-___-___ / Technical Support ___-___-___-___ / Customer Service ___-___-___-___
Charting				Technical Support ___-___-___-___ / Customer Service ___-___-___-___
ISP				Technical Support ___-___-___-___ / Customer Service ___-___-___-___
Phone				Technical Support ___-___-___-___ / Customer Service ___-___-___-___
Cell				Technical Support ___-___-___-___ / Customer Service ___-___-___-___
Other				Technical Support ___-___-___-___ / Customer Service ___-___-___-___
Other				___-___-___-___ / ___-___-___-___

Market Indicators

Market Direction	INDU DOW JONES Industrial Index (Daily Change)	COMPX NASDAQ COMPOSITE Index (Daily Change)	VIX CBOE Volatility Index (Daily Change)	TRIN NYSE Arms Index (Actual Value)	TICK NYSE Tick Index (Actual Value)	TIKQ NASDAQ Tick Index (Actual Value)	TIKI DOW JONES Tick Index (Actual Value)
High Reversal Probability				0.55 or Lower	1000 or Higher	600 or Higher	25 or Higher
Extremely Bullish	75 or Higher	20 or Higher	-1.20 or Lower	0.70 to 0.55	600 to 1000	475 to 600	20 to 25
Bullish	35 to 75	15 to 20	-0.80 to -1.20	0.85 to 0.70	300 to 600	300 to 475	12 to 20
Neutral	35 to -35	15 to -15	-0.80 to 0.60	1.00 to 0.85	300 to -300	-300 to 300	-12 to 12
Bearish	-35 to -75	-15 to -20	0.60 to 1.0	1.15 to 1.00	-300 to -600	-300 to -475	-12 to -20
Extremely Bearish	-75 or Lower	-20 or Lower	1.0 or Higher	1.30 to 1.15	-600 to -1000	-475 to -600	-20 to -25
High Reversal Probability				1.30 or Higher	-1000 or Lower	-600 or Lower	-25 or Lower

powerzonetrading.com

GLOSSARY

+R Advantage +R Advantage is achieved when a trading system makes more money on each winning trade than it spends on its losing trades.

Adaptive Price Zone The Adaptive Price Zone is a technical indicator that creates bands on a price chart; the majority of price action tends to stay within the upper and lower bands of the zone. When price deviates significantly from its average and crosses out of the zone, there is a tendency for price to push back towards the statistical average.

Anti-Martingale Betting System An anti-martingale betting system dictates that traders take greater risks when trading with profits than with initial capital. As the account size grows, so does the bet size.

Ask The ask is the price a seller is willing to accept for an instrument, and is therefore the price that retail traders will pay to buy an instrument. The ask price is always a little higher than the bid price.

Average Trade Net Profit The average trade net profit is a performance metric that measures the expectancy of a trading plan. This metric represents the average amount of money that was won or lost per trade, and is calculated by dividing the total net profit by the total number of trades.

Backtesting Backtesting, or historical modeling, refers to the testing of trading plans on historical market data.

Backtesting Application A backtesting application is a type of software that applies trading systems to historical market conditions and calculates performance characteristics.

Bid The bid is the price that a buyer is willing to pay for an instrument, and is therefore the price that retail traders will receive for selling an instrument. The bid price is always a little less than the ask price.

Bid-ask Spread The bid-ask spread is the difference between the bid and ask price of an instrument at any given time.

Bracket Order Bracket orders are multiple orders placed simultaneously in the market using a combination of stop and limit orders. They allow traders to lock in profits (when a profit target is reached) or limit losses (when a stop loss is reached), without having to constantly follow the position.

Channel Breakout A channel breakout occurs when price breaks out above or below two parallel (or close to parallel) trendlines. The price will often stall at the trendline that it broke out from before making a dynamic move away from the price channel.

Compounding Compounding refers to the reinvesting of profits and dividends in additional shares of stock.

Conditional Trade Orders Unlike basic market, limit, or stop orders, a conditional trade order will be automatically submitted or canceled only if specified criteria are met. Conditional trade orders must be specified before placing a trade, and are entered directly through the order entry software.

Countdown Meter A countdown meter is a type of indicator used to display the number of ticks or volume remaining in a current candle bar.

Counter-trend Strategy Counter trend strategies rely on frequent market oscillations to make consistent gains. Each winning trade often reflects price moves that are many times smaller than the preceding trend. This type of logic anticipates the possibility of price reversing in the opposite direction.

Data Indicators A data indicator is an index of short-term trading data that is collected from the major stock indices.

Day Trading Day trading refers to the active style of trading in which all positions are closed by the end of the day.

Direct Access Brokers Direct access brokers are broker that allow clients to trade directly with a stock or futures exchange. This is often the broker of choice for active traders who want to focus on speed and order execution.

Downtrend A downtrend occurs when prices form lower swing lows and lower swing highs, creating trendlines with negative slopes and a downward price channel.

Duration The duration of a trade order (sometimes referred to as time-in-force) defines how long an order will remain active in the market.

Equity Curve An equity curve provides a graphical representation of trading performance by charting the number of trades versus the running total of trading profits.

ETF Exchange Traded Fund. ETFs track an index, a commodity or a basket of instruments, but are traded like a stock on an exchange.

Expectancy Expectancy expresses the average amount that a trader can expect to win (or lose) per unit of risk. In order for traders to have any chance of making money, their system must have a positive expectancy.

Fibonacci Retracements Fibonacci retracements measure the strength of an initial price move by establishing the beginning and end of the price move using the swing highs and lows. Once these points are established, prices are projected that represent different percentages (based on Fibonacci sequence numbers) of the original move.

Fill Fill refers to the action of satisfying a trade order for an instrument. Placing a trade order does not guarantee that it will be filled, or if it will be filled at the intended upon price. Fill price is the price for which the transaction is completed.

Fixed-percentage Betting Fixed-percentage betting refers to risking a consistent percentage of capital (2% for instance) on any given trade. As an account size changes, so will the trade size.

Forex The foreign exchange market, also called "forex" or "FX", is the arena where one nation's currency is exchanged for another's.

Forward Performance Testing Forward performance testing, sometimes referred to as paper trading, is the stage in trading plan development where trades are placed via an order entry simulator or on paper. No actual trading takes place during this stage.

Front-end Software Front-end software allows its users a certain level of strategy automation. The advantage to using front-end software is its ability to automate complex exit strategies that may include multiple profit targets, multi-level stop orders, or pyramiding (adding shares or contracts to a winning position). This tool can significantly speed up the order placement process.

Full Service Brokers Full service brokers are broker whose services include research and advice such as trading recommendations, retirement planning, or tax tips. In exchange for their services, full service brokers typically charge substantial commissions.

Historical modeling See Backtesting.

Input Values Input values are user-defined variables (such as look back period or type of price data) that modify the behavior of an indicator. Changing input values can give an indicator much different values and point out different market conditions.

Inside Bid and Ask Inside bid and ask are the best prices currently available for buying and selling.

Investing Investing refers to the buying and selling of instruments with the goal of building wealth over extended periods of time.

Leverage Leverage refers to the increased buying power available in margin accounts. Leverage allows traders to enter larger positions than could be afforded with the money in a trading account alone. Leverage magnifies both profits and losses.

Limit Order Limit orders allow traders to specify the price they are willing to get for a trade, known as the limit price. A limit order to buy will be filled at or below the specified price, while a limit order to sell will be filled at or above the specified price.

Liquidity Liquidity is characterized by a high level of trading activity allowing traders to enter and exit positions easily without affecting the instrument's price.

Live-market Performance Testing Live-market performance testing is the stage in trading plan development where traders must put real money on the line to test the system. Live-market performance testing should only be conducted with a minimum position size. The focus of this phase is to establish a correlation between the live-market trading results and the previous development steps.

Margin Margin is essentially a loan that a broker provides traders and investors towards purchasing stock shares, futures contracts, or foreign currency.

Margin Call A margin call is a demand from a broker that money be added to a trading account in order to meet the minimum margin requirement. If this demand is not met, the broker will close out any positions (without consulting the account holder) in order to ensure that the account is brought up to the minimum maintenance amount.

Market Analysis Platform Market analysis platforms create price charts and display price quotes that allow traders to see market action graphically. Market analysis platforms require a data feed into the market that allows access to current information (typically, in less than a second).

Market Order A market order is the most basic type of trade order and instructs the broker to buy or sell at the best price currently available. The advantage to using market orders is that a trader is guaranteed to get the order filled.

Market Trader The market trader defines one role of a trader (the other being the strategist). The market trader's role is to follow the trading plan exactly.

Mark-to-Market Mark-to-Market (MTM) is an election that active traders may choose to elect for tax purposes. This is the only designation for traders that allows deductions for trading related expenses, such as platform fees or education.

Maximum Drawdown Maximum drawdown is a performance metric that measures the greatest difference, or loss, from a previous equity peak in a system's equity curve.

Online Brokers Online brokers offer access to the markets via the Internet and charge significantly smaller commissions than do full service brokers. Online brokers typically offer only stock/ETF trading and do not offer advisory services, but may include online or software research tools for their clients.

Optimal Risk Optimal risk, sometimes called optimal f, refers to the method of estimating the optimal percentage of risk for a trading system, so that the system achieves the highest net profit possible.

Optimizing Optimizing refers to the process of modifying values in a trading plan with the goal of achieving better performance. Once traders develop the tools to assess a trading plan, it is possible to change part of the plan, such as the length of a moving average or ADX value, to create better historical results.

Order Execution Software Order execution programs allow an advanced level of strategy automation through fully automatic order handling for trading systems, strategies, and indicators.

Oscillator Oscillator is a general term for technical indicators that bounce between two extreme values to define overbought and oversold conditions.

Over-optimizing Over-optimizing refers to excessive curve fitting that produces a trading plan that is unreliable in actual trading. An over-optimized plan will often show outstanding performance statistics, but will only work well on the historic data on which it was tested.

Pattern Day Trader Pattern day traders are those traders who make four or more day trades within a consecutive five-day period, where the number of day trades accounts for more than 6% of the total trades taken during the time period.

Pattern Recognition Pattern recognition is a strategy type that relies on regularly occurring price patterns for trade entry or exit rules. Individual markets often display a tendency to move in a particular direction following the formation of reoccurring price patterns. Pattern recognition can be done visually or with the help of a computer.

Percent Profitable Percent profitable is also known as the probability of winning. This statistic is calculated by dividing the number of winning trades by the total number of trades for a given trading period.

Performance Metrics Performance metrics are statistics that can be used to evaluate a trading plan. Traders often develop a preference for those metrics that are most valuable based on their particular trading style or business goals.

Pip Pip refers to the smallest price change that an exchange rate can make.

Pivot Points Pivot points are a type of technical indicator calculated by averaging a previous day's high, low, and closing prices. Originally calculated by floor traders and market makers at the exchanges, pivots points project support and resistance levels.

Position Size Position size refers to how many units a trader is buying or selling, or the dollar amount that a trader is going to trade. Short-term traders often refer to position size in terms of lots.

Position Trading Position trading refers to a relaxed style of trading in which trades are taken over a period of months to years. This style of trading attempts to identify technical trends in stocks or commodities where large price movements are likely to occur.

Price Bands Price bands are formed by adding and subtracting a user defined distance from a moving average. The result is a channel with upper and lower lines that are projected onto a price chart.

Price Breakout Price breakout refers to price moves resulting from a break of an established trend line. These moves can by very dynamic, especially when confirmed on multiple timeframes.

Probability Probability can be expressed either as a decimal from 0.00 to 1.00, or as a percentage from 0% to 100%. A probability of 1.00 or 100% means an event will always occur, while a probability of 0.00 means the event will never happen.

Probability of Ruin (Risk of Ruin) The probability of ruin refers to the risk of losing all of the invested capital.

Probability of Winning The probability of winning is the inverse of the probability of loss or ruin.

Profit Factor The profit factor can be thought of as the R advantage for the complete trading plan. While the R advantage is only used to measure the risk ratio of individual trades, the profit factor is defined as the gross profit divided by the gross loss (including commission) for the entire trading period.

Profit Target A profit target defines when an open trade will begin to take profits.

R The amount of trade risk can be expressed in risk units, or R.

Real Equity Curve A real equity curve is constructed by combining the data from live trading and from the development phases of a trading plan.

Risk Risk is the probability of losing money or trading capital.

Risk-adjusted Expectancy Risk-adjusted expectancy (ERA) expresses expectancy per unit of risk, instead of as a dollar amount, and is often useful in comparing different systems. Multiplying ERA by the average dollar amount of risk (average loss) brings us back to the dollar value in which expectancy was originally defined.

Routing Instructions Routing instructions refer to the ability to choose which exchange will fill an order.

Scalping Scalping refers the trading style that involves frequent buying and selling throughout the day. Scalp trades target the smallest intraday price movements and take place within seconds or minutes.

Sell Short Selling short, or short selling, requires traders to begin a trade by borrowing shares of a stock or futures contracts from a broker (using margin) and then selling them. Traders must then buy back the stock or futures contracts (known as buying to cover) when they wish to flatten or close out the trade. In this way, traders can profit from falling prices.

Signal Exit Signal exits refer to a condition occurring in the market that indicates when traders may want to exit, or flatten, their open positions. Signal exits are based on the adverse action of price, an indicator, or an outside market relationship.

Slippage Slippage refers to the difference between the price a trader expects and the price he or she actually gets in a transaction.

Stop Exit A stop exit refers to any type of trade exit that attempts to follow the movement of price. The goal of a stop exit is to protect profits by moving the stop exit level in the direction of the market. This type of exit includes breakeven and trailing stops.

Stop Loss A stop loss is a simple limit to how much capital a trader is willing to risk on any one trade.

Stop Order A stop order to buy or sell becomes active only after a specified price level has been reached (known as the stop level). Stop orders work in the opposite direction of a limit order, with buy stop orders placed above the market and sell stop orders placed below the market. Once a stop level has been reached, the order will be immediately converted into a market or limit order. In this sense, a stop order is not really an order in itself, but a trigger for either a market or limit order.

Strategic Plan A strategic plan leads traders from where they are now to where they would like to be in the future. This type of planning allows traders to build a comprehensive model for their trading businesses as well as providing the most direct path for getting there.

Strategist The strategist defines one role of a trader (the other role is the market trader). The strategist must see the "big picture" and is responsible for the overall planning of the business, including the development of the trading plan.

Support and Resistance Support and resistance refers to areas where prices have previously stalled or reversed. Support can be thought of as a floor under trading prices, while resistance is the ceiling.

Swing High Swing highs are price movements characterized by inverted Vs on a price chart; swing highs are points where price has risen and reversed, forming an inverted V shape.

Swing Low Swing lows are price movements characterized by Vs on a price chart; swing lows are points where price has dropped and reversed, forming a V shape.

Swing Trading Swing trading refers to the trading style that involves taking trades (or positions) that last a few days or weeks.

Symbol Symbol refers to the abbreviation for an instrument that is being traded.

System Trading System trading allows traders to develop specific rules that establish both trade entries and exits. Similar to front-end software, system trading requires software that is linked to a broker.

Technical Analysis Technical analysis is the method of analyzing market movement based on past price and volume activity.

Thermometer Indicator The Thermometer Indicator acts as a temperature gauge for intraday price movements and is intended to function in real time. It works on all intraday charts and registers a value as a percentage price difference.

TICK The TICK stands for the NYSE Tick Index and measures the difference in stocks currently trading positively on an uptick and stocks currently trading negatively on a downtick.

Tick Chart Tick charts plot prices for a specific number of transactions. For example, a 144 tick chart will print a bar for every 144 transactions that have occurred.

Time Exit Time exits are a type of trade exit. Time exits close a trade after a set amount of time or after a number of candlestick bars have passed. This type of a trade exit is used to establish the maximum time horizon in which a trade will take place. At the end of this time, the trade will be closed, with or without a profit.

Total Net Profit The total net profit represents the bottom line profit or loss for a trading plan over a specified trading period. This statistic is calculated by subtracting the gross loss of all losing trades (including commissions) from the gross profit of all winning trades.

Trade Filters Trade filters define the setup conditions that will allow a trade to occur. Trade filters should not be confused with the trade trigger. Trade filters simply define the conditions for when the trade trigger is active. Trade filters can be thought of as the "safety" for the trade trigger. Once all of the conditions for the trade filters have been met, the safety is off and the trade trigger becomes active. Trade filters must occur before the trade trigger.

Trade Trigger A trade trigger is the line in the sand that defines precisely when a trade will be entered. While there may be several other conditions that will further define a trade entry, known as trade filters, the trade trigger tells traders exactly when to act.

Trader A trader is one who places frequent trades in the markets with the intention of profiting from the trades. Within the scope of this book, a trader is part strategist and part market trader.

Trader Alerts Trader alerts are audio or visual alerts that are set to activate when certain conditions in the market occur. Traders can customize these alerts within their market analysis platforms.

Trader-assist System Trading Trader-assist system trading is an alternative form of investing that allows traders to purchase or lease commercial trading systems that are traded and monitored by a broker.

Trading Trading refers to the frequent buying and selling of stocks or commodities with the goal of generating returns that outperform buy-and-hold investing.

Trading Journal A trading journal is a record of individual trades and acts as a trading diary.

Trading Plan A trading plan is an essential element of a strategic plan that addresses the specific trading aspects of the business. This plan is based on thorough research and addresses the implementation of all of the previous goals.

Trading Style Trading style refers to the time frame or holding period in which stocks, commodities, or other trading instruments are bought and sold.

Trading Volume Trading volume refers to the number of shares that have been bought and sold during a particular time period.

Trailing Stop A trailing stop is a dynamic stop order that follows price trends in an attempt to lock in profits. A trailing stop will incrementally increase in a long trade to follow the rising market, and will decrease in a short trade to follow the declining price.

Trend Following Strategy Trend following strategies attempt to catch the largest price moves in a market. Trading plans that use trend following typically have a lower percentage of winning trades, offset by the winning trades being much greater than the losing trades.

Trendlines Trendlines are straight lines drawn on a chart connecting points where prior price reversals have occurred. They typically project into the future, or the right-hand edge of the chart.

Triangle Pattern A triangle pattern forms as two trendlines converge, creating a consistently smaller support and resistance channel in which price can move.

TRIN The TRIN, also known as the NYSE Arms Index, is the NYSE Trader's Index. It measures the intraday direction of the market by comparing the number and volume of NYSE stocks that are advancing to those that are declining. The TRIN can be a helpful tool for assessing market strength, and, while based on the NYSE, often represents the broad market.

Undercapitalized Being undercapitalized is the risk of not having enough money to trade with in order to become profitable.

Uptrend An uptrend is price movement with higher swing highs and higher swing lows. Two trendlines can be drawn (one connecting swing highs, one for swing lows) that both have positive slopes and form an upward channel of price movement.

Volatility Volatility refers to the amount of price fluctuation in a given instrument.

Volume Chart Volume charts record the prices for a specified number of contracts or shares traded. For example, a 250 volume chart will print a bar for every 250 shares/contracts that have been traded.

INDEX

and profit availability, 153–54

in stock exchanges, 48–52, 53

See also ask prices; bid-ask spreads

BP (British Pound) futures, 71–72

brackets, 162–63, 167–69, 204

breakeven stops, 165–66

British Pound (BP) futures, 71–72

brokers

backup broker, 240

choosing, 87–88, 91–92

commissions, 70–71, 224–25

for day trading, 90–91

direct access brokers, 84, 90–91, 150, 151

full service brokers, 89

margin account with, 63, 65, 92–96, 149, 181–84

online brokers, 89–90

order routing systems, 152

proprietary order execution software, 84, 91, 152

simulators for learning trading, 85, 171, 231

statements from, 246, 269

and system trading, 172–73

trade durations available from, 152

trading account, 91–96, 249

bullish reversal patterns, 100, 101

business. *See* trading as a business

business entity decisions, 268

business expenses, 44, 45

buying (going long) currency pairs, 70

buying to cover, 94, 148

buy stop orders, 162–63

C

cable Internet connections, 80

candlesticks, 98–101, 204–5. *See also* charts

capital

    equating to inventory, 27–28, 37, 249

    potential for losing, 9, 19, 28

    and probability of ruin, 12–14, 20–21, 219–22, 223–24

    and style of trading, 5, 7

    and trading plan, 249

    undercapitalization, 11, 45

capital, protecting, 27–31, 32, 274, 276. *See also* position size; stop losses; trading plans

capitalization-weighted indices, 56–57

cash indices, 56, 57

catastrophic losses, 218–19

CBOT (Chicago Board of Trade), 61

CCI (commodity channel index) oscillators, 127–28, 129–31, 132

cell phone, 80

central pivot point, 115, 116–17, 287–90

Certified Public Accountant (CPA), 270–71

chain of technology, 75

channel breakouts, 112, 113–14

charts

    bar charts, 98–99

    candlesticks, 98–101, 204–5

    curve fitting, 226–27

    daily charts, 101–3, 139–42, 201

    equity curve, 183–84, 256–57, 259

    Fibonacci retracements, 117–20

    and multiple moving averages, 123

double exponential moving average (DEMA), 122–24, 125, 197–98, 290–91

Dow Jones Industrial Average (DJIA), 56–58

Dow Jones Tick Index (TIKI), 135, 137

downticks, 136–37

downtrends, 110–11, 131, 132, 137

drawdown, 214–15, 221, 249, 262

drawdown troughs of real equity curves, 260, 261

DSL Internet connections, 80

duration of a trade order, 151, 152

E

Eckhardt, William, 180

ECN (electronic communication network), 152

economic calendars, 266

ED (EuroFX futures), 71–72, 113

educational path

    avoiding losses, 28–29, 250

    broker-provided simulators, 85, 171, 231

    competency model, 34–35

    deciding on, 33–35

    forward performance testing as, 178–79, 230–31

    need for, 31–33

    on-the-job learning process, xi, 9, 31–37, 241, 262–63, 276–77

    See also trading journal

electronic communication network (ECN), 152

electronic trading, 65, 66–67, 156. *See also* technology maximization; trade automation

EMA (exponential moving average), 122, 124

emergency numbers list, 237–38, 302

E-mini index futures, 66–67, 94–95, 116–17, 154

E-mini NASDAQ 100 (NQ), 66–67

maximum historical drawdown, 262

optimizing and over-optimizing, 225–27

software for, 83–84, 210, 211, 212, 226, 259

using in-sample and out-of-sample data, 227–29

value of, 25–27

holding period, risk and, 7–8

horizontal trendlines, 110

I

Important Numbers worksheet, 302

independent trading

benefits of, ix–x

challenges and responsibilities, x–xi

profit and loss statement, 44, 45

surfer to yacht comparison, 1–2

See also trading styles

indices, stock market, 55–58, 136–38

initial margin, 93

input values, 120–23, 128–31

in-sample data, 227–29

inside bid and ask, 52, 63, 153–56

instrument symbol for futures contract, 62, 63

intelligent order routing, 152

intentional trading errors, 253

Internet connection, 80

intervals

on candlestick charts, 98–99

data-based, 103–6

data points, 98

multiple chart intervals, 111–12, 120, 187, 189–90

multiple interval charts, 101–3

    time-based, 101–3, 105

intraday charts

    applying stochastics to, 129, 130

    choosing interval for, 105–6

    data-based charts, 103–6

    DEMA analysis, 122–24

    overview, 142–43

    time-based charts, 101–3

    and trendline triangle pattern, 114

intraday market, data indicators for, 134–38

intraday traders. *See* day trading; scalp trading

intraday trades and margin account, 93, 94, 95

investing vs. trading, 2–4

iShares Russell 2000 Index (IWM), 58–60

J

Japanese Yen futures (JY), 71–72

journal. *See* trading journal

L

Lambert, David, 129

Lane, George C., 128–29

Level 2 screen, 51–52, 59, 152, 153–54

leverage

    in forex markets, 68–69

    in futures contracts, 63, 65

    margin account and, 94–95, 181–84

limit orders, 156–58, 189, 192–93

liquidity, 8, 49, 59–60, 66–67, 153

M

R

R (trade risk units), 9, 16

R1 resistance level, 115, 116–17

R2 resistance level, 116–17

R advantage, 16, 17, 216–17, 254

+R advantage

    in counter trend strategy, 204

    maximizing, 20

    overview, 10, 14–18

    from recognizing entry or exit points, 106–8

    from relationship of stop loss and profit target, 193

    with stop losses, 30–31

+R advantage ratios, 16, 18

real equity curve, 258–61, 262, 263

record keeping, 265–71. *See also* trading journal

reevaluation criteria, 250

Regulation T (Federal Reserve Board), 92, 93

research, 42, 175–76, 267–68. *See also* trading plans

resistance, 106–8, 110, 115, 116–17

retracements, 117–20

reversal patterns, 100–101, 124, 205–7

revisions to trading plan, 176, 178, 179

risk

    assessing amount of, 210

    individual risk tolerance, 20, 277

    of individual stocks, 53–55

    length of holding period and, 7–8

    from misuse of technology, 76

    optimal percentage of risk, 210

SF (Swiss Franc) futures, 71–72

short gap entry, 283

short selling. *See* short trades

short swing entry, 282

short-term buying/price drop, 52

short-term goals, x, 4, 35, 42, 43

short trades

    currency pairs, 70

    of ETFs, 60

    futures contracts, 63

    long trades vs., 147, 149

    margin account for, 94, 149

    orders for, 148–49, 163–65

    overview, 148–49

    and trailing stop levels, 160

signal exits, 194

simple moving average (SMA), 121–22, 124, 131, 139–40

simulators for learning trading

    broker-provided, 85, 171, 231

    forward performance testing as, 178–79, 230–31

slippage, 146, 153, 154–56, 193, 224–25

smart order routing, 152

SMA (simple moving average), 121–22, 124, 131, 139–40

software

    application program interface, 90–91

    for backtesting, 83–84, 210, 211, 226, 259

    chart setups, 138–39, 140–42

    Excel spreadsheets, 211–15, 256–57

    front-end, 167, 170–71

    indicator formatting window, 120–21

trends

    assessing strength of, 128, 139–40, 261

    daily change in indices and, 57

    in forex markets, 197

    identifying changes in, 128

    indicator value and, 138

    and moving averages, 123

triangle patterns, 113, 114–15

TRIN (NYSE Arms Index; NYSE Trader's Index), 135, 138

troubleshooting list, 238–40, 247–48

TTO (threshold triggered order), 168

the Turtles, 180–81, 183–84, 185–87

typical price (TP), 131

U

undercapitalization, 11, 45

unintentional trading errors, 253–54

uninterruptible power supply (UPS), 80

uptick rule, 60

uptrends

    and CCI values, 131, 132

    and stochastic oscillator, 128–29

    trendlines showing, 109–11

    value of TRIN and, 138

user-defined ruin%, 220, 221

V

volatility

    diversification and, 185–87

    of E-mini market, 67

Trading Resource Guide

RECOMMENDED READING

JACK SCHWAGER'S COMPLETE GUIDE TO MASTERING THE MARKETS
by Jack Schwager

Imagine having an in-depth conversation with not one-but dozens of the world's greatest traders. Jack Schwager has, and his three best-selling "Market Wizards" books reveal intimate secrets of the trading superstars. Now he's filtered years of in-depth research into an amazingly comprehensive home study workshop. This workshop is now on DVD and repackaged to make it easier for you to maximize the profit potential of this course. With Schwager's trademark thoroughness, easy-to-follow instruction, and real-life examples, this complete trading resource-hailed by the "Market Wizards" themselves-will send you into the trading world armed with proven techniques, insider knowledge, elevated self-confidence, and winning methods.

Item #BCJFx4352093 - $799.00

STRATEGIES FOR PROFITING ON EVERY TRADE
by Oliver Velez

An accessible, reliable course for the trader looking for profits in the competitive, dynamic world of trading.

Each section of the book offers clear examples, concise and useful definitions of important terms, over 90 charts used to illustrate the challenges and opportunities of the market; and how you can take advantage of patterns. Written in the parlance of the day trader's world, you'll enjoy the experience of being taught trading skills by the best of the best.

This focused and effective trading resource features seven key lessons to further a trader's education including market basics, managing trades, psychology in trading and planning, technicals, utilizing charts, income versus wealth building producing trades, and classic patterns. It truly is as Paul Lange says, "Many of these lessons have been taught to students worldwide over a span of 4 years. These lessons contain powerful information that goes far beyond the basics you may find in many introductory trading books."

Item #BCJFx5031652 - $49.95

BREAKTHROUGH STRATEGIES FOR PREDICTING ANY MARKET
by Jeff Greenblatt

Breakthrough Strategies for Predicting Any Market is sure to be considered one of the great trading books of the 21st century. In this landmark work, Jeff Greenblatt will teach you how to understand the time dimension of the market and take your technical analysis to the next level.

With extensive case studies and charts, Jeff will reveal his high-probability pattern recognition system; one that will give you a deeper understanding of how the markets really work and will make whatever methodology you use ten times better. Following in the footsteps of the great W.D. Gann, Jeff will help you gain greater precision in any instrument you trade, on any time frame.

Item #BCJFx5150460 - $149.95

THE COMPLETE GUIDE TO TECHNICAL INDICATORS
by Mark Larson

Traders have used the power of technical indicators to put significant gains in their account. Now you can easily carve through the hundreds of indicators and get right to the ones that make money most often and help you achieve success in trading. In this comprehensive guide to cracking the code of technical indicators, best-selling author and acclaimed presenter, Mark Larson, shows you how to find the indicators that best fit your trading style and reveals which indicators work in which markets. With this experience, you will have the power to increase your winning percentage, no matter what the market does.

Item #BCJFx5197572 - $795.00

ABOUT THE AUTHORS

JEAN FOLGER

Jean Folger is a stock and futures trader who began her trading business while searching for dynamic portfolio diversification. She is a system researcher and developer for PowerZone Trading.

LEE LEIBFARTH

Lee Leibfarth is an independent futures trader who designs, tests and implements his own trading systems. He is president and founder of Power-Zone Trading. His articles on trading have been featured in The Technical Analysis of Stocks & Commodities, Futures, Active Trader and Trader's Journal magazines.

This book, along with other books, is available at discounts that make it realistic to provide it as a gift to your customers, clients, and staff. For more information on these long lasting, cost effective premiums, please call us at (800) 272-2855 or you may email us at sales@traderslibrary.com.